MW00356022

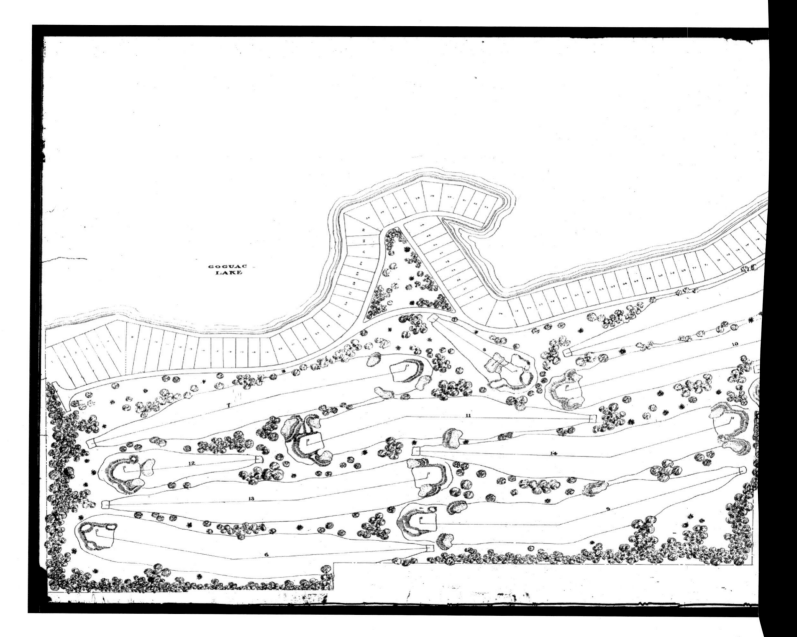

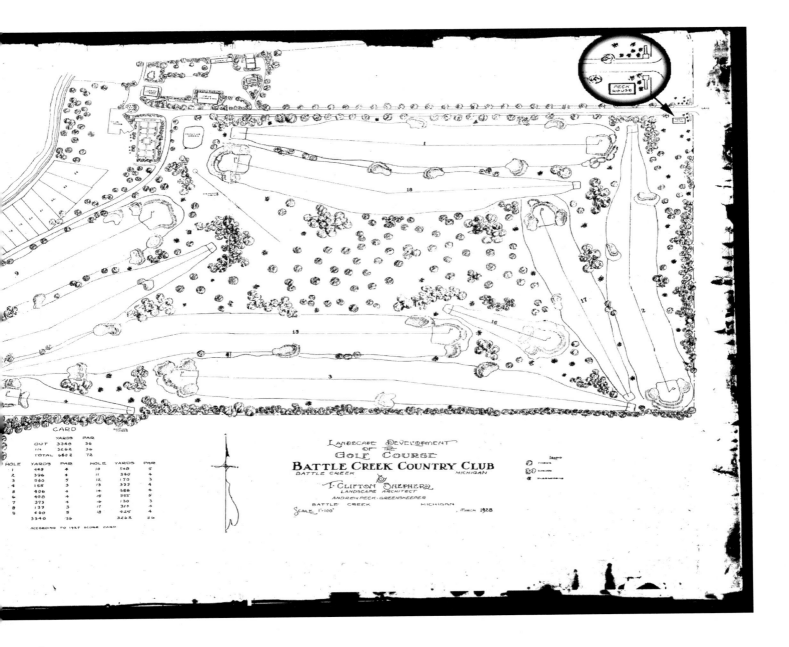

PECK
HOUSE

CARD

	YARDS	PAR
OUT	3340	36
IN	3262	36
TOTAL	6602	72

HOLE	YARDS	PAR	HOLE	YARDS	PAR
1	448	4	10	540	5
2	396	4	11	380	4
3	560	5	12	170	3
4	155	3	13	332	4
5	406	4	14	580	5
6	408	4	15	355	4
7	373	4	16	130	3
8	137	3	17	328	4
9	460	5	18	425	4
	3340	36		3262	36

ACCORDING TO 1927 SCORE CARD

LANDSCAPE DEVELOPMENT
OF THE
GOLF COURSE
BATTLE CREEK COUNTRY CLUB
BATTLE CREEK   MICHIGAN
BY
T. CLIFTON SHEPHERD
LANDSCAPE ARCHITECT
ANDREW PECK · GREENSKEEPER
BATTLE CREEK   MICHIGAN
SCALE 1"=100'   , MARCH 1928

Above – Original Bylaws for the first Battle Creek Country Club – 1908 to 1919

Inner Spread – 1928 Blueprint by T. Clifton Shepherd showing Landscape Development of BCCC. Note "Peck House" in upper right corner.

Back Cover - Andy Peck with Ray Lampke at the wheel of the golf course's new Roseman Turf Tractor in 1925.

Cover / Above – Elm Trees line Country Club Drive after ice storm in 1924.
One Country Drive home is off left at mailbox.

With many thanks to my dear friends who helped with ideas and proofing, to the Battle Creek Country Club members and staff, to Willard Library for local historical images,

and to my editor – Judy Steininger.

Copyright 2019 by Marty Peck. All Rights Reserved.

Certain imagery © Willard Library or Alamy.com

No part of this book may be used or reproduced without express written permission of the author.

Published by BookBaby

ISBN: 978-1-54397-685-4

Library of Congress Control Number: 2019907915

ONE COUNTRY CLUB DRIVE

STORIES ACROSS THREE GENERATIONS OF GREENSKEEPING

By Marty Peck

bookbaby

David & Ed
Thanks for
all your help
and support,
and for making dreams
happen

Dedicated to my father, Harold Peck...

...who taught me many things, and that I could do any thing...

...and to my mom, Jayne, who gave me the inspiration.

CONTENTS

PREFACE

"Playing" Golf...

Imagine, perhaps with a bit of envy, a child who grows up playing on almost one-hundred-twenty lush acres of a golf course with hills, woods and a swimming beach. Picture the child who gets to operate all sorts of machinery for maintaining the course. Relive the experiences of a child who gets to spy on adult antics and the craziness behind the scenes of that private country club.

That child, just now revisiting his lucky lot in life, was me. I had the privilege of growing up in a house right off the second tee of that golf course because both my grandfather and my father were greenskeepers, charged with keeping the grass green and the members happy. Three generations of Pecks occupied that four-bedroom Dutch-colonial house for almost 100 years, including my dad and his six siblings. Grandmother took care of them while Grandfather and his crews built the original course using teams of horses. After my dad took over, I grew up there too, along with my older sister. The address, appropriately, was One Country Club Drive.

My family packed a lot of living into that sturdy frame house on the corner. Over the decades we watched as some of the greatest names in golf played in our yard, witnessed the escape of slot machine bandits and the national scandal of a horrific crime, and experienced fires and floods, while I played at climbing giant trees, wrestling with gophers and trying booze. My family saw wars come and go, survived the depression and built a golf legacy. You see, the house I was raised in is on country club property, and that private golf course was what we all knew at one time or another as our backyard.

Look in on our family, learn a bit of history behind the country club and its care, and listen to our behind-the-scenes "caddy shack" stories from across three generations of greenskeepers.

An Old House with a Few Mysteries…

Nobody knew the age of the house. For a young kid, its old rafters held many curiosities along with the roof. The stair to the attic led to a big trap door at the top that swung down on a rope to cover the opening. I'd always thought it was to keep the flies and bats from getting downstairs, since my tough grandma had once caught a bat with her bare hands in her bedroom. Outside there were brick chimneys on both ends of the roof, but oddly, inside the attic there was only one; where the other chimney should be there was nothing but wood with buckets there to catch the erratic leaks where the brick stopped. Old antenna wires were strung around from when, as a boy, my dad had a shortwave radio. Piles of unusual dusty junk that had accumulated over decades became a treasure trove for a kid.

Under the floorboards were old electric wires that went through ceramic tubes in the rafters called knob and tube wiring. My dad said they used to go just to a single light bulb socket in the middle of every room. When he was growing up, they ran cords across to the center of the ceiling to plug things into the sockets like fans and irons and radios, creating a giant spider web of wires. When my parents moved in my mom's first fix up project was to have my dad and her brother install new outlets and switches. But the old wiring was still there under the attic floor looking like Thomas Edison himself might have put it there.

It looked like the Phantom of the Opera would have been at home in the basement with big round cement patches in the floor hiding some cave-like underground cisterns. Old abandoned pipes resided in the basement walls; one went to an old sewer that had backed up at the worst times. According to my dad, another water pipe used to supply drinking water to the house from the golf course sprinkler system. That always grossed me out because it was pumped out from the lake, and the idea of drinking *lake* water right out of the faucet was pretty disgusting.

But as a kid, the biggest mystery was the bullet hole. I can thank that bullet hole for any story telling skills I might have. On one end of the house was a big porch complete with three round columns and two doors leading into the living room. In my lifetime nobody ever used the porch because it fronted busy Capital Avenue, so the only time the porch doors were ever opened was when a Christmas tree got dragged in. Smack in the middle of the porch between those two doors was an old leaded glass window visible from the outside. Curiously inside the living room there was no window – it had been

The leaded-glass porch window had a mysterious bullet hole through one of the diamonds.

completely covered up as though it never existed. I found out later that my mom was the someone who had ordered it covered up, as she thought it looked too old-fashioned. My curiosity peaked, I decided to take a look to see how it was covered up. Looking closely at that window from the porch, in the middle of one of the small diamond-shaped panes of glass, I found a neat round hole. A bullet hole!

After that discovery, I made up story after story about how that bullet hole came to be, involving gangsters, robbers and spies. My dad had always said that he didn't know anything about it, but I wasn't so sure. Someday, I told myself, Agent Marty would crack the case.

But there was another mystery! Like a vain mistress, our house had kept its age a secret. My dad had grown up in that house, but no one knew when the house was built or who built it. I always took our family home on the corner for granted, so imagine the surprise when we found out that our house didn't even exist, officially anyway, on any map or tax roll. We didn't learn about its invisibility until the seventies when the new city sewer was being installed right next to the foundation. My dad asked the crew why they weren't hooking the sewer up to the house. The foreman looked at his plans, then looked at the house and said, "that house isn't supposed to be there." My dad was amazed to discover it was not on the tax rolls or on any city maps. The big house right next to a busy road was hidden in plain sight as far as the local township was concerned. In all those years it had never been assessed, and there had apparently never been any taxes paid.

Looking south in 1924 on the Lake Road (now Capital Avenue) with our Country Club Drive home on the left.

I always thought that someday, when I was a grown-up and living in that house, I'd shake its old bones and solve those mysteries. Maybe I'd start with that big white hollow banister at the top of the stairs. Surely there would be a note in an old bottle hidden inside it, or the plans for the house rolled up inside. When I was older, I would tear apart that banister, or find something written inside the walls, or maybe find the bullet lodged in the wall somewhere. I now know, 100 years after my grandparents moved into the house, that I'll have to find those answers another way. But I did find out a lot, and here's just a beginning of what I did find…

The house was built soon after the turn of the 20th century, as it was the home for the caretaker of the Post country estate known as Calmary Farm. Yes, that was the same Post family who'd invented Post Toasties and Grape Nuts. It was situated a few miles out of town on the corner of a quiet country dirt lane which eventually became known as Country Club Drive. Over the years the house had at least four different addresses, finally ending up with the house number of 'One' because it was about as close to the corner as any house could get. It was almost a gatehouse except it was a big, solid two-

www.onecountryclubdrive.com

story, four-bedroom Dutch Colonial-style home. The white clapboard siding and large porch had a barn-like charm which fit well into the rural country. The house was discreetly built on the grounds of the Post estate, I'm guessing without any permits or approvals. This explains the continuing mystery about when the house was built and by whom since there is no record of its construction and it never officially existed.

My grandpa Andy Peck is plowing the field across Country Club Drive from our house.

It became the Peck family home in 1919, when the private country club purchased the site of the Post estate and started building their new course there. Seen here, plowing the field on the other side of Country Club Drive is my grandpa Andy Peck, the first Peck to live in the house. As a teamster he had been working at the old nine-hole course in town, mowing and maintaining the course with his team of horses. Because he was well-liked by members of the old course, he was asked to stay on as the greenskeeper to help build and maintain the new golf course. Grandpa Andy had just married my

grandma, Rena Post, in the fall. In the spring, the new couple, along with their three step-children, moved into their new home, the former estate caretaker's house on the corner.

One Country Club Drive in 1921, with Everett, Philip and Shirley Peck in front yard

The house had a porch along the east side, and inside paralleling the porch was a large living room. The entry hall and stairway to the second floor were in the middle. The dining room and kitchen on the west faced the course just off the second tee. Upstairs there were four bedrooms and a bathroom around a central hall. The lower level exterior was clad in white clapboard siding, while the second level was sided in dark green shingles; the roof had light green shingles. When built, the home had a coal furnace, wood stove, electricity and running water - pumped up from the lake. In the photo above, the biggest bedroom and dining room are closest; the kitchen is toward the right. When they were married, Andy

had four-year-old Philip and six-year-old Andrew II (known by his middle name, Everett), and Rena had one-year-old Shirley, the three shown here in the front yard. Andy and Rena had four more children together, raising seven children in that home. Three of their kids, Roy, Harold and Les, became Golf Course Superintendents.

That house at One Country Club Drive would become our family's home for the next 91 years!

But like I mentioned our family home wasn't really ours. Since it had initially been part of the C.W. Post summer estate and was quite literally on the golf course, it technically belonged to the club.

Growing up I never realized that my folks didn't own it because to me it had always been "our" house. My dad, Harold Peck, grew up playing in that same big yard as I did - the golf course. My father was born there, worked there and lived almost all of his 88 years there, right off the second tee. At one time or another, we all played, worked and lived at One Country Club Drive.

And a Family Legacy...

You might think that growing up on a private golf course with so much family history would inevitably lead to a career in golf; becoming a famous golf pro, or a greens superintendent, or a landscape architect, or maybe even owning a golf club. Spending my formative years on a golf course should have undoubtedly been a golden opportunity to become

Harold Peck posing for a photo next to #18 Green.

7

involved in the ancient sport. That's what happened to my dad, and I thought he had the best job in the world. He got to be outside as much as he wanted, surrounded by beautiful scenery. He got to be the boss and tell people what to do; building and fixing things, driving all sorts of complex equipment and having a lot of fun. As a young kid, I couldn't imagine doing anything else when I grew up. I always pictured myself being the course superintendent, living in the same house, raising my own family there, and becoming just like my dad (even though I hated the part about getting up early in the morning). I probably should have grooved a perfect swing too, but I thought I could figure that out later. To me, the adult world could wait; right then I was having some crazy adventures or another, in a backyard that was bigger and better than most…my dad's golf course.

My dad didn't actually own the golf course; it was really just the opposite. The course owned him…and us. To me, it always was and always will be Dad's golf course. As the Golf Course Superintendent of a private country club, he was in charge of making the grass grow and then cutting it down to make a perfect playing surface. The Superintendent is a buck-stops-here person who gets blamed when the grass isn't green, or when it's too wet, or too tall or doesn't lay right. When the ball didn't go where it was supposed to, which is most of the time, it was easy for golfers to blame the playing conditions. If the greens are too fast or too slow, it was my dad's fault. There's an old saying: when you're the one in charge, you get the blame. He never complained about that aspect of the job, but I know it was always there with him.

Nevertheless, he relished his work, and especially loved the trees and being outdoors. He enjoyed keeping the course beautiful, maintaining the equipment, supervising, planting, trimming, building and remodeling the turf, and the appreciation of the players. Like a happy warrior, he had to battle bugs, weather and disease, all with a tight budget. The biggest challenge was keeping the entire membership happy, all three hundred of them!

Amazingly, not only did he manage to keep them happy most of the time, but he also stayed good friends with most. This was the era when the care of the golf links had transitioned from the old-style instinct and artisanship of the Greenskeeper to the science and technology of the Golf Course Superintendent. In the early history of golf and in the old English tradition, knowing how to play the game was nothing special, but to be the keeper of the greens was to be revered and honored. In modern times, the profusion of private clubs had turned the sport more elitist, and those who maintained the

course became less respected and more subservient. If there was an overly wet or a dry year, or an outbreak of a disease or fungus diminishing the beauty or playability, the superintendent took the blame and was occasionally let go because of it. Through his hard work, congeniality and steady emotions my father was able to remain at his job, from the time he took over after my grandfather's unexpected death, till the time he retired at age 65, for a remarkable 41 years.

I didn't realize any of that as a kid growing up on the golf course. I only knew that my dad got to work at a place where most people came to play. We didn't get to go on vacations like most families, since most of the year my dad always had to stay home. Spring meant winter cleanup, spraying, getting the water system turned on, planting flowers, and preventing eager players from damaging the new grass. Summer required constant mowing, raking, watering, more spraying, getting ready for tournaments, and keeping a close eye on the weather. Fall included mowing, watering, tree work, still more spraying, aerating and remodeling. Winter was about painting, fixing and sharpening. I was in school during winter, and besides, we didn't have the money for a big vacation. But that was pretty much okay with me; I had the best yard to play in that a kid could ever hope for.

This story is about our family, and about growing up and working at a private country club. In a way, it's a testament to those who work behind the scenes on the game of golf. Yes, I experienced a lot of "Caddy Shack" escapades, but this is no epic about winning a golf tournament. Rather, it is about living around the game of golf, in the shadows, and the fun and misfortunes while working and playing around on the course.

My name is Marty. This is my tale about three generations working on the same golf course, and about deciding whether to follow a father's footsteps and preserve a family legacy…

Marty Peck working on course in 1975.

A THIRD GENERATION ON COUNTRY CLUB DRIVE

Pounding Holes and other Early Memories…

I am going to start these stories in the middle. That's when I "started" near the end of 1954, joining my older sister as the third generation of Pecks in the house. My father Harold was born there in October of 1922. He married Jayne Hosimer on the last day of 1944, a date selected for two reasons: their friends were home on leave from the war, plus very conveniently their reception merged with New Year's Eve celebrations. They lived in the other house on club property called the 'cottage,' while he worked as Grandpa's assistant. When Grandpa died unexpectedly in 1947, my dad was asked to take over the course. The young couple moved in at One Country Club Drive along with their new daughter Andrea. They joined the household of my Grandma Rena, my Aunt Winifred and my Uncle Les, who were still living in the house after Grandpa's death. The situation was chaotic time with my young mom taking over household duties from my grandmother who had ruled the roost for years.

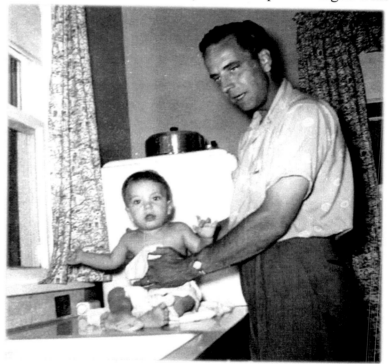

Harold is giving son Marty a bath in the old kitchen.

By the time I came on the scene seven years later, the house was less crowded since my Uncle Les and Aunt Winifred had moved out, giving my grandma, my sister and me our own rooms. My mom told stories about my dad running out the front door to show off his newborn son to people waiting in their car at the corner. With the front door

just twenty feet from the stop sign on Country Club Drive, there was a unique intimacy between cars waiting at the intersection and my family. He must have done that a lot since he knew just about everyone driving on the road.

The first memory I have of the house, like many first memories, is one of fright. I must have been three or four, when for the first time my dad took me down in the basement to the "men's" shower. Talk about a rite of passage! This shower was a simple and crude arrangement with three walls, a shower head, and a hole chopped in the floor for a drain. It was time for me to be a man, so with some excitement and even more anxiety, into the basement we went. I was finally grown up enough to take a shower, rather than bathing like a baby in the tub in the single upstairs bathroom. My initial excitement at being a big boy was slowly turning to fear as we went into the dark, creepy basement. I'm sure desperation drove my grandpa to cobble up the shower; no doubt he was tired of sharing the single bathtub in a house that held ten people. As if the rough cement floor, exposed ceiling wood joists, rust marked walls, and lots and lots of cobwebs were not enough, it was where the water went when my dad turned on the shower that really set me off…

It disappeared down into a hole in the floor; a simple, raggedy-edged GIANT hole. He told me not to step in it; no problem! No way would I even go near it. The water swirled around on the floor and went into the hole, carrying soap bubbles and all down under the house. It seemed big enough to suck me down under the floor, into who knows what dungeon: I was terrified. Then there seemed to be a cataract of water gushing into my eyes so now I couldn't see the hole. I was petrified, frozen in the corner of that blasted shower with my face jammed against the wall trying to keep from getting water in my eyes. I was horrified that I couldn't see the hole and might get washed down under the house. Tears mixed with the water as I cried, angry mostly at myself for being afraid!

Marty helping build the "Back Room" onto the house

11

My first remodeling project was helping my dad build an addition on the back of the house. My mom had always wanted to get the laundry room out of the basement and have more storage for the kitchen and our many kid coats. And could my dad please create a decent back door and patio space. The back door from the kitchen originally led to an awkward tiny vestibule with a tacked-on step. My parents were constantly having company which always came through that narrow back door. At about four-years-old, I got to help my tolerant father, as he built this snug little sixteen by fourteen shed addition on the back of the house. I remember trying to pound nails and hitting my front tooth with a hammer, causing some momentary panic, right as the photo on the previous page was taken.

This additional room became vitally important to my mom and dad, not only as the laundry room and coat closet but also as the primary entertainment focus – the cocktail bar. Whenever there was a party, which seemed like all the time to my childhood self, the booze came out of the cupboard there and was set up right on the washer and dryer. The "Back Room" became the main entry and first stop as everyone came into the house.

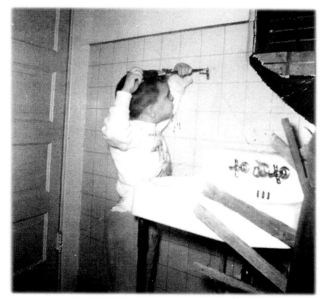
Marty pounding holes to help remodel the bathroom.

A year or so later I got some revenge of sorts on my scary basement shower. With much childhood glee and destructive satisfaction, I was "helping" my dad remodel the bathroom by pounding holes in the house. He was going to add a real shower to the upstairs bathroom, and I insisted on helping — no more spooky basement shower for me. Being a typical little boy, I went at it with a vengeance, pounding holes into the walls with my tiny hammer: dust, plaster and old plastic tiles flew everywhere. Of course, I caused more damage than I helped, but I think that was alright with my parents.

My dad was typically frugal, always trying to save the club money, and he was probably told he couldn't spend anything anyway. For our remodeled bathroom, he re-used the matching blue toilet, sink and tub taken from the other house on club property, the cottage. He built a big cabinet for the

sink vanity by hand. With seemingly very little effort (to me), the bathroom was quickly completed. For years I thought all there was to remodeling was pounding holes in the wall and the room would magically complete itself. After that, I came up with all sorts of grand remodeling schemes for my dad like putting a fireplace in the living room or fixing up the kitchen.

I can see why my grandpa built a shower in the basement out of desperation. My teenage sister was nine years older, so as I grew up, I frequently waited to get into that single bathroom. It's hard to imagine ten people (my grandparents and seven kids plus a boarder) surviving out of one bathroom, but it was common back then. Even with just five of us that single bathroom was a bottleneck. When my parents had friends over for a party that single bathroom became a huge issue.

What was worse, it seemed like every time during parties and on holidays, the sewer or the toilet would plug up; a spectacularly disruptive and smelly event. This caused my mom, who I always thought of as a neat-nik, no end of consternation. To her, whatever was wrong was always my dad's fault. Many times, I remember flushing the toilet and watching it overflow out onto the floor, but in my defense, I don't remember doing it on purpose. When the toilet overflowed onto the bathroom floor, it had to go somewhere, often staining the

Kitchen cleanup at a family house party, about 1960.

ceiling in the entry hall downstairs. The worst I remember was sitting at the kitchen table when someone flushed the toilet upstairs, and brown water came bubbling up out of the kitchen sink all over the counter and into the silverware drawer. Of course, my mom totally freaked, and my dad spent the rest of the day cleaning out the pipe and then cleaning up the smelly mess in the kitchen. I couldn't help but start to warbling: "Up from the ground came a bubbling crude…black gold, Texas tea." for the next few days because it looked just like I had seen on TV. That mess caused more than a few harsh words between my parents. Not surprisingly, my dad's next project was the installation of a new septic tank system.

Friends, Family and Parties…

Almost every day there would be friends or family stopping by to visit. With the house at the beginning of the drive right next to the intersection, everyone passing by couldn't help but think of my folks. They all knew my parents would make them welcome. Any cars in the driveway served as magnets so even more people would stop in believing something was going on at the Peck house. Our guests might be relatives, club members or old friends, but almost every day someone was visiting. It seemed most of the time they stopped by unannounced, even walking into the house

Three cousins in a tub

without ringing the doorbell. I don't know how many times I'd be watching TV in the living room at the other end of the house when somebody would walk into the room unannounced. Tinkerbell, our

Shirley, Andi, Jayne with granddaughter Jennifer, Winifred and Rena at garden, with #2 Tee behind

little dachshund who was always in my mom's lap or curled up at the hot air register, would let loose a barking barrage. My mom kept our house spotless, and all my toys were picked up right away. I grew up thinking that it was normal to leave your door unlocked and have people just walk right in.

My mom said they had so many visitors because they were midway between everything, Chicago and Detroit or down south and up north, but I didn't believe that was really it. I know it was because my folks always made everyone feel so welcome! It wasn't so much like we had a huge family, but I think everyone felt very close to my parents. It seemed everyone was always coming to visit Aunt Jayne and Uncle Harold, and my folks loved every minute of it.

Growing up I always wondered if the big attraction was the golf course or riding the golf carts. Sometimes friends and family would go out golfing, either just hitting a few balls or playing 9 holes. Me? I was convinced the real attraction was going for a ride in my dad's 3-wheeled utility Trucksters, and I was happy to oblige by taking everyone for a tour. At gatherings years later, everyone still talks about the time they toured the golf course on the Cushman Trucksters.

My niece Jen is ready to take Cousin Kelly Cook and sister Steph (on fender) for a ride.

My parents had tons of friends who always visited, like my mom's sorority Beta Sigma Chi and her church circle. Whenever I went anywhere with my dad, I was amazed that he seemed to know everyone in town; we couldn't go anywhere without him stopping to talk with old friends. Even the salesmen that called on him became more than work friends.

Family and Friends – A Huge Cast of Characters…

I really should mention all the names of our family and friends here, as they helped make One Country Club Drive such a warm and happy place. Hopefully those I've left out understand that it would take a book to mention everyone and not be offended.

My dad grew up with his brothers Roy and Les and sister Winifred. Roy's kids are Ron, Randy and Brenda; Les' kids are Debbie, Tim, Nikki, Tammi and Mitzi; Winifred's family is Linda, Rick, Karen, Amy and Melanie and their many children. My dad's stepsister Shirley was there often, sometimes with her kids Russ and Bill. My dad's stepbrother Phil died when I was young; Stepbrother Andrew ran Peck's Rock Shop nearby, which was a favorite visit.

My mom's brother Bob and his wife Ruby, and their kids Bobby, Sandy and MaryLynn and nieces and nephews visited often. My mom's cousins, Gloria (Dody) Cook and Joan Wiant, were like close sisters, and we were always getting together with their extended families; Dody and Glenn and their kids Steve, Ed, Doug, Ray and Kelly Cook; Joan and Dave with their kids Mike, Chris, Eric and Su Wiant. You can see we hung around a lot in that photo of three babies in the bathtub; myself and cousins Su Wiant and Steve Cook.

Numerous close friends included Smokey & Mickey Stover, Rock & Lee Martin, Margaret & Wayne Jordan, Ken & Evelyn Ellerton, Norma Mayo, the Kools, the Clarks, the Nesbits, the Burnhams, the Radebaughs, the McNallys, the Scotts, the Kerrs, the Morses, and the Dukes, and many, many others…

*Peck "golf course" cousins (CW from left) -
Marty, Andi, Tim, Ron, Randy and Deb*

My parents were also great friends with many club members. Some of these were hunting buddies who stopped regularly. At Christmas, everyone visited to see the Big Tree and my mom's tasteful decorations. Many dropped off a fifth or two of Seven-Crown or Martini (my namesake). By the end of the holiday, their bar in the back room was overflowing with new bottles of booze.

And then there were the real parties, big affairs that amazed me with lots of food and drink. My mom was great at organizing fancy parties; she had the right serving dishes, great food and decorations. Sometimes they borrowed the club's ornate decorations. Cleverly, my mom often organized a

party soon after a themed affair was held at the club (never let Valentine decorations be underused). I don't know if they had "beatnik" parties at the club though, but I was shocked to see them like this...

Harold and Jayne are getting in character for another party.

16

Sad to get sent away for the big Halloween party

One memorable party was on Halloween. I was sent to my Uncle Roy's maintenance shop at the Kalamazoo Country Club to help pick up his coffin – yes, a real coffin. My dad and I set it up right in our living room. Mom had stuffed clothes to fashion a person with a pumpkin head lying in the coffin. I was also commissioned to carve a bunch of giant pumpkins that my dad grew in the garden. As usual though, I was sent off overnight to someone's house and missed out on the real fun. It always amazed me the number of people they could fit into that house. As a kid, I wondered if it might collapse…

A Few Firsts...

Until my sister Andi moved out when I was nine, my bedroom was the smallest one, in the quietest corner of the house toward the golf course and away from the roads. One of my earliest memories in that bedroom is of a dream I had during the mandatory afternoon naps. It was my first crush, although an imaginary one. In the dream I was on a magical old street with brick buildings and sidewalks, standing next to a very old decorative streetlight. It was nighttime, I think when the most beautiful girl I'd ever seen rode up on a horse. This dream was particularly unusual for at this very early age I had no interest whatsoever in girls. But this girl fascinated me. She was like a princess with blond hair riding this big horse, and I was totally infatuated. She spoke to me though I don't remember the magical words. I woke up astounded and so moved that I was in tears. I ran downstairs to tell my mom all about it, and then I spent the rest of the day in frustration trying to get back to sleep so I could see her again. I think, later on in life, that I did really meet her, but that comes later in the story.

One of the favorite things in my bedroom was an ancient phonograph player I'd found in the attic, quite a treasure for a six-year-old. Late one morning it was raining, and I had to stay in, so I was playing a record and watching the storm out the window. Suddenly, I was knocked off the bed by a huge explosion and blinding flash. I was sure the house had been hit by lightning and ran screaming "We've been hit; we've been hit." I got to the top of the stairs and almost...and I remember thinking this through in slow motion...I almost jumped down the long stairway to get to the bottom landing, so desperate was I to quickly get to safety. But something stopped me, and I ran down the stairs lickety-split to the kitchen where my mom and grandmother were working, still screaming "We've been hit." That terrified little kid was sure the house was going to burn up or explode.

Bolts of Lightning Damage Houses Here

The bolt that struck the home occupied by Andrew Peck, country club caretaker at the main entrance to the club, about 5 p. m., followed wiring into the residence to a second floor bedroom and down the electric light wire above the bed and into the bed, setting fire to bedding and mattress. The room was unoccupied at the time.

My mom and grandma were cool as cucumbers; they'd been through this before and knew the house hadn't been hit; instead, lightning had struck one of the towering elm trees surrounding our house. Sure enough, when I went outside later there was a naked strip of bark spiraling down the elm across the driveway from my bedroom, not twenty feet from where I'd sat. That was the first of many close encounters with lightning. Grandma tried to calm me down telling me the story of when lightning did strike the house years ago, coming in an antenna wire my dad had put up, and causing a small fire. I did not calm down!

And there was a day my dad was elevated to super hero status after he came home to pick me up and said we were going for a ride. He made it sound like a big deal, but all we did was drive across the golf course. Why that was anything special; I would soon learn. Just past the Halfway House and #5 Tee, sitting near the edge of the course was an honest-to-gosh helicopter. I'd never even seen one before since they were very unusual in the early sixties.

Scarcely believing my ears, my dad said we were going for a ride! One of the member's sons was a pilot and had asked Dad if he could land it on the course while visiting. Amazed and excited, I climbed in and sat in the middle

A helicopter awaits Harold and Marty next to the 5th Tee.

Helicopter view of One Country Club Drive, surrounded by giant elm trees, in 1962

19

between my dad and the pilot. The engine started with a whine. I couldn't believe it as the rotors over my head started spinning around, and then with a roar, we quickly sprang up in the air. I was inside this little flying bubble hovering above the golf course. Dad was pretty excited too, taking pictures every couple of minutes.

We flew around over the course, Goguac Lake, my school - my entire childhood world. And then the pilot pointed to the stick and motioned for me to take it. I wrapped my hand around the grip, but fear kept me from moving it much at all. Cautiously, I wiggled the stick, but I still regret not pushing it around to really fly the helicopter and see what would've happened. But I did indeed have a great story to tell my friends.

Always a Big Christmas…

Of course, there were many other wonderful memories of growing up on One Country Club Drive. Christmas was always a big event, crowned by a massive 9-1/2-foot-tall tree that

Maybe bigger wasn't always better…

Marty helping decorate about 1956.

seemed to fill a quarter of the living room. My mother supervised its decoration more tightly than the Macy's Christmas windows designer. During the holidays all of my parent's friends and our relatives stopped by to see it and marvel at my mom's artistic decorating.

20

Mom didn't allow any clumps of tinsel on her tree. When I was really little and anxious to get the tree finished, I'd toss handfuls onto the tree. Mom removed the messy wads and reapplied one strand at a time. Each year I begged for a bigger tree, even pestering my dad to cut a hole in the ceiling to have the top stick through into my bedroom. From the time I was a toddler until my dad could no longer put up the tree, our Thanksgiving weekend ritual was to pick out the tree from a nursery; for over 50 years. I consider myself most fortunate...

Artfully wrapped presents always filled the living room.

Every year, my mother wrapped the mounds of presents so artfully that it was really a shame to tear them open. She thought nothing of spending an hour on one present, gluing on little somethings or making fancy bows and ribbons. She set up her wrapping room set up as early as September. With my dad's help, she'd install racks of ribbons, boxes of bows and decorations and dozens of rolls of paper. My mom bought presents all year and stashed them, but rarely could she successfully hide them all. One year I "discovered" a few and she explained how finding them ahead of time spoiled the surprise and the giving. I never snooped again.

A tree of my own

It seemed every year there were more and more presents, stacked all around the living room and even spreading into rooms beyond. Like all good fathers at that time, one Christmas my dad built me a terrific train set; an American Flyer S-gauge set with two loops, an X crossing and two switches - I was in 6-year-old heaven. Spreading Christmas cheer, a few years later I got to have my own Christmas tree for my bedroom.

Christmas decorating was always a Peck family tradition. My Uncle Les was almost maniacal. Les took strings of colored bulbs used to light the skating rink at the beach in the winter and strung those lights in the oak tree at the corner next to the house. In the early 1930s, the house had one of the earliest outdoor light decorations around.

We didn't have a fireplace to hang stockings, but this bookcase my dad built for the front hall was always filled with Christmas decorations. It always worked really well to hang our stockings, and there was plenty of room for all the goodies that spilled over.

Stockings in the bookcase at the bottom of the stairs were always well-stuffed at Christmas.

Andy and Rena's 1940 Christmas featured a faux fireplace.

In the '60s, Dad started building large cutout decorations based on patterns he could buy from Popular Mechanics. He'd pasted them onto big sheets of Masonite and then cut out the characters. The cutouts included a big Santa in a sleigh with all the reindeer. Every year, my dad - the greens keeper turned Santa - hauled those up on the clubhouse roof. For our house, it became a tradition to "put out the carolers," five half-size cutouts of Dickens-like characters which survived fifty years and two, short-lived abductions. In the photo on the next page, their heads are barely visible above the snow in the spotlight to the left.

The "Christmas Carolers" under the light at left were almost buried in this 1973 snowstorm.

Soon after I graduated, Dad and I brought a new tree decorating scheme to town, and we began the yearly ritual of wrapping the branches of the dogwood tree next to the driveway with a couple thousand lights. Every year we spent hours going over that tree to fix or add lights. The compliments my folks received made it well worth the effort. I am always amazed at how many people in town remember that tree and the carolers.

Why was Christmas so special for my parents and why did they make it so special for my sister and me? My mom didn't have much when she was young. Both grew up during the Great Depression when a gift of anything was exceptional. Christmas was always very special for both my parents, and every year I knew they were remembering their childhood holidays, making sure we had an even better one.

Getting Too High...

As a kid, I'd always wanted to string Christmas lights in the golf course trees, especially the three giant spruce trees between the house and the #2 Tee. Grandpa Andy and Aunt Winifred planted them, and I always thought maybe they were symbols for the three brothers, Roy, Harold and Les. By the time I was around, they had grown into incredibly tall trees perfect for climbing. They were at least three times taller than our house, with branches spaced just right for stepping up. We could climb up between them, lean against them or sit on them to rest. I named the trees the "Three Brothers."

One day when I was probably 10 years old, my cousin Steve Cook was visiting. Like a typical kid, I decided to show off and see who was more fearless. We started climbing one of the trees, pretending we were on Mt. Everest or something. We even packed snacks for the excursion.

The Three "Brothers". Cousins Steve and Marty climbed nearly to the top of the tree "brother" on the right.

Higher and higher we went. Soon the roof of the house was below us, but we were still far from the summit. It was exhilarating. I could see for miles over other trees all the way to downtown buildings and boats on the lake.

24

I made it about three-quarters of the way up, sixty feet off the ground and still going, when we were busted. My mom came out the back door and started hollering for us, wondering where we were? I should have kept quiet, but being proud of our exploit I yelled down to her. She looked up and almost fainted! She started screaming and yelling that we had to get down from there - Right Now! For a short moment I thought how free and independent we were, and she couldn't make us climb down. Wrong. She threatened to call the fire department…you know, the "if you don't get down from there right this minute, I'm going to call…" etc. tone. She called in reinforcements - my dad, who rushed home from work to convince her that we were okay as we climbed down as slowly as possible. We got the chewing out we deserved, but Dad calmed her down and made me promise not to climb that high again. A few days later I noticed the bottom branches had been trimmed off.

Gang of Three…

Long before I was old enough to work with my dad, I was part of a gang of three boys growing up on the course. Pictured here is Bobby LaParl (right), son of golf Pro Ron LaParl, Lon McNally (middle), the (then) club president's son and me, the greenskeeper's son. Our dads were all best of friends, so of course we were best friends too. I don't recall the gang forming… it just always was. Lon lived in a big house in the woods between the lake and dad's maintenance shop. His home was newer and quite fancy, but as a kid all that meant anything to us was the cool secret room off Lon's bedroom closet. Bobby's house sat on the same short, private road along the lake, next to the clubhouse and just across the

The Three Stooges of Country Club Drive - Marty Peck, Lon McNally and Bobby LaParl (right)

parking lot from the shop. His home was a drafty old two-story house called "the cottage," part of the original estate on which the club was built, just like my family's home.

Looking back, my dad was amazingly tolerant of the mischief we three cooked up, and we cooked up a lot of it. No doubt he remembered what it was like to grow up on the same 120-acre backyard, with tractors and trucks, a beach and a big lake. Later I learned from my dad's stories, he too had a couple of best friends - his own gang of three.

Dad called us the Three Musketeers, Three Stooges or a few other names depending on what we were up to. I was a grade ahead of Bob and Lon, but only because my birthday was on the very last day you could get enrolled. So, I started school a few months after everyone else feeling like an outsider, which didn't help me get over my shyness. Even though we were basically the same age, the three of us rarely hung around together at school because of that great divide between grades.

After school was a different story though. We were always building something, or tearing something apart, or planning to do one of those things. We had our own clubhouse, many forts, and even our own private golf cart to drive around to keep watch over our supposed territory. At the early age of nine, I was just getting out into the neighborhood, with the new-found independence of a bike. Even though I was not allowed play out on the course and was under general orders to stay out of the members' sight, we were three imaginative kids who still got into lots of mischief and found plenty of unusual places to explore around the country club.

"Marty's Gonna Die..."

Give a kid a dog; what could possibly go wrong? When I was about five, my parents took me on a long drive to their close friend Shelloy's house in Indiana, where we picked up our newest family member, Tinkerbell. She was a cute miniature dachshund who was supposed to be my dog - teach me responsibility and all that stuff. Tinkerbell never got that memo. My mom did all the care, feeding and training. Despite coaxing her to sleep in my bed, she was devoted entirely to my mom, and vice versa. After bringing her up to my bed, Tinker would tunnel under the sheets to escape back downstairs as fast as her short little legs could go, anxious for popcorn or whatever snack might be happening

downstairs. However, one thing that disgusted my mom was taking her sweet Tinkerbell out gopher hunting. When Tinker and I walked on the course, gophers dove for the nearest, deepest hole.

Tinker loved gopher hunting more than eating. I'd get a bucket of water or a hose, and we'd go out in the backyard (which could be anywhere on the golf course) looking for little heads sticking up or listening for the distinctive chirrup sound. Gophers and golf courses are not compatible at least not from the human perspective. Dogs try to dig them out of their holes by making major excavations foot deep or more. The gophers also leave substantial mounds of dirt around their holes, which are sometimes so large golf balls roll down into them. We two brave little hunters would approach a hole, or Tinker would find one and stick her long snout down the hole and kind of point. That sweet little dog trembled a bit with excitement as I poured water down the hole. When that gopher's head popped

Jayne is holding our dachshund, Tinkerbell, who was a veteran "gopher-hound".

up, faster than you could blink, Tinker snatched the head, pulled it out of the hole and violently shook that rodent. The hapless gopher was dispatched to the big golf course in the sky with a resounding crunch.

Once it was dead Tinkerbell was all business; the gopher was dropped, and she moved on quickly to the next hole. Usually she stuck close to me, but one particularly memorable day she caught a gopher all by herself while tied up next to the house. I was upstairs as my mom went to let her in. Very proudly, Tinkerbell showed off her solo kill; she was holding a dead gopher in her mouth. My mom, who wasn't in on our usual routine, grabbed that dog and shook her, yelling at her and trying to get her to drop the dead rodent. Tinker wouldn't have any of that because that just wasn't the way we did

things. Instead, she swallowed the dead gopher – whole! Mom freaked out, screaming at the dog, and at me. She finally calmed down and let her little killer lap dog inside.

That is not the end of the story… A few minutes later, my mom started screaming again…Tinkerbell had tossed up the slimy dead gopher, right on the living room carpet! …Didn't hear the end of that for a long, long time…

Lon and Bob also enjoyed the hunt with us. I was down near the clubhouse with Tinker one afternoon, and Bobby had an idea to put one of the big five-gallon glass water jugs used for distilled battery water on the back of a golf cart for a portable supply of water. We strapped it in and drove out to the practice tee, where Bobby stuck a rubber garden hose down inside the bottle and started filling it. We were standing nearby as the jug was almost filled, when suddenly there was a big explosion and water and glass were flying everywhere. Apparently when the hose was turned on it expanded enough to effectively seal the top of the glass jug, and the pressure built up, bursting the bottle and sending shards of glass flying all over the Practice Tee.

Shocked and astounded, we looked around and gathered our wits. I was worried that Tinker had been hit and bent down to check on her. I saw my own bloody hand but thought at first that Tinker had been hurt when Lon pointed to my shoulder and said: "Man, you're bleeding all over the place!" Suddenly I didn't feel too good, but my buddies quickly mobilized and took charge, so to speak. Lon hopped in a cart and went racing home to my house to tell my parents. Soon after, Bobby grabbed another cart and followed taking me back with Tinker clutched in my arms.

By the time I got home, boy and dog were both quite the bloody mess. Lon had gotten there a few minutes earlier, screaming those infamous words that my mother will never forget - "Marty's gonna die; Marty's gonna die!" Apparently, a cut near the shoulder joint bleeds very well. I remember even my underwear was soaked. My folks got me cleaned up and off to the emergency room for a few stitches, and a scar that I still carry. Someone was definitely looking out for me.

For many years, Tinker and I continued to catch gophers. As I got older and needed spending money, I worked out a deal with my dad to get a 10-cent bounty per gopher. I'm sure dad expected that to add up to a dollar or so. Not so; with potential wealth in sight, I streamlined the process. Instead of dragging the hose around or running back and forth with a bucket, I put the big water tank on the Truckster and

drove around the course with a few hundred gallons and a hose for our bazooka. It was a drive-up massacre. I cruised from one gopher hole to the next, sometimes not even getting off the seat; just inserting the hose in the hole. Tinker's nose would follow the end of that hose like a bloodhound. We made quite a team, clearing out not only the area behind our house but also nearly the whole front end of the course. In one record-setting afternoon, we caught over a hundred gophers! Tinkerbell was exhausted, but I think she would have kept on going until she dropped.

Stump's Shack and Big Jim…

Between Bobby and Lon's houses on Jennings Lane next to the clubhouse was club member Howard Rich's house. Only adults lived there, and, therefore, we stayed away from their house. But on the other side of the road were some extensive woods where we always played, and a big yard and gardens that had at one time been elegant but were now mostly overgrown ruins. Our ideal adventure world was filled with ancient impenetrable secrets. Rich's father was one of the original members who had helped move the country club to its current lakeside location. Naturally, he selected a choice location on the lake next to the clubhouse. (C.L. Post intended to build a new home there but got angry at the club organizers.) I suppose Howard was rich, too, because their yard extended way back to the dump behind the tennis courts. As a kid, we didn't think in acres, but in today's real estate parlance it would be listed as a 3-acre lakefront estate.

An overgrown dirt drive led from my dad's maintenance shop into that woods. The spot included what was left of an old vegetable garden and a giant cherry tree we climbed up and picked cherries. The drive ended deep in the trees near two old shacks. One was really a large shed for gardening tools and mowers that were still used at the formerly grand estate. The other resembled a cabin, bigger and two stories tall with a dirt ramp leading up to the front door. It had some barn doors below the front entrance, with cow paddocks inside. That seemed outlandish to us because there were no fields for cows, only woods filled with dense smaller trees. The cabin was known famously as Stump's Shack. Stories circulated it was haunted, because it was overgrown and looked creepy, but also because a man with a perfectly scary name had once lived in the shack.

When I was older, Dad told me he had known Cal Stump, and the scary stories were simply stories, more fun than reality. Mr. Stump had worked on the golf course and apparently cared for the cows (or maybe pigs) kept in the shack's lower level. As young boys, we chose to believe the scary stories instead.

Stump's Shack was visible from Lon's house. When I slept over, we'd pretend to see ghostly lights there. Which turned out to be real lights, but not for ghostly reasons. The first summer playing in those woods we met Big Jim. Big Jim was a bit scary, because he was big and because we didn't know any black men other than through our parents. At first, we thought he was a bit creepy, but after we got to know him over the summer, we learned he was just a regular old guy. Big Jim was the current caretaker for what was left of Rich's fancy yard. He hung around Stump's Shack a lot, sometimes taking naps. He let us play around there, and we kept an eye out for him in case anyone came around. We did find a couple of girlie magazines of his which was very enlightening at our early age. Lon and I even got a couple of kerosene lanterns from there that must have been headlights from an old car.

Early course workers Cal Stump, Herman Verdine and Dave Harper are sifting dirt at bunker between #1 Fairway and Country Club Drive in 1943.

Once upon a time, Stump's Shack must have been nice inside with its little kitchen and toilet. By the time we arrived, it smelled awful; a terrible combination of sour, mold and fuel oil. The oil smelled so bad because someone had broken the pipe leading to the little oil burner in the middle of the shack. Still, being at that age where staying out of sight was critical, a hangout for our gang was needed. The shack would make a magnificent fort, so one summer we started to fix up the place by cleaning out the trash. After a couple of days of work, everyone began to realize that repairs would not be simple and it would always stink of fuel oil, so a different grand plan was needed. While the three of us were great at planning all sorts of projects, we were somewhat short on perseverance and action. We needed another fort, so we could plan for an even better fort.

Defending the Fort…

In the woods nearby were the remnants of an ancient tree fort. At our young age, anything that wasn't from the present was prehistoric. Up in this giant oak where the branches spread were some time-worn boards, with steps nailed into the tree to reach the fort. With new boards, nails, saw and hammer from the maintenance shop, we went to work on the next phase of our small empire. Soon we had a real fortress of two-by-fours that were the barest hint of walls and seats. Its most important feature was a first-class view of the tennis courts, the drive and the first hole. Progress at last!

With the hangout at Stumps Shack all but forgotten, we made new plans to build up the tree fort with camouflage and other defenses to keep out the Vikings, Martians or whatever else we imagined might invade us. We cut branches and strategically placed them to hide the boards from our imagined enemies – other kids and especially anyone at the tennis courts. After a few days, we realized those dead branch leaves were more obvious than the boards. Our next logical step was to dig up live trees and move them into the tree fort to hide things. Watering the little trees turned out to be another problem, so we moved from stealth to defense.

To stop the occasional missile from being lobbed into our fort (AKA a tennis ball), we knew we needed to retaliate. Using true kid logic, we had a Eureka moment when we thought of the best ammo: the almost inexhaustible supply of range golf balls. However, golf clubs are difficult to swing in the woods,

and at our age we were inaccurate, so a novel method of delivery was conceived…an inner tube slingshot!

I think Lon came up with the idea. It was one of our best inventions yet, an old bicycle inner tube tied between two sturdy branches that formed a 'Y.' The ball fit perfectly in the tube, and we could pull the slingshot way, way back – especially with all three of us pulling. By our calculations, we slung the ball almost as far as a tee shot and with much better accuracy. We could hit Country Club Drive which crossed our target range at least three hundred feet away. Practice ensued to target the passing cars with the assumption that if one were hit, the driver would think the ball came from the course and not notice it came from the opposite direction. Luckily for us, the combination of range and timing was beyond our abilities.

Yet another line of defense was apparently needed in case of hand to hand combat, so we made spears. We never discussed who they would be used on though, but our only casualty turned out to be a case of friendly fire. Many straight little saplings grew in the woods, so we cut some down to make six-foot-long spears and carved the ends into sharp points. Hefting them down the hill toward the tennis courts like junior Olympians tossing javelins worked well enough with decent range and accuracy. During maneuvers, I ran down the slope and was retrieving my spear right when Bobby chucked his. I heard Lon yell and looked up just in time to see Bobby's spear jab into my calf muscle. I was speared! The wound looked worse than it hurt though. The wooden spear remained stuck in my leg for a moment until Bob and Lon ran up to me. I pulled it out dramatically and asked Bobby about his thinking capability (not quite those words). I proudly notched another childhood scar, but that concluded our offensive defense.

On Rich's Ponds...

One neighborhood artifact particularly appealed to our gang. These were relics of history deep in Rich's yard - ancient fish ponds. We discovered them at an early age, and those ponds fascinated us through our childhood years. Situated a long way behind Rich's house and overgrown with shrubberies, we didn't pay any attention at first. One day Lon mentioned there was something weird about the bushes, and I started checking out a strange little crack in a mowed part of the yard between

the bushes. Curiously, the crack looked like a fissure in the earth, lined with flat sandstone rocks on both sides. We soon became like archeologists unearthing an ancient civilization. Like true adventurers, we braved the almost impassible groove through the dense, very overgrown arborvitaes. Finally, after numerous scratches and wounds, we found ourselves standing in a depression of flat concrete! We were really on to something big now. Could Martians had landed a millennium ago? What else could be so far out in the woods?

Nevertheless …in true junior scientist form, we began to study our find; I uncovered a fascinating round hole which looked like a drain in the middle of the concrete. Our vital research would need to be delayed, however, because I was already late for dinner. We made a pact to work only on solving the mystery together and agreed to meet early the next day.

I'm sure the next morning my mom wondered what was up when I left after a quick breakfast to renew our adventure. I told her I was going to the shop, so she thought I was working on something with my dad. I did stop at his shop to get necessary archeological supplies such as gloves, rakes, shovels and a trimmer, but we had a much bigger date with destiny than anything on the golf course. At the site, we began to dig out the leaves and trim back the branches to see what we had found. Over the next few days, we gradually realized that it was an old dried up pond of some sort, and, as more branches were cut back, we discovered that at one time it must have been really elaborate. The depression was surrounded by thick flat sandstone rocks arranged in layers with a stack like a tiny mountain with a hole in the top that must have been a pipe for a fountain. A little more digging unearthed a higher basin next to the stack to create a waterfall which would flow into the biggest pond. We had discovered an ancient garden pond from before time began - at least 40 years old!

About then we also realized that we had a problem. We'd made a colossal mess on Rich's land with piles of mud, leaves and branches lying out on the lawn. Even though they never used that part of their property, they did have the old caretaker Big Jim who would surely notice. We'd be in trouble. We spent the next day dragging the branches and stuff off the grass and dumping them in the nearby overgrowth. Once again, we could have been in serious trouble, but Mr. Rich knew our dads well and was apparently tolerant of us playing in his ponds when he did eventually find out. Over the rest of the summer that tolerance wore out as our continuing attempts to restore the water feature to its original glory became our mission.

Being highly industrious, I was determined to figure out where the source of the pipe that supplied the fountain at the top of the mountain. We all wanted to fill the pond with water in the worst way and would do anything to get things working. We began digging around and hunting for pipes looking under rocks and in holes, and finally…Holy Cow; I discovered a valve! But it wouldn't budge by hand. A quick run to the shop for the necessary tools and we were back at work like plumbers and managed to turn the valve. Water started bubbling out of the top of the fountain and down the side of the tiny mountain in a glorious cascade. We celebrated as the first basin began to fill with muddy water for the first time in centuries and really whooped it up when the waterfall started its cascade into the pond. We'd cracked the secret code of the ancients, and we were thrilled!

Once we plugged the drain, the pond took absolutely forever to fill. As we were cutting branches away from around the edge of the first pond a few days later, we had our first serious setback. The branches neatly hid a large nest of bees', and after we got too close, they became angry and did what bees do. Somebody started yelling, and we ran as fast as we could, swatting at bees and getting stung. Each of us archeologists-in-training needed our moms to nurse those stings. That painful episode put a severe damper on our restoration efforts.

Common sense didn't last long, and we couldn't resist the temptation of the ponds. We were back at it after a couple of days. This time we knew where their nest was, but being typical, unwise young boys, we got them stirred up again. Although too scared to finish cleaning out the branches, once they settled down, we turned the water back on, thinking that might drown them out. After a long wait, the big pond finally began to fill up, but we realized then that it still could take days to completely reach the top.

Bravely deciding to leave it on overnight, we all got up early the next day and returned to see the waterfall still working and the pond almost filled with water. It was then we discovered that the mysterious crack that began this whole epic was actually a small stream, and the water began flowing through it from our pond to lead into another pile of dense, impregnable prickly shrubs. This time we got wise; rather than wading through the thick brush and getting scratched, a wide plank was found to lay on the branches to climb over them. Slowly we edged along the board to see another set of even bigger ponds and an even higher tower of rocks. This second pond even had a wide dam across the middle with places for the water to cascade down into the lower half. Discovering the Pyramids of

34

Giza wasn't half as important as this find. It was like we had found a buried tomb full of treasure, but what happened next delayed our adventure until later that summer.

Bobby said it looked like I was trying to fly, flapping my arms up and down and spinning around. I was inside the newly discovered pond just beginning to fill with water; he was walking up from the shop with some tools. Watching me dance about he started laughing hysterically, but I didn't see anything funny about it because I was getting stung again; it was really hurting. I was yelling at Lon and Bob to get away and was angry that they were laughing. They quickly figured out what was happening when the bees found them, too. Either the water or I had stirred up an even bigger nest of bees; as messengers of the Evil Spirit guarding the pond, they were telling us to get lost. This time it was a trip to the doctor's office for me, and another week before we got up the courage to return to the ponds.

Wisely, the remaining branches were left untrimmed, but our curiosity in seeing all the waterfalls and fountains working remained. Undaunted but perhaps a little more careful, I investigated the new tower of rocks and found another hole from a pipe outlet inside. A day of excavation revealed yet another valve but opening this one did nothing; we were devastated. And now the valve for the first pond did not work either. Another setback in our quest, but we did not give up.

Being curious kids and having grown up around sprinklers and pipes, I led the investigation to fix the source of our water supply. We followed a series of wooden valve-box covers in the lawn back toward Rich's house, confirming in each that the water had been turned off. Finally, we got all the way down by the lake to the pump manhole! This was a large concrete slab with a metal cover in the center opening into a dark pit. After some debate and dares, we got the courage to climb down in, although I'm not sure who was first. Of course, the last one down threatened to close the cover and lock us in, but that was to be expected. There was just enough light to see a valve on a pipe that went to the backyard; it was closed. Of course, I opened it to the satisfying rush of water, but the sudden noise of the pump turning on had us all scrambling out of the hole. I never did find out if it was Big Jim or my dad who had turned off the water in a futile attempt to dampen our interest.

Our World in the mid 1960's - One Country Club Drive is 1/4 mile to the right; Rich's Ponds are hidden by trees.

At last, we had achieved success! Both ponds were filling slowly, but then I realized that the water and Rich's pump had to stay running to keep them flowing. We decided to risk it and hope that when they saw how beautiful the somewhat restored ponds were, the Rich's would leave them on. For the ponds to be at their finest, they must have fish, so our next task was to become ichthyologists. We were skillful minnowers; quickly lifting a towel held underwater in the lake to catch schools of minnows. Soon we had caught dozens. We stocked our ponds with the minnows and even caught a few larger fish to enjoy. All was perfect, until a few days later the water stopped. After some quick checking, we

realized that the adults had finally turned the power off to the pump from inside the house. Our summer's beautification efforts, and soon the fish, were sadly at an end.

Spy vs. Spy…

Between *Mad Magazine* and *The Man from U.N.C.L.E.* TV show, my friends and I grew up in the middle of a spy craze. We thought of ourselves as secret agents, protecting the neighborhood and golf course from a disruptive malicious element. Often that disturbing element was, in fact, the three of us, rather than the rare someone who did break into the Halfway House concession stand or cause some vandalism. Carving up a green or driving cars on the course were about the only things that really upset my dad. About once a year something serious like that happened, but most of the time he could repair any damage to make it as good as new within a few hours. I witnessed one serious incident that caused him to get really mad, and that is when we decided to become unofficial neighborhood spies.

He got a phone call early one morning and was visibly upset, so I wanted to go along to see what the trouble was. We drove out to the green on #3, and I saw that it was a mess of torn up grass, dirt and tire ruts. The back apron of the green had even been cut down into deep grooves. My dad described to me what he thought had happened as he studied the destruction. Apparently, a car had driven past the end of the nearby dead-end road and out on the golf course, and up the full length of the green. It had gotten stuck on the steep bank trying to go over the back apron of the green. To make things a whole lot worse, a heavy tow truck with dual wheels had then backed up the entire length of the green and pulled the car loose. All of this had happened overnight, and Dad was just finding out about it from the neighbors along the course. Naturally, Dad called the police. They came out and then told him

Harold is inspecting tow truck damage on #3 Green.

no one had reported the incident, including any tow truck company. Dad was furious; that was the angriest I'd ever seen him!

Later the police investigated and found the tow truck driver, and ultimately the vandals. The kids who did the initial damage had called their dads, who had apparently paid the tow driver a little extra not to report the incident. The story ended up in the newspaper since both the vandals and the tow operator got in big trouble and paid for the repairs and fines. Several weeks passed before the green returned to perfection.

That event caused the three of us to become secret agents! We were kind of in the middle of this mess anyway because our fathers were all very involved in the club. It was essential for us to help our dads keep the peace as well as learn what sort of mischief was going on. On the other hand, our friends were often the cause of the trouble. Sometimes, we were the ones at the root of whatever was going on. We had great fun being between the "good guys" and the "bad guys."

As everyone knew from television, spies need hi-tech headquarters, so building one was our first priority. Lon had a storage room in his basement which we used to assemble various equipment for our communication HQ. He had a train set with a realistic control panel that had lots of switches, dials and knobs, so we started to build around that. Lon's dad had been a pilot, and my dad had tons of cool looking junk in the shop and at our home. Our attics and basements were raided, and every imaginable space age-looking gadget was added to the mix: an unused TV, radios, wires, electrical devices, gauges, and even bubbling jars of colored water. We soon ran out of space and had to move into Lon's dad's workbench which probably didn't sit well with him, but our enthusiasm won out.

With an impressive array of electronic gadgetry stitched together with tubes and wires and even a little working television, we could begin to gather information about the goings-on in the neighborhood. Although knowing that none of these things really worked, in our wild childhood imaginations we believed that somehow when it was all put together it would magically start to function, telling us everything we wanted to know just like on TV. When that didn't happen, a new strategy was required; we needed to recruit spies and informants to be our eyes and ears around the club.

So began a program to solicit a crew of informers into our gang which was necessary to become useful spies, but turned out to be quite a challenge. A group of gullible younger recruits was needed who would believe we were, in fact, secret agents in the employ of some even more secret agency. They needed to believe that said agency was actually concerned about the activities of disruptive youths roaming the golf course and beach. By necessity, these recruits needed to be significantly younger and

fooled by the vast array of hardware at our headquarters which looked somewhere between a junk heap and a mad scientist's lair. Since we were preteens ourselves, that left a rather narrow age group old enough to be out playing without their parents around but young enough to believe what they were told. Several interested candidates were found and brought down to headquarters where we attempted to explain to them that the complex, hi-tech communications technology was disguised as a pile of junk to fool our parents. Invariably our bluff was called even by the youngest kid when they eventually asked us to make the hardware do something. We soon gave up on the recruitment plan and had to do the espionage ourselves.

TWO "GOLF DEPUTIES"

Special deputy sher..fships were granted today to E. W. Harber and Andrew Peck, for the purpose of policing the Battle Creek Country club grounds, the county clerk's office records show. Their authority does not extend outside of the club property.

The Golf Pro and Greenskeeper were deputized as early peace-keepers of the golf course in 1927.

Down at the beach we were recognizable as the sons of either the pro, club president or greenskeeper, so it was difficult to hear any tidbits or gossip from anyone. Those kids belonged to the club and weren't likely to be involved in anything terribly wrong anyway, but in our enthusiasm, everyone was a suspect. The older kids knew other older kids who weren't members, so we tried to eavesdrop, which didn't turn out so well, either. However, one day I was riding on the course with my dad and noticed a trail leading onto the golf course from a section of woods that was an entirely different neighborhood. It was near #3 Tee, part of an area at the end of the course far away from the clubhouse and shop that we hadn't yet explored. I was sure I'd discovered where all the trouble was coming from – that trail.

We decided to investigate, and that, of course, required planning. Since we were secret agents, this newfound hotbed of malicious activity needed an official designation, known forever after as Area RA. The R stood for red because it was a top-level threat and the A because it was the first. That initial step completed, we could begin assembling the necessary survival and investigation materials to take on our expedition. Every possible item that might be needed was collected and piled in Lon's attic room over the garage: rope, canteens, magnifier lens, matches, bags, notebooks, spare clothes, knives;

everything we could possibly think of was heaped up. At some point, we realized the vast mound could not practically fit into our backpacks, necessitating a few days' delay while we debated what equipment was critical enough to be required on our mission. Then we had to wait for the right day to be out on the course which was any day except Wednesday, Thursday, Friday, Saturday and Sunday.

As a gang, we'd never crossed the golf course before, so it was an excursion. Since Area RA was nearest to my house, we gathered there for lunch and another planning session. Our backyard was really the rough between the second fairway and a busy road, so we had a good excuse to be out there. We dashed around the second green and across the #3 Tee to the trail. The narrow path twisted through that woods much like our own woods then opened up into a narrow scrubby field of tall grasses and occasional small trees with houses along both sides. The trail actually ran all the way down to another road where our exploration stopped due to a lack of the required parental permissions. We weren't totally empty-handed; we found deer tracks and a little trash. Disappointed, we never did see any evidence of malicious activity coming onto the golf course from that trail, only an occasional bicycle and frequent deer, but the designation was never downgraded to yellow or orange, and there never was an Area RB. But a few summers later, I would explore that area much more quickly on the Truckster.

Radio Daze...

My interest in radio was inherited from my dad. When he was young, he had sizeable curiosity in electronics and built several gadgets. His collection included an old shortwave radio which I discovered in the fruit cellar. The radio was a beauty, a big wooden box with an ornate speaker grill and lots of tubes inside. I cleaned and hauled it up to my bedroom. When I turned it on, the tubes came to life with a respectable glow. Soon it gave off that stale hot dust smell that old electronics always smell like when they haven't been turned on for many years. Really odd noises came out of the speaker, but no voices or music like I'd expected. My dad told me I'd have to hook up an antenna wire, which all sounded very technical and exciting. I discovered a bare wire strung down the length of the attic ceiling, and my dad explained the radio was his and he'd set up the antenna when he was a kid. He said the wire even ran outside at one time, but when lightning found it, the wire became the source of the small fire mentioned earlier.

My Einsteinian alter ego was soon in business…I found more wire and ran it from the antenna in the attic through the attic stair, down the hall and into my bedroom. I turned on the old set, and after a few minutes, I could hear all sorts of fascinating new sounds; beeps, warbles and foreign voices. I was listening in on the world! I could hear really fast Morse code and other unknown codes that I was sure were spies. There were voices whose pitch rose and fell through the atmosphere sounding like science fiction, and odd gibberish that didn't make any sense.

Tuning the radio, I realized I was getting only a couple of stations that sounded like what I thought a radio station should sound like. Because I wanted to show off this neat technology and my knowhow to Lon and Bobby, I decided to tune it up. In our museum-like basement was an old tube tester my uncle had made from a kit; I hauled it out and pretended to know what I was doing by testing all the tubes. The flaw in that plan was that I needed to buy new ones and I didn't know where to get them. Genius that I supposedly was, I proceeded to take apart the radio set thinking that any faults would miraculously appear to my young technical eye. Didn't happen. The unfortunate end of this radio is that the pile of parts I created never did get put back together, and after a while, the beautiful old shortwave became a pile of junk that eventually got thrown out. My dad wasn't very happy about that. Years later I realized having that old radio would have been a classic antique and a perfect memento of my dad's youth.

Still interested in electronic gadgets and a couple of years older, I was browsing through an electronics catalog and saw an AM radio transmitter. This was really cool; I imagined operating my own radio station! When the package arrived, I opened it to find a pile of parts - it was a kit. There was something to be said about coming full circle, and this time I'd have to learn how to put it together. Undeterred, I got a soldering iron; my dad showed me a

The heart of Radio Station W-A-S-S

few tricks, and I got to work. After a week of assembly and some trial and error, I plugged it in and the tubes began to glow. I was in business…again.

I hooked a microphone and record player to the transmitter. Firing up the popular song *In-A-Gadda-Da-Vida*, I grabbed an AM portable radio and ran outside to see how far away I could transmit.

Nuts…not far at all – only a hundred feet! Remembering my dad's advice, the next step was to make the antenna larger, as the kit said by FCC regulation it could be ten feet long at most. Never one for regulations, I soon had a mile of wire running through the attic of the house, just like my dad once had. That helped a lot, but needing still more range, I played around with an antenna amplifier. At last, my range was almost a half mile! Then it was time to get into the act and become a DJ just like the real radio stations. Call letters were needed, and in a moment of true juvenile brilliance, the perfect not-so-subtle station name hit me. No one could mistake it for anyone else's but mine: W-A-S-S.

I spent the next few weeks that summer pretending to be a radio station. Unfortunately, the radio at the beach house rarely received my weak signal. And as far as I knew, Bobby was the only one who ever listened to me, which was probably for the best as I had two records and little worthwhile to say. That endeavor ended abruptly when lightning struck nearby; nothing ever worked the same again. Dad comforted me by reminding me about the wires he'd also run through the house and yard when he was about my age. He, too, found out the hard way how important grounding the antenna was so the radio wouldn't get fried due to lightning, not to mention fires. My respect for storms got a lot more respectable.

Gamblers Anonymous…

Stuck inside one rainy day, we decided to build a casino! Playing outside was no fun, and we had relocated to Bobby's basement when inspiration, fortunately, struck while playing pool. Recently the clubhouse had hosted a casino night; one of those parties where they had roulette wheels and card games set up and everyone gambled with play money. My dad had shown me the tables and games during one of our frequent lunches in the clubhouse kitchen. A famous vaudeville magician named Monk Watson had been the entertainment that night; we kids knew him because he had performed at Bobby's birthday party and was a good friend of Bobby's dad. Looking over the game setups, Dad told me there used to be several real slot machines in the clubhouse. My grandpa had even brought them home every winter and stored them in the attic.

I was fascinated with the idea that there were once slot machines in our attic. As the three of us played pool, I mentioned the machines, and a plan to build a casino formed in our collective minds. The pool

table was the centerpiece, and one of us had a toy slot machine bank. The basement room wasn't much larger than the pool table, so it was no wonder Bobby accidentally shattered the fluorescent overhead lamp with a pool cue, creating a shower of glass and mercury in his hair. That fixed the stark light fixture above the table which was too harsh for a real casino, but we made up for it with a couple of lamps. Bobby brought down his mom's toaster oven, so we could create *hors-d'oeuvres*, and I placed my toy soda dispenser along the back counter. We hung sheets to hide the rest of the basement rooms and used posters and crepe paper for décor. Our dance band was a radio.

Then we had to figure out how to gamble. None of us were that good at pool, but Bob and Lon both had tables, so they were much better players than I. We found a book to learn how to play blackjack. This was new and exciting - spending the afternoon pretending to win or lose. We learned how to play poker and had even tried craps, but that game was entirely beyond us. We practiced cheating because that's how we thought casinos worked. Now if only we had some customers…

The nearby beach at the club provided some likely clientele. To be able to pull off our scam, our victims needed to be younger than the three of us and have some cash money. With the promise of riches, we found our first gullible kid and talked him into coming down into our basement casino. I don't think he was fooled, but maybe the peer pressure from the three of us convinced him. We pushed pizza, ice cream and pop from our own make-believe restaurant, for an additional charge, of course. Not content with letting the house odds at blackjack give us the edge; we played poker with one of us peering at the kid's cards. We won little money, but the word got out quickly that everyone came away a loser. That ended our casino venture, and none of us were very happy with the result. I'm guessing Bobby's mom was happy to get her toaster oven back in one piece.

Racing Stickers for Sale…

We should have named our little gang "The Persistents"; when one venture failed, we started another. Lon's dad owned a motor parts warehouse store, and he had access to the promotional stuff that came with the world of cars and racing. He brought home advertising stickers of every size and shape, promoting motor oil, spark plugs, air filters, manifolds, carburetors and shifters. Neighborhood kids

were envious of his vast collection and always asking him for some. We decided to make money by selling these stickers, but first some advertising was required.

Let me backtrack a little... As the golf pro, Bobby's dad Ron rented out golf carts to the players. Parked in his cart barn there was an old Victor cart used mostly for parts or emergencies. The light blue cart still worked but it was a little scratched up, had an old style 'T' arm for steering, and the batteries were weak. It hadn't been rented out in years, but it was good

Our personal ride, "Victor", was completely plastered with dozens of racing stickers.

enough for our gang, so we commandeered it as our "ride." The dirt was scrubbed off; a headlight and horn from some old tractor were dug out of a junk bin in the shop and then installed on the cart. To make it go faster, we *might* have even swapped the batteries out with some of the newer ones on the regular rental golf carts.

But the *piece-de-resistance* was the stickers. For our advertising, we plastered the cart with dozens of large Pennzoil, STP, Hurst, Fram, Purolator, Holly, and Edelbrock stickers and emblems, so you could hardly see the paint. Some were huge, like the two-foot-tall Champion sticker down the middle of the back. We thought it was the coolest thing; like our own Indy car – with a top speed of eleven mph - and we appropriately named it "Victor." Lon carried his little suitcase filled with stickers for sale. We

drove up to kids in the neighborhood or along the beach and if customers saw a sticker they wanted, they bought it on the spot.

You can imagine how garish and obnoxious that cart looked, with very little of the light blue paint seen through all the stickers, and Bobby's father was not pleased. Near the end of that one great summer driving the cart around the club, his dad had had enough. Ron was especially careful with appearances, always immaculately dressed. Everything associated with the Pro Shop had to be perfect. And here was this ugly old golf cart that we were joyriding. No doubt quite a few members made comments, and our fathers were of course very sensitive to that. Early one morning, without any advance notice, our unique, personalized ride just disappeared. We were devastated, and Bobby was furious with his dad. Bobby had made this unique contribution to the gang that made him a bit special; now it was gone. We no longer had our custom ride and had to use our bicycles like other ordinary kids.

The loss of our special wheels was a severe blow to our freedom and eccentricity, and we really missed it. Over the winter we planned and planned; by spring, we had, you guessed it, a new plan. We'd badgered and convinced our dads that we deserved another cart. The good news is one of the suppliers brought us another old vehicle; the bad news is it had no motor or batteries. Undeterred, I found an old lawn mower engine with a little transmission built in that could change from forward to reverse. We figured out how to bolt that in the back where the bags usually went, found some gears and a chain to hook it up. My dad gave in and helped us by welding the motor in place. Soon we had the chain connected, and to change direction we hooked up the levers for the clutch.

The gas engine started right up, and the three of us thought we were back in business - wrong! We hopped in, pulled the clutch and the cart quickly jerked forward. It kept moving ahead at that same speed - very, very slow! Someone yelled to give it the gas. The engine revved, but the speed barely changed; it increased but only a fraction. Our new cart, at top speed, traveled as fast as a very slow walk, but had so much power it could probably climb a tree. A significant engineering error had been made: the assumption that hooking up the motor to the driveshaft with a couple of gears and a chain would be all that was needed. Things like RPMs and gear ratios were a little above our young minds.

So, it was back to the drawing board, again. We needed new gears and might actually have to spend some money to buy them. Then came the final straw... A couple days later Bobby was driving the rehabilitated cart behind the shop and had bypassed the governor to run the engine as fast as possible.

The little gas engine was never intended to run that fast, and it blew up. Bobby was very nonchalant about it; I was furious. I had put a lot of time into making that cart work, and my dad had helped too. Now it was toast. That was the last of our gang's efforts to build our own set of wheels.

Electric Beach...

Where the land meets a lake is magical - the views, the waves and the fun all working together. The beach at the country club was shaded with oak trees that were big even when the old clubhouse was part of the Post family estate. A broad expanse of lawn reached between the clubhouse windows and two steeply banked terraces that followed the old concrete seawall. The flat areas between hills were perfect for lounge chairs and low enough for some privacy from the clubhouse windows. The wide sidewalk from the clubhouse stopped at two sets of stairs that followed the terraces; those same old stairs are seen on these next two photos. Those stairs and the Beach House were set into the double terrace and had a distinctly older look as they were built with the original clubhouse. The two buildings

A view of the beach when it was the Post's Calmary Farm, *with the carriage house far left*

46

seen in this early photo of the beach were later combined into the one Beach House with locker rooms, a concession stand and pump house under one long deck. The beach was a favorite hangout for kids and teenagers, one of those few places where the age groups sometimes mingled.

That pump house fascinated me with its array of giant pipes, two big pumps, and two huge water tanks as big as cars set into the walls. The room was always hot and damp with dripping water and smelled of oil and ozone. As a little kid, it was always a thrill when I got to go there with my dad, and he let me turn the switches that brought the pumps to life, with a whine that slowly rose in pitch to a deafening drone.

Sometimes at night when he was checking on the pumps, Dad would open the door to the concession stand and I got to pick out an ice cream or candy bar. That stand was the best part of the Beach House

One of many family gatherings at the Beach, with Brenda Peck and son Jessie at left, Linda, Karen, Melanie & Amy Ott, and Andi's daughters Jen (towel) and Steph at lower right.

with a freezer full of ice cream and frozen candy bars, hot dogs, chips, a pop dispenser, and shelves full of all kinds of candy. Soon enough I realized these childhood luxuries could be had by merely signing a piece of paper, charging them with my dad's member number. I still remember that

number...1410-0. A kid could live there for the rest of his life! I had my first taste of "the country club life," surely this was the best part of it.

Occasionally the older kids running the stand wanted to take a break or just got lazy. Being one of the younger kids, I was always trying to act older and get noticed, so I'd offer to run the stand. You gained instant prestige with the easy job of handing out candy, soda and hot dogs, but I pushed for more. The lifeguards were always yelling at customers to stop hanging over the metal half door to the stand since that would break the hinge. One day I came up with an idea to fix that for good.

Being a junior electronics geek, I thought I knew more than I really did. I had a small battery charger gizmo that put out some low-voltage current, and my idea was to give people a little zap when they touched the metal door. I hooked up one lead of the charger output to the door and stuck the other wire in a puddle of water on the ground. Since most people at the beach were barefoot, I thought it would work pretty well.

After standing there trying to hide my grin for a few minutes, an unsuspecting kid came up, and I quickly reminded him not to touch the door. Of course, he did anyway; he almost flew into the lake. After a few more people got zapped really well, I thought I'd better try it myself... and Wham! That was quite a jolt. I suddenly realized the assumption I had made that my battery voltage setup was safe was, in fact, incorrect. I got a meter from the shop and discovered that the charger, while putting a low voltage onto a battery, actually had 120 volts between the one lead attached to the door and the ground. I could have electrocuted someone with my hijinks, and once again my guardian angel was looking over me.

One Slip-n-Slide Too Far...

Besides sunbathing on the terraces and munching at the concession stand, the beach had other amenities. There were the "normal" slides: a little slide for the little kids and the big slide for us big kids that seemed at least 20 feet above the water. While the small slide was relatively new, the big slide had been there when my dad was a kid. I remember him telling a story about his friend's dog learning to go down that slide.

As kids, we had lots of ideas and energy, and when that is coupled with all sorts of junk stored in the shop, the sky's the limit. While watching a commercial for a new water toy, the Slip-n-slide, I came up with a brilliant idea that would surely be loads of fun and get some of that all-important attention that twelve-year old's crave. Those two steep ten-foot-high grassy terraces along the beach would be a fantastic place for a super slip and slide! I envisioned a slider even sliding beyond the bottom hill right over the seawall and splashing into the lake.

Rummaging through the shop, I found a seventy-five-foot-long roll of heavy plastic sheet and rolled it out from the clubhouse lawn down both the terraces, across the sidewalk at the seawall and into the lake. Using some yellow cart path stakes, I fastened the plastic down, got out some of the big hoses that were stashed everywhere and staked the end of those to the top of the plastic. When the water was turned on, a healthy little river ran down the plastic, creating a magnificent waterfall right into the lake.

My slide was ready. By now, everyone at the beach had gathered around to watch what I was up to. Walking up to the top of the plastic I could tell it was especially slippery with the water running down it. I carefully sat down then sheepishly realized I was too far away from the slope. Several willing hands gave me a quick push, and with a speedy swoosh-bounce-swoosh-bounce, I was in the lake. It was really fast; much faster than the stationary big slide, although I hit hard on the bottom of each terrace. Everyone at the beach quickly lined up to take a turn, and my slide became a big hit.

Alas; as with most of my ideas, eventually something had to go wrong; my slide was no exception. We all realized right away that it helped to get a running start back up on the lawn. I began to get worried when the bigger kids started showing off, running from further and further back. Soon, it became a challenge to see who could go the fastest, but added speed came with a jarring whump when the slider hit the flat bottom of the terrace. Some of the oldest kids were starting to go airborne over the slope and hitting hard down on the flats. One of our swaggering lifeguards decided to really show off so he started running from way back at the clubhouse, jumping onto the slide as fast as he could go. He slid so quickly he completely missed the first slope, flying through the air and landing so hard on the flat middle part he *bounced* up again. He completely missed the second slope and flew through the air again to land spectacularly hard on the concrete seawall at the bottom. Ouch!

Another couple of feet further and that big bounce would have taken him safely into the lake, but as it turned out, he ended up with a broken tailbone. The accident spelled the end of my Slip-n-Slide. I

realize now how lucky I was I didn't get into big trouble, or that my dad, the club or both didn't get sued.

Battleship vs. Battleship...

At the beach, a wide dock stretched out at least seventy-five feet into the lake, with short spurs on both sides for swimming lanes. A big raft extended another thirty feet out into the lake. It was a major production each year to put-in and to take-out all the docks and everything. It all had to be ready before Memorial Day weekend, and sometimes the lake

The "little slide" at the beach, seen from the dock. The sloped terraces are at right.

was very, very cold in May when Dad and his crew put them in. I'd really looked forward to being old enough to help, only to find out what a frigid chore it was. They brought in special heaters to warm up the locker room because they could stay in the water only for about 20 minutes before going numb. All the crew was very relieved when my dad convinced the club to let him get a couple of wetsuits, but even then it was cold work.

Right next to the beach, just outside the roped off area, was the boat launch. The launch was in fact only seventy-five feet of lake frontage with a sandy beach where members could park their boats while they stopped at the club. It was a popular hangout with the young member kids whose parents had boats. Usually, several kids were there with their boats hanging out, taking their friends and other cool kids skiing or cruising around the lake. It was totally like a drive-in with boats instead of cars, except

50

the drivers could be under 16. Everyone was showing off all kinds of craft: float boats, sailboats, small outboards, ski boats, and larger inboards. Kids cruised around the lake, then swam and hung out. Me? I was younger and definitely not one of those cool boat kids. I wanted desperately to be part of that crowd, and was hearing the typical ridiculous teenage complaint that there was nothing to do. You can guess who came up with an idea for a new escapade…

I had just read about something called a tennis ball cannon. The article reported these were simply beer cans taped together, and lighter fluid was used to set it off in order to shoot a tennis ball. The easy part to figure out was cutting the tops and bottoms off the cans and taping several of them together. The hard part was getting it to fire. I experimented with squirting fluid into the cans first, but how to light them? Next, I put a small hole in the bottom can and lit a match near the hole. With a pop, the flaming tennis ball came out - but not very far. Knowing a little bit about how a cannon worked (Doesn't every kid?), I realized it needed a combustion chamber, and tried stuffing a rag in first to hold the charge; it shot out flaming rags. After more experimentation, I hit on the right combination…the bottom can was kept intact with its top on, making a perfect combustion chamber. A small hole in the side of that bottom can allowed for ignition, and the pop top opening was the perfect size to let the explosion drive the tennis ball out at tremendous speed. Eureka! With a bit more testing a stack of five cans was found to be the perfect combination of distance and accuracy, sometimes shooting the ball as far as 80 yards. (Writer's Note: Today's aluminum cans will rip apart and send shrapnel flying, so don't even think of trying this.)

After perfecting the tennis ball cannon, I started showing it around; it was instantly a hit! Everybody wanted me to make them one, but I really didn't want anyone else to have one. (Plus, I didn't want to be blamed if someone got hurt, having learned a bit of wisdom from an earlier lesson.) My teenage desire to be with the in crowd won out over common sense though, so an idea began to form. What great fun could be had by bombarding kids on the beach from tennis ball artillery located on board the boats? One of the member's kids had a slick mahogany inboard, so I went out with him to try our hand at playing Battleship. Butch was on the tennis team and had a seemingly endless supply of tennis balls. We lobbed most of them at the beach crowd that first day.

In the days that followed, the Boat People became armed with tennis ball cannons, and each boat sped toward the beach swerving while the gunner shot a broadside at people on the beach. The Beach People

hid behind lawn chairs, returning cannon fire of their own at the marauding boats. Those without cannons or those running out of ammo resorted to a ready supply of apples from the old club orchard. It was war!

Moms spoil everything! After a few of them complained, the lifeguards told us to quit attacking the beach. No problem. Those of us in the boats turned on each other. Two boats ran at each other in a game of chicken, then each swerved to the right, exposing each to a broadside volley of fire as we popped up to shoot and then duck. This maneuver was incredibly dangerous and stupid, all sorts of bad things could happen, but that's what teenagers do. The boats could have collided or caught fire from the lighter fluid, but, as it turned out, there were only minor injuries. A broken windshield became the major fatality, and that's when we finally realized that something worse could happen, so the war ended in a draw.

More Forts and Flying Cucumbers…

As a group of three pre-teens, Lon, Bobby and I were still big on forts and hangouts. Building our own private spaces and hideouts was something primal and hugely satisfying. We would outfit them with everything needed for survival, making and accumulating a long list of necessities from flashlights and food to comic books and compasses. We could imagine ourselves as the good guys spying on others, or, in some cases, the bad guys hiding out. We had all kinds of secret places … a cave-like hole in the lake bluff caused by a rotted-out stump where we watched other kids at the beach…or a shelter under the bows of a big pine in the woods where we could imagine being stranded in a snowstorm… We hid out underground in the pump pit where we'd be safe from the impending Armageddon…or that commanding tree fort in a giant oak overlooking the tennis courts.

In the fall, Dad would get out the "Turf Groomer," which consisted of a tandem rig of two large Jacobsen orange trailers pulled behind a tractor. The first trailer had a 4-cylinder engine powering a vacuum to rake and mulch an eight-foot-wide swath of leaves and then blow them into the second, a giant dump trailer. He emptied the collected leaves out in the dump behind the tennis courts, leaving giant monolithic cubes of compressed and mulched leaves. The gaps between these squares provided trenches that we could sneak through without being seen, perfect for young make-believe soldiers. By

covering the top of the larger gaps with plywood or branches, we laid out an ideal rabbit warren of hidden passageways and forts.

When winter came, we soon realized a major benefit of our semi-underground habitat… Our "Mulch City" was thoroughly heated! The big squares of decaying leaves gave

The giant orange Jacobsen Turf Groomer was a sure sign of fall, and a favorite, rare implement that Harold kept running for over 20 years.

off a considerable amount of steaming heat, enough so we could take our coats off and be completely comfortable. We carved out seats and benches from the compressed leaves and made quite a relaxing hangout for the winter. We even tried to convince our parents to let us sleep overnight in our fort. I'm sure our mothers did notice us coming home smelling like decayed leaves, but that was their problem; we didn't mind.

The following winter we upgraded to a more elaborate fortress, completing a major construction effort to build our fort within a three-sided concrete storage area. One of the sides was the wall of the old maintenance barn; the other walls were about eight feet tall because topsoil was sifted into there in the summer. Using some old wood pallets and plastic sheeting we built the fourth wall across the front opening. We covered the top of the fort with boards and more plastic sheeting to keep it dry. The front opening was disguised with junk so no one could see anything (although it's a safe bet my dad knew it was there). To enter we had a secret trap door and ladder in the back. We scrounged lockers, a couple of old upholstered benches, tables, and even installed electric lights and an electric heater. For us, it was the fanciest fort yet, although thinking back the only exit was out the top, and it could have been a fire trap. It became our base of operations that one winter; we could hide out, warm up, eat lunch, and make more plans. Many times we talked about staying in the fort overnight, but none of us had the nerve to do it.

But we did camp out in our backyard in my dad's old army tent. One summer, I had decided to dig a fish pond in the back of our yard after we had given up trying to restore Rich's ponds. I dug out a large hole under the lilac bushes near the end of Grandma's garden and lined it with flat rocks and even made a waterfall. After filling it and stocking it with minnows, I learned very quickly why the pond should be lined with plastic or cement because with nothing to hold the water in, it would leak out by the next morning. I needed to keep the water running from the hose all the time – too much and the pond would overflow, too little and it would dry up. I asked my folks if I could stay out all night and keep an eye on the water filling the pond. That also meant I needed the use of my dad's old tent. Next to the pond was a little, sheltered place in our backyard, hidden between a couple of cedar trees toward the road and some lilac bushes toward the course. It was one of many hangouts for my friends and me. We thought it would be a great place to pitch the tent and camp out. Apparently, my dad had done that before and he proudly showed us his surplus army 5-man tent and helped us set it up.

Of course, I wanted my friends to stay with me. Dad told me it was the same canvas tent that he used to camp out in when he was young. It had no bottom to it and was supposed to fit five people, although it was just big enough for the three of us kids. I had his army cot set up in it, and we had most of the comforts of home with all kinds of snacks. We built a fire and roasted hot dogs and marshmallows. Being inventive and crazy, we began daring each other to eat silly things. Retrieving several cucumbers from the garden, we filled one with peanut butter, marshmallows and mustard for starters and decided to roast the cuke in the fire. After several rounds of "dare ya's" failed to come up with a taker, we elevated the dare to throwing the gooey

Andi Peck is posing in front of the Grandma Rena's garden, which extended all along to the back yard and hid our tent.

54

cooked up mixture at cars passing by on the nearby street. One of us (I honestly don't remember which.) used a pair of tongs to send the mushy cucumber mess flying in the air over the hedge and onto traffic on the busy street. Right after it went flying, we suddenly realized how stupid we were, and ran before seeing if it hit anything. We quickly doused the fire and flashlights and hid out for a while, although we would easily have been discovered. That was our first and last flying cucumber.

The Locker Room for Old Ladies...

Our last and best ever hangout was the old, ladies' locker room. We always said "old-ladies" locker room like it was the locker room for old ladies, but the space was really the old, abandoned ladies' locker room. It was originally the carriage house and staff rooming house for the Calmary Farm Post Estate. I was very surprised to find out later that our part of the building was built as the original men's locker room. It was used for the first four years after the club opened. It had only 80 lockers, so the club soon sold lots along the lake and used the money to build the new men's locker room and pro shop in 1925. That's when the ladies took it over until 1960 when the new clubhouse was built with a comfortable locker room for them. When the three of us moved in, the carriage part was still used for cart storage and some of the seasonal clubhouse staff lived in rooms

Our 'Best Hangout Ever' was in the old-ladies locker room at the right half of this building, originally the carriage house for the Post Estate.

upstairs. We took over the locker room part downstairs, on the right side of the photo, and made it our own private clubhouse, party and game room.

The entire space was painted that pale, sickly green popular in the Fifties. My dad even tells about selecting that color in a later story. It smelled musty with an overlay of mold and vermiculite which was stored there. Showers, sinks and toilets ran along the back, but the main room where we hung out was surrounded by original lockers. Exposed wiring and pipes ran all over that were painted the same color, with lots of peeling paint adding to the ancient creepiness of the place that was perfect for us.

We got the lights and water working and cleaned the place up just to the point of being acceptable to us. We had all the luxuries of a grand clubhouse, old furniture, an ancient pop cooler, rickety tables, couches of ripped vinyl upholstery, bare light bulbs hanging on cords, and plenty of lockers for storage. Grand that is if you didn't mind all the vermiculite bags, old pro shop displays and assorted junk; did I mention the awful smell. Being deviously inventive we even made one locker into a torture chamber, pounding nails into it from the surrounding lockers and threatening to put our perceived enemies or each other into it. Beneath all this was a really smelly, dark basement filled with old lumber which became our dungeon.

The locker room fort became our headquarters where many of our crazy schemes were hatched: spying strategies, sticker sales, imagined getaways and such. Occasionally, we brought someone else in to show off, but it was mostly our private hangout where we talked, drank cokes and played cards. We spent more time planning ways that we could fix up our clubhouse, building a wall here or painting this, than actually doing anything. I think Lon and Bob were there more than I was because it was close to both their houses.

By the next summer we started outgrowing our interest in forts, probably with good reason. A fire truck went down Country Club Drive with its siren blaring. I jumped in the pickup with my dad to run down and see what was going on. As we got near the clubhouse, we could see the fire truck was stopped at the old ladies locker room door – the entrance to our fort – and firemen were running a hose inside. What happened? I found out that Bob or Lon had been there playing at smoking and threw something into the vermiculite which started smoldering. Luckily, Bobby noticed it and ran to the pro shop where they called the fire department. I always admired him for doing that as I think most kids that age would have just run away. If it had really caught fire, the golf carts and the staff's rooms would have been

destroyed. The close call spelled the end of our clubhouse hangout, and I think the gang grew up a little that day realizing what could have happened.

Snowmageddon…

In the mid-'60s, both my friends' dads, Ron LaParl and Bob McNally pooled their resources to buy a Boatel Snowmobile. It was an early model and might have been the first one in town; it was certainly the first one I'd ever seen. After much pestering, the three of us were allowed to drive it. Of course, we drove it slowly and carefully at first, with due parental supervision. We got comfortable driving after a while and cruised around the course at full speed, sometimes going airborne over bunkers. By today's standards, it was slow at probably 25 MPH tops, but we sure had a blast. Now they are common, but for a couple of years this was the only snowmobile anyone had ever seen on the golf course.

In late January of 1967, the upper Midwest had a surprise blizzard, and our town got almost 30 inches of snow. When it started snowing hard, my dad realized it might be a fierce storm, and I bugged my parents to let me stay overnight at Lon's. They relented, and my dad drove me to Lon's house. Dad drove the tractor with the snowplow back home that night. Plowing was another one of my dad's many duties, but one that he really enjoyed – most of the time.

With much excitement Lon and I watched it snow heavily all night; in the morning it was still snowing and blowing hard. We were up early, celebrating and preparing for the day's excursions by cooking an entire pound of bacon, after which we got down to some serious playing in the drifts. A little later I called home and Mom said that Dad was out trying to plow a path down to the shop, so Lon and I thought to meet him over there. My dad worked long into the afternoon just to clear that single lane the one-third mile from our house to the clubhouse. Finally, he made it to the shop where I helped him gas up, then rode with him back home on the back of the tractor.

Nobody moved anywhere for several days. It was all he could do to keep a little section of Country Club Drive and our driveway from drifting shut. The only thing moving around for the next couple of days were a few military tanks and our neighborhood snowmobile. My dad plowed out a small parking lot next to the house for people who made it to the drive but couldn't get their cars home; fortunately,

no one had to stay the night at our house. Over the next few days, our dads all took turns contacting the people living on the drive to take orders for groceries. They drove the snowmobile a mile up Capital Avenue to Steadman's Grocery to pick up supplies, then made food and mail deliveries. Over the next week, the town slowly dug out from incredible snow drifts. Next to the clubhouse entrance, there was a ten-foot-deep drift at

Club secretary Sharon Treadwell at a deep snow drift burying the club entrance

the flagpole, where my dad wrapped a piece of tape around the flagpole (at the top left corner of photo) to mark the spot that we would marvel at for years.

After spending almost all day plowing a path to the club and the winds were still blowing, my dad realized he could not move enough snow with the club's equipment. So, he called in a favor from Clark Equipment where he had worked many years ago and where he had many member-friends. The day after the snow stopped, as the main roads were just starting to get plowed, a colossal front-end loader - one with five-foot-tall tires and a bucket that could pick up a golf cart - was delivered to our house. He'd gotten preferential treatment because anything capable of moving that much snow was in big demand. My dad was in a snow plow heaven with this big machine. It took him only about a day

to plow the club and everyone else out. What a good dad; he even let me drive it, a little. That's him in the photo making fifteen-foot-high snow piles in the parking lot near the lake.

A few years later, in 1976, I was home from college on Spring break, and we had a massive ice storm. The ice coating was

Harold digging out with a borrowed Clark Equipment loader. The Paddle Tennis courts at right also had to be cleared, by hand, every snowfall.

measured in inches and branches were down everywhere across the state. Of course, power was out just about everywhere, but when my dad and I began surveying the damage, we noticed the power lines were ripped right off the house by falling branches. Dad knew it would be days before power crews could get down to repairing wires to the individual homes. All the hotels were full and nearby friends that we knew were in the same cold, dark boat. Then I remembered that the club had a very small electric generator attachment for a Toro trimmer. I walked down to the shop and brought it back home. We hooked it up to the furnace and started the engine to try to get some heat on. It turned on the burner but wasn't powerful enough to run the blower fan. Then, with a stroke of luck, I found a window fan that Dad saved from the old clubhouse would run, and it fit perfectly over the furnace filter opening. We were fortunate that for the next five days the power was out, we were able to heat the house to almost 60 degrees by switching electricity between the furnace and the refrigerator. My dad and I thought it was fun, kind of like camping, except indoors, but my mom could barely keep warm. That was a Spring break adventure when we read a lot of books.

Famous Friends...

The golf course where I planned so many shenanigans is located in a small town famous for its cereal manufacturing. As the fanciest meeting place in the city, the private club hosted many events for these manufacturers and other organizations involving celebrities and famous golfers. While I remembered most of the golfers, I took celebrities for granted and have forgotten most, but I do recall being introduced to Michigan football coach Bo Schembechler - I liked his name.

There was one big celebrity event that I will never forget. Being in the "Cereal City," the club hosted many cereal icons like Tony the Tiger, but the coolest thing ever was when I looked out our living room window late one morning and saw the Beverly Hillbillies turning onto our drive in their famous old truck. They weren't even twenty feet away; right there next to our house was Jeb, Jethro, Granny and Ella May.

The Clampetts made it all the way to Country Club Drive in 1963. (Used with permission)

I got really excited and took off out of the house after the jalopy, running all the way down the drive. By the time I got to the club that old jalopy was sitting at the entrance and the Clampetts were already inside the clubhouse. At eight-years-old, I didn't dare just go in on my own, but then I found my dad and bugged him till I got to meet them...sort of. That afternoon Buddy Ebsen and Max Baer played

golf; I stood behind my dad as they were introduced. Kellogg's was their sponsor, and they were in town in 1963 for a corporate luncheon at the club, and a variety show the next night.

Over the years I also met some of golf's greats like Gene Littler, Don January, Gardner Dickinson and Chi Chi Rodriguez, but I

Arnie Palmer giving an exhibition at the 1st Tee, with Bob Nesbit.

especially remember meeting Arnie Palmer. The cordial Arnie was at the club for exhibitions, and I was thrilled to shake his hand. I especially liked him because he was the son of a golf course superintendent; naturally, he was always generous with compliments and appreciation for the grounds crew. He grew up just like me, playing on a golf course, although with a slightly different career result.

Arnie was friends with the club Pro, Ron LaParl, who had also helped build and operate a miniature golf course called the Arnold Palmer Putting Course. It was not far from home next to the Interstate. The gang could bike over there, but it was much easier to bug our parents for a ride. The three of us occasionally descended on the place because Bobby's mom often worked there; we hung out like we were really important. Bobby sometimes got to run the cash register or be asked to do some cleanup work, and we would "assist." Probably more like goof around, I think. We had a game where we stood behind the counter in the Pro Shop and when the customers weren't looking we'd dive through the hidden trap door behind the counter and climb down a ladder into the basement. Then we'd run around outside and nonchalantly walk back in one of the doors to the Pro Shop. We'd sometimes get a few double takes, but we thought we were much funnier than anyone else did.

On Two Wheels...

One great thing about the dirt path to Stumps Shack was that it was easy to drive down it from the shop and then disappear quickly. I was totally addicted to driving the green, three-wheeled Cushman Trucksters, and sometimes took off on one even if I didn't have a good reason to. I was so anxious to learn to drive that my dad relented after my persistent begging and taught me how when I was seven, before I could hardly reach the pedals. Next summer, at age eight, I was driving without help and could shift; the following year, age nine, I was driving them every chance I got. At first, my dad turned down the governor to limit my speed, but I soon figured that out and would crank it back up as soon as I was out of sight. For years my dad complained I didn't avoid or slow for bumps, since I almost always drove at top speed even when he was riding with me.

Before I was officially working on the course, I found excuses for driving the Trucksters by begging for things to do. The dirt path that leads into a trail through the woods had some thrilling mounds of dirt - perfect moguls - and I often went over them too fast for my own good. Sometimes Bobby also snuck a golf cart away from the pro shop, and we'd have a road race or demolition derby back there, during which we were usually careful. The Truckster always won because it was much faster.

I recall only one time when Dad really blew up at me. I suppose there was a bit of a rivalry between Bobby and me. I thought it was because he was jealous of the Truckster that I got to drive and the keys I possessed to the shop and concession stands. Years later I realized he might have been

A young Marty is giving mom Jayne a ride in a brand-new Truckster.

62

jealous of the relationship between my dad and me. Sure he could drive his dad's golf carts, but it was frowned upon while I could drive the Trucksters even when I didn't have a good reason. I think his dad was always worried about what the members would say if they saw his kid goofing around or being reckless. I don't think my father cared nearly as much about what the membership would think; plus, he had much more faith in me. That is a trust I was perhaps reckless with and sometimes came close to jeopardizing. I was either very, very lucky, or I had a guardian angel, probably both.

The Cushman Trucksters were much faster than golf carts because they were powered with a 22 HP gas engine. A three-speed shifter allowed the driver to quickly accelerate, because first gear was rarely needed unless hauling something. By adding something I called the Lightning Speed Device (more about the LSD later) I could get the Trucksters to go almost forty, and I became an expert, typically invincible driver at a very young age. I was good at all sorts of stunt driving like slaloming, high speed banked turns and jumping sand traps.

However, on one particular day, I was driving a golf cart past the maintenance shop with Bobby seated next to me. He had brought the cart to the shop and was showing off. Not to be outdone, I decided to show him I was no slouch either driving the carts. This was a regular EZGO golf cart with six acid-filled batteries and a one-horse motor. I was showing off too, driving fast around the tight turn on the dirt service road to the back of the shop when I took the left curve at speed, bringing the left wheel off the ground as high as possible without going over. While getting up on two wheels is easy to do with a three-wheeled cart, keeping it there around a turn is not so easy. Bobby was hanging on next to me watching the dirt and grass fly past much closer to his head than it should be. The hardest part was bringing the cart back down smoothly without flipping over, which I did, barely, manage to do.

Apparently, my guardian angel was on vacation that day. My dad and Bob's dad, Ron, were just driving up in my dad's truck; they had watched the entire stunt! My smugness at accomplishing the maneuver quickly changed to horror and trepidation as I turned around and saw them. I was caught recklessly driving one of Ron's golf carts and could have easily flipped it over, wrecking the cart and hurting both of us. I realized I was in seriously big trouble, but what I immediately knew was how much I had totally embarrassed my dad in front of his friend and co-worker. The trust I had enjoyed was shattered; I thought my dad would never forgive me. Worse yet, he and Ron might not be good friends anymore. I felt terrible…

My dad didn't yell at me, but I knew I was toast. He had to punish me in front of Ron, and I knew I had it coming. He was livid, and there were words and some grounding and maybe threats that I'd never drive anything again until I was 16 or something like that. But I had the feeling that what he really wanted to do was hug me, grateful that neither of us had gotten hurt.

Firework Dreams…

Every Fourth of July was a huge deal around our house. That was because *my dad* set off the fireworks display for the country club …yes, *MY DAD*! Starting way back in the winter, just after Christmas, he started getting firework catalogs in the mail, and I would start pouring over them, oohing and aahing at the various aerial and ground displays. I was always quick to point out what he could get if he spent "just a few more dollars." I recall he usually paid $450, but I pestered him relentlessly to spend more, not realizing that he had a budget and limited manpower but knowing that more was always better. I could not wait until the year when I was old enough to help him (or so I thought).

We always had a crowd at our house that day. Friends and relatives from out of town came to watch the display; some of them were drinking a lot and insisting that my dad should let them help set off the fireworks. Club members, who were essentially my dad's bosses, also insisted he let them help shoot things off, and some had been drinking and getting obnoxious by the evening. But Dad knew how dangerous fireworks could be... They were quite literally playing with dynamite, and he knew many people had been killed setting off the colorful shots. He was always very strict and would not let anyone but his men near the fireworks.

A couple of years later, I saw just how dangerous they were when the pro shop staff set off a firework called an Aerial Report for a shotgun start. They dropped the firework into a mortar pipe that always set in the ground, not realizing there was water inside. The firework sat there for a while and water soaked through, so the aerial part got wet and didn't go but the report part, the big bang, went off - in the ground. It blew a big hole in the earth, sending shrapnel from the metal pipe across the street to stick into the side of the Pro Shop! I didn't realize until years later, but Dad was very nervous during fireworks and never drank any alcohol until the show was over.

At that time, the club had the most prominent display of fireworks in the city. Cars lined the streets around the neighborhood, and people flooded the golf course in droves to watch my dad and his crew set them off on the driving range. First, they watered the whole area ahead of time and covered everything with tarps to keep sparks from setting things off prematurely. He and his men lit their flares, then dropped the firework shell into to the mortar pipe, pulled the cover off the fuse, touched it with the flare, and ran like hell!

Their display was more modest than those of today, and almost every burst was applauded. Dad also had some ground displays every year: spinners, the American flag, and one called Niagara Falls. One year I talked him into purchasing a few more, especially one called a whirligig or something. It started off spinning horizontally like a top or helicopter, then it suddenly flew right up into the sky with a loud whizz. It took everyone by surprise (including my dad) especially when this big disk of still-burning lumber fell back to the ground, scattering the audience.

Every year included a few duds; aerial bursts that didn't, or some that stayed in the mortar. One year a couple days after the Fourth, Dad's long-time employee, Glen Eggleston called me into the shop to show me something in his locker. He pulled out a little pear-shaped piece of rock-hard paper and gunpowder – the bomb that caused the loud report. He had saved it out of a dud, and I honestly thought he was giving it to me. I said, "Gee, thanks, Glen," and left with it. At home, I devised what I thought was a safe way to set it off and placed it on the top of the picnic table next to a lit sparkler. A few long minutes later the charge lit, and it surprised me by quickly scooting across the table. My breath caught as I thought it would take off across the yard, but before that happened, it exploded! That little acorn-sized charge blew a hole right through the two-inch thick top of the table! Later that day my dad asked what had happened; Glen told him he didn't mean to give it to me and was very worried.

That was as close as I ever got to setting off my dad's fireworks. The year I turned thirteen, the very first year that I could start working for my dad, he convinced the club to stop their annual fireworks display. He was older, wiser, and warier of the risks, and the liability for him, his men and the Club. Frankly, I think he didn't want me anywhere near the fireworks and didn't want to argue with me about it. When I found out, I was very disappointed and angry, but we're not to that point yet in this story.

Chemistry 101…

My dad's shop was loaded with various chemicals; tanks, drums and bottles of nasty smelling things used for treating all the diseases and bugs that afflict grass. Hubert Dull was the one who usually mixed the powders or liquids in the spray rig, a big tank with a pump and long arms. The spray rig was pulled behind a tractor and used to cover fairways and tee boxes using the outstretched arms, or a nozzle and hose on the greens. There was always a pungent chemical smell and a cloud of green, blue or orange dust when the rig was being filled or washed. The tanks were always rinsed out into the large drain next to the shop, along with grass clippings and everything else. As kids do, we soon found where this drain went: it simply dumped out into a small wet area behind the tennis courts. Back in the '60s dumping like that was not uncommon, but for us, that was the perfect, genuinely toxic dump. An incredibly smelly, nasty, colorful, bubbly soup to explore.

Watching these chemicals get mixed up appealed to the little mad scientist in me, in addition to all the electrical stuff. In my young years, I thought it would be really cool to become a scientist and make new things or invent some innovative gadget. A few years later I signed up for Latin as a high school freshman because I thought it was the language of scientists. Next to the hardware store my dad always took me to, there was a hobby shop specializing in science gadgets, stuff like model rockets, microscopes, electronics kits and chemistry sets. Lon started his adventure early

A geeky Marty setting up his chemistry lab

with chemistry since his dad had majored in it in college. Soon both of us began to buy stuff. We did it mostly because it looked cool and like we knew something no one else did. We started with a few chemical bottles, test tubes, and simple experiments that turned red liquid to white. Quickly we were obsessed and Lon took over a little room in his basement with a countertop he called his laboratory. We thought we would soon solve the mysteries of the universe.

Having a laboratory was amazing, so I wanted one, too. After bugging my parents, it turned out to be surprisingly easy to talk them into building one for me. Probably, they figured if there were any chance that my interest was genuine it would be worth it, and, besides, it was a project I could work on together with my dad. I was just getting to the age where I could actually be helpful, even though he did most of the work.

So Dad and I got started by demolishing that crude old shower stall in the basement built by my grandpa. Since that shower was the cause of some early childhood trauma, wrecking it was sweet revenge. We built a small ten-foot-square room next to Dad's workshop with counters along two sides, a small sink with hot and cold water and a drain that ran down into the infamous hole under the floor. Dad taught me about carpentry, drywalling, painting and plumbing. We even did the wiring together, installing lights, outlets, and an exhaust fan. Though it was built using mostly leftover materials, I had a first-class laboratory, the envy of any junior scientist.

Now both Lon and I began to collect chemicals and apparatus with a passion; we were kind of competing with each other. For a year, almost every spare dollar we earned was used to buy new stuff, mostly because it looked cool but not because we knew what to do with it. We'd go to the hobby store and imagine how elaborate our setups would look with all the cool stuff. My dad and I built racks for beakers, flasks, test tubes, glass coils, and I even learned how to bend glass tubes. There were alcohol burners and glassware stands, hoses and valves, and all sorts of Frankenstein mad-scientist looking equipment. Lon and I collected bottles of chemicals like they were trading cards, based on how colorful or combustible they were. Our quest became more about building up each of our labs, than actually running experiments.

When I got to nearly 100 bottles of different chemicals, almost all that could be purchased at the hobby store, our enthusiasm weakened as we both kind of realized that neither of us really knew what we were doing. I had the bigger, fancier laboratory, and in my oblivious youth may have even bragged about it. Looking back with the experience of age, that boasting could've also ended our shared quest and might have hurt our friendship, but it didn't.

Although my interest faded, the lab didn't gather too must dust as I experimented in it occasionally over a few years. Learning about the characteristics of chemicals, I made up a dry compound that flared spectacularly when water was added or when I spit on it. As a thirteen-year-old freshman, I thought showing this stuff could be an ideal way for me to become cool and accepted by my classmates in the marching band. One evening, just before marching band practice, I decided to mix up a new batch to take it with me. Down in the lab,

Marty showing off his JV Band uniform before getting toasted in an explosive chemistry experiment

while wearing my band uniform, I began to grind up the powdered zinc, phosphorus and whatever using a mortar and pestle. I did not realize how volatile this compound could be. There was just enough moisture in the air to set it off while I was mixing. With my fingers an inch away, there was a sudden explosive flash with sparks flying everywhere! The skin on the side of three fingers was severely burned. My face was sunburned, my glasses pitted, my uniform slightly damaged, and even the ceiling in my lab was peppered with marks. I ended up in the emergency room instead of band practice that night, hearing doctors talk of a skin graft. But it could have been much worse if the compound had gone off in my pocket in the car. Once again, I thought someone was looking out for me.

Digging Up History...

I will never forget one fateful day when my dad came home at lunch with an exciting discovery! He was holding several old bottles that had just been dug up near the clubhouse by a crew putting in a new gas line. My dad explained how contractors were digging through an old foundation buried near the putting green by the clubhouse, which was probably the old greenhouse of the Post estate. I thought that was just the coolest thing and couldn't wait to dig up more of this buried treasure on my own.

After lunch, I fairly flew down to the club only to find I had to wait until the workers quit for the day. But nothing would stop Marty, AKA Indiana Jones. For the rest of the day, I sifted through piles of dirt looking for intact bottles and other artifacts.

My dad said C.L. Post raised and sold orchids and poinsettias in that greenhouse. When the club bought the farm, Post took the greenhouse with him. Dad

Marty (in mirror) with start of antique bottle collection

figured the foundation was filled in with all sorts of junk and garbage when the country club purchased the property. I spent every minute of an intense weekend at my newest hobby of pseudoarchaeology, sifting and digging through all the dirt I could get in to. My treasure hunt was highly successful, and I

A 'Coca-Cola of Battle Creek' bottle and the old light bulbs I dug up that really worked!

amassed a collection of over one-hundred old medicine, liquor, ink and perfume bottles; together my treasure was worth perhaps three hundred dollars. The most amazing find was three fragile Edison-style light bulbs. They each had a little glass tip at the top, and, as the dirt was carefully cleaned off the glass, I could see a single big loop of carbon filament inside. Amazingly, two of them looked like they were still intact. With much care, I wrapped them up and ran home to show them to my

1935 photo of Golf Course looking east; Goguac Lake and Clubhouse are off left.

70

dad. He was as surprised as I was; we quickly screwed them into an old table lamp he'd built in shop class – and discovered the light bulbs still worked, each giving off a dim, warm glow! I was fascinated to think of people using these years ago, and what that must have been like.

That short step back in time opened my eyes to a whole new world - the history of my family and the club. Afterward, I had many questions for my dad and my grandma. Throughout the summer, I found out there were more ancient secrets throughout our house, and around the golf course. Digging through Grandma's old articles and scrapbooks, I found some fascinating history which always led to more questions. I knew my grandfather had worked on the course before my dad, and I vaguely remembered the old clubhouse. I wanted to know what it looked like; what else was scattered here and there? What did the course look like back then? What was it like to live back then? Did Grandpa build the course with his horses? Did my dad work for my grandpa?

I discovered there were once big stone pillars standing next to our house on either side of the entrance drive. The old white house across the street was once a restaurant called the Windmill Inn; people could rent horses there to ride down to the club. I also found out an 18-hole mini-golf course had been built somewhere near the main clubhouse in 1930, and that there was a skeet shooting range and an archery range built in 1935 between the tennis courts and our house, complete with a tower for launching the clay birds. And, in the early days, caddies had competed in something called a "greasy pole contest."

MINIATURE COURSE OPENS

The 18-hole miniature golf course at the Battle Creek Country club was opened for use today after a month had been allowed for the sod to set. The course was started about the middle of June and was to be opened July 4 but at that time it was found that the sod was not in proper condition so the opening date was put off. Chick Harbert, son of E. W. Harbert, professional at the club, has been placed in charge of the course. One of the rules to be enforced is that no one is allowed to play while wearing high-heeled shoes.

Skeet shooting along Country Club Drive

71

Having been a member of the Indian Guides, I was also very interested to find an article mentioning an archeologist who claimed there was an aborigine Indian burial mound "at the south end of Goguac Lake, east of Mingus Brook, which was leveled and is now part of the Battle Creek Country Club."

Those bottles my dad brought home started an interest in family history that would set me on an anthropological path of sorts that I am still traveling on today. The trip has been a fascinating journey of discovery filled with family and country club historic details that I am eager to share. Here is as good a place as any to start...

At Country Club Hills

Horses for Adults
Ponies for Children
for Rent

Windmill Inn

A Delightful Place to Eat—Home Style Cooking

Phone 3534
for Reservations

Mrs. Nettie McElroy
Hostess
At Country Club Hills

All his life Charles Marsh has been interested in archeology, botany, and nature study in general, and he has a fine collection of arrowheads and other Indian relics which he intends to turn over to the Kingman Memorial Museum in due time. Some of his arrowheads are at Rae McCoy's establishment 35 West State street. Most were obtained in what would be called surface explorations, but some are from Indian burial mounds of this and other localities.

Mr. Marsh tells of a former Indian burial mound at the south end of Goguac lake, east of Minges brook, which was leveled and is now a part of the Battle Creek Country club's golf course. He worked in it over 40 years ago. There were then mounds on both the Kalamazoo river and Battle creek, but they are now effaced. He uncovered some of his rarest specimens in Georgia.

Prehistoric Indian Mounds might have once been on the golf course site.

The Windmill Inn was cattycorner from One Country Club Drive, and offered a tea room, riding stables and dining from 1926 through the 1930. The house is still there.

EARLY HISTORY

A Real Teamster...

I was fascinated to find out that like his father Lester before him, my grandfather Andrew (Andy) Peck was a teamster. He had his own team of horses for hire around the small town of Battle Creek for jobs like hauling and construction.

Andy Peck (right) with his Team. Wonder if that is his first wife Mabel at left?

Andy with his team, shown on the right of this postcard, lived with his parents as a young man in a house in town. They probably kept the horses in a small barn nearby. There was a lot of building going on in the area with the ten-story Post Tavern, an eight-story bank building, and the 10,000acre, Fort Custer military camp being built between 1914 and 1916. Apparently, people moved around a lot then, as Andy married his first wife Mabel in 1908 and lived with his in-laws for a while. He then built a house, sold it and bought a sixty-acre farm in the spring of 1912. That farm didn't work out, so he sold it in the fall and built another house, only to sell it in 1914. Grandpa lived in two more homes over the next few years, and according to his war draft record owned a farm again in 1918. He lived in eight different addresses over ten years, gradually moving ever closer to his (apparently) favorite job of cultivating and mowing grass – at the golf course.

The Old Course...

Grandpa Andy started his golf course career in 1914 by helping to maintain the nine-hole Country Club of Battle Creek. He showed how he could manage his team with the somewhat delicate task of mowing. He had always used horses to do the heavy work, carrying loads of cinders, lumber, earth and stone, so pulling the heavy mowers was undemanding but delicate work. Harold remembers, *"My dad*

GENERAL GROUND RULES.

1. Hunting or shooting on the grounds is strictly forbidden.
2. Building fires on any part of the grounds is forbidden except by the permission and under the direction of the Grounds Committee.
3. Members or visitors must not pluck the blossoms or flowers growing on the club premises; neither shall they be wasteful of the fruit growing in the club orchards, or pull any of the fruit while green or unfit for use.
4. Members wishing to camp on the grounds must first obtain permission from the Chairman of the Grounds Committee.
5. Parties using the grounds for camping out or other entertaining must not leave papers or other refuse on the grounds.
6. All horses must be hitched to the hitching rack provided for that purpose, the hitching of horses or letting them stand in any other parts of the grounds being strictly forbidden.

An excerpt from the early country club Bylaws

always had horses, and his brother, Uncle Lou, had mules. The mules worked hard, but only when you could get them to work. Dad got more work overall for less trouble with his horses, but both types of animal worked on the old course." The horses easily pulled the three-unit, reel-type mowers down the short Par 3 fairways, and, if the weather was good, they could mow three holes a day. Greens and tees were cut by hand; backbreaking hard work was usually done by two men on one mower. The rough bordering the fairways was cut twice a year with a mower called a sickle bar, pulled by a team hitched to a seat for the driver next to the giant scissors that moved with a characteristic clackety-clack.

Creek Golfers Cannot Golf.

Battle Creek, Mich., April 30.—For the second season, the Battle Creek Country club will be unable to play golf this summer. The club laid out its links last summer, but had to "wait until spring" to let the grass grow. The grass hasn't grown sufficiently, and this season the club will again have to content itself with tennis, croquet or bridge. It is planned, however, to take advantage of the Kalamazoo river, which flows back of the clubhouse, and canoeing will be developed. Plans are under discussion, too, for building a small Mississippi flatboat to carry passengers up and down the Kalamazoo on short excursions.

From the Detroit Free Press, 1907

Golf was becoming very popular. Around 1906, golfers were using an early 9-hole layout called Merritt Commons, and had raised $20,000 to build a new nine-hole course and clubhouse west of town. In the early 1900s, the growing popularity of the Battle Creek Sanitarium brought the wealthy and famous to town for

Original Country Club of Battle Creek clubhouse. In 1920 it became a casino and speakeasy after the club moved out.

rejuvenation and lessons on healthy living, including Thomas Edison, J.C. Penney, Amelia Earhart, and President William Howard Taft. At that time, cereal was an offshoot of the very celebrated Sanitarium. The fancy retreat helped the wealthy and famous to purge themselves (literally) of the poisons of an affluent lifestyle. The retreat offered many bizarre treatments such as electrotherapy exercise beds, electric baths and the colonic irrigator, along with a healthy program of diet and exercise. The cereal that made the town and C.W. Post famous was just becoming a favorite part of that healthy diet. But outdoor sports and recreation were already widespread and growing. Far and away, golf was the most popular and convenient because it was social as well as active.

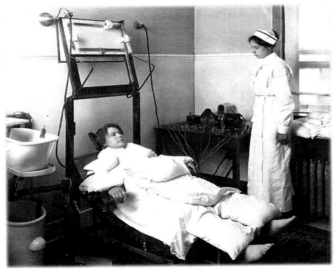

Electrotherapy bed at the Sanitarium

Built on the edge of town, the new nine-hole course was easily accessible by club members and guests of the Sanitarium. This picture shows that the streetcar tracks ran right by the clubhouse in the background. One of Grandpa's stories relates to an evening in October of 1918, when this convenience turned into a catastrophe. That night right along the golf course a spectacular head-on collision occurred between the heavy interurban train and the much lighter streetcar that shared the tracks. The article from the local paper on the next page gives some details…

Interurban stopping in front of original Clubhouse along Main Street

I loved hearing my dad tell about Grandpa's version of the story, as there were indeed some "hooligans" Grandpa knew had messed with the switches and caused the accident. Apparently, he had had some trouble with the same group and knew something about what was going on.

The resulting crash destroyed the streetcar and caused the interurban to roll down an embankment and right across the 4th Green. The wheels of the car severely sliced up the green. As my dad related the story, the accident and the car's recovery required almost a week, and then another week of work to rebuild and repair the green. Nearly a month passed before the green would grow in and be playable.

TWO CARS COLLIDE IN HEAD-ON WRECK; 15 ARE INJURED

Interurban and City Cars Smash Together Near the Country Club Switch.

SAY SIGNALS CONFUSED

Various Theories Offered as to Cause of Accident.

Motorman of City Car Received Broken Hip—Injuries to Others Not Serious.

Fifteen persons were injured, one seriously, when city street car No. 412, bound for Urbandale and Jackson-bound interurban. No. 2 met in a head-on collision at Ridgmoor, just west of the Battle Creek Country club, at 11 o'clock last evening.

Scrapped the Equipment.

The city car was almost completely smashed. The interurban car was badly damaged, almost the entire front vestibule being torn away. Traffic was tied up from the time of the accident until noon today, although a work crew of 17 men were busy through the night and early morning.

The accident happened on the slope of a hill just west of a gulley beyond the Country club and east of the Burney home on West Main. The view of the interurban motorman was partly obscured until he reached downgrade about 10 rods from the place of the accident.

Hunt for the Cause.

Two theories were advanced as to the confusion in signals which caused the accident. The place was between two switches. One theory was that both motormen threw the light signal at exactly the same time, showing "clear" at both ends of the line, a synchornism that might happen once in a million times. Another was that boys had tampered with the light switch at Urbandale. Some street car men said that this was a favorite pastime with some boys and gave the motormen trouble on several occasions.

A Romance...

Many auspicious events occurred at that former country club, but none more so than when my Grandfather Andrew, the greenskeeper, met my Grandmother Rena, a waitress at the clubhouse. The actual detail on how they met is only speculation, but she

The Original Clubhouse was on the Kalamazoo River, where Rena met Andy.

was a pretty 24-year-old, and he was undeniably handsome. When they met Andrew was likely still married; he had two sons, and Rena had an illegitimate daughter. Whether or not he was separated from his first wife when they met is a secret lost from history. They married on Thanksgiving Day 1919, four months after he was divorced from his first wife, Mabel.

Rena Post, at about 19 years old

My Grandmother's first daughter, Shirley, was born on July 1, 1918, but no one today knows who her father was. Little has been passed on about this other family secret, but we were always told that Shirley was from Andy's first marriage along with his sons Everett and Philip. However, Shirley's birth certificate and marriage certificate both list Andrew Peck as father and Rena Post (her maiden name) as mother more than a year before he was divorced from his first wife. This might suggest my grandfather had an earlier affair with my grandmother, and that Shirley was a full sister. Interestingly, the birth certificate was made later at the start of WWII listing Andrew as the father. It turns out this was a fabricated, gracious effort on

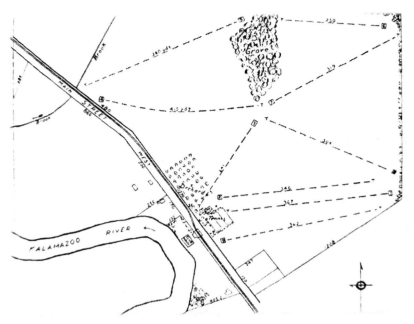

Andrew and Rena's part to legitimatize Shirley's parentage. My grandfather was, in actuality, not Shirley's father. My Aunt Shirley really was my dad's stepsister. Speculation is that when my very religious grandmother visited her brother Floyd in Saskatchewan in 1917, she had a naive romance with someone, rumored to be a pastor, and got pregnant before returning home that fall. Very complicated and curious...and a family secret no one wanted to discuss.

Original 9-hole course layout, now the site of Leila Arboretum, with streetcar track running along Main Street.

Shirley was the kindest, most generous person I knew; the one who always came to stay and care for one family member or the other who was ill. I was heartbroken to hear that my aunt had grown up burdened with that era's stigma of being illegitimate. I can't imagine what it was like for her when, as a little girl she was told to hide up in the attic when company came over.

That was even more ironic considering Everett and Philip, Grandpa's sons by his first wife, came to live with their father and stepmother right after they were married. According to a legal notice in the local paper, Grandpa had a letter from his former wife in April 1920 giving the newly married couple custody of her first child, Everett, so Grandpa petitioned the court to stop his monthly $2 child support payment to his former wife. This time frame is soon after Andy and Rena moved into their new, larger house at the country club. Perhaps the reason he divorced Mabel was that she did not want to raise her own children, a task my Grandmother Rena willingly took over.

Rena with daughter Shirley

Some New Digs...

During the fall of 1919, Andrew was caught in the transition between courses. A couple of months before they were married on Thanksgiving Day, 1919, my grandfather was told the club would be reorganized, dissolving the old Country Club of Battle Creek and eliminating his job there. The club was moving to a new site a couple of miles out of town where a new 18-hole course would be built. Grandpa continued maintaining the old nine-hole course for the members who wanted to play golf there, and he kept picking up contract work as a teamster-for-hire that winter while awaiting confirmation that he would be named Greenskeeper of the new course. The announcement would be hugely important to the Pecks and surely a worrisome time for the newly married couple. Grandpa would have been very anxious to become involved with the operation of the new course.

The new clubhouse was the former summer home of C. W. and C. L. Post.

Not only was this the time of a big transition for my grandparents and their new combined family, but also the time of a big change for the country club. Club history confirms the old course membership had grown to well over 100 active members in less than twelve years, and demand for guests and new members were increasing. The old course was small, consisting of only Par 3 holes, and it was landlocked, so expansion would be expensive. The quaint three-story clubhouse on the bank of the Kalamazoo River where my grandparents met was also inadequate, built for a smaller membership and difficult to heat. While the private club was convenient to the city and growing commerce, it was simply too small. Even before my grandfather had been hired as Greenskeeper, there was heated debate among the members about expanding and moving the club once again.

After several years of discussion, late in the summer of 1919, club members S. J. Rathbun, L. J. Montgomery, W. I. Fell, A. O. Jones, G. R. Rich and W. T. Bobo finally did something about it. They started negotiations with Carroll. L. Post for the purchase of his 103-acre Calmary Farm. The site had 1400 feet of lake frontage on Goguac Lake; a large lake two miles south of town lined with summer cottages and an

C. W. Post and C. L. Post - Original Site Owners, Cereal Magnates and Industrialists...

Charles W. Post was born in Springfield, Il and started out selling and manufacturing farm machinery, but suffered a mental breakdown and moved to Fort Worth to invest in real estate. After a second breakdown he traveled extensively in search for a cure and came to the Battle Creek Sanitarium. Here he founded Postum Cereal Co. in 1895 with the coffee-like Postum beverage, soon inventing Grape-Nuts and Elijah's Manna (Post Toasties). To undercut competing startups, he sold his same cereal at a cheaper price under different names. In 1904, C. W. divorced his first wife, Ella Merriweather, and married his 27-year-old secretary Leila Young. In 1906 C. W. invested his substantial earnings in a 225,000-acre development in Texas he named Post City. A few years later he purchased the 100-acre parcel on Goguac Lake that became the golf course "front nine". C. W. Post's daughter, Marjorie Merriweather Post would undoubtedly have spent time there, and she later married E. F. Hutton and became the wealthiest woman in the United States, eventually building the Mar-a-Lago estate in Palm Springs that Trump now owns.

When C. W. took his own life in 1914, his brother Carroll L. Post took over the Goguac Lake property and named it Calmary Farm, raising pigs and poinsettias. He expanded the beautification of the grounds, and according to the offer to sell he had invested $82,000 into the property. With all his other duties including running Postum Cereal, a bank, a land company, a box company and the Post Tavern, C. L. Post was apparently getting tired of farming, so he agreed to sell the property to the club members in the fall of 1919.

amusement park and known as a recreation spot. They also purchased 100 acres of the Henry Coe farm, which would become the back-nine.

That Post property itself had quite a history. As the summer estate for the Post family, Calmary was the site of many society gatherings. The property had its own heat and electricity-generating plant for lighting, and boasted a long tree-lined beach, manicured gardens and numerous buildings including the "sash house" (greenhouse). The prime real estate had many previous owners; Goddard, Gillet, Smith, Jennings, Rice, and was finally purchased from John Reasoner by C. W. Post., with his brother C. L. Post taking it over in 1914 when C. W. died.

Postum Cereal Company

MAKERS OF
POSTUM CEREAL, INSTANT POSTUM,
GRAPE-NUTS, POST TOASTIES, ETC.

Battle Creek, Mich., U.S.A.
Aug. 20, 1919

Mr. Stephen J. Rathbun,
C i t y.

My dear Steve:

In reference to the sale of my Calmary country place. I have actually invested in this property at the present time over $82,000. The survey shows that there is approximately 103 acres. The survey overlaps into the site of the house adjoining the property on the north side about 18 inches, and there may be some little question as to it. The survey also shows, I think, approximately 1400 ft. of shore line. I would be willing to sell the place for country club purposes only for $60,000., retaining a plat of approximately 3 acres commencing on a line with the south back-stop of my tennis court running east and west, and to the north line of the said property, to include the small house now occupied by my chauffeur, but not to include the two story house occupied by my gardener; the said reservation to extend from the lake east until there were approximately 3 acres reserved. This would extend partly into my present orchard, and would naturally cross the road loading into the woods, but in doing this I would grant an easement to the Country Club for so much of the road privilege as may be necessary, and if the Country Club did not care for my present greenhouse I would make a further allowance of $3000. for it, and move it off its present site.

So far as terms are concerned, I should want 25% in cash. The balance I would be willing to extend in equal yearly payments running from one to twenty years, with 6% semi-annual interest.

I will grant to the Country Club the privilege of considering this offer up to Oct. 1st of this year. If they cannot consummate the purchase by that time

2.

I shall make other disposition of it.

I do not believe that there is another site in the United States where there are greater possibilities of making a beautiful country club, and it is practically the one and only site for the Battle Creek Country Club. It is also the last opportunity to purchase a site if they ever want to have a country club near this city where there will be enough social interest in conjunction with the golf interest to maintain it.

Yours very truly,

CLP*C

P.S.
Where reference herein is made to the Country Club, I would grant the same privileges to you or your associates so long as it is understood that the ultimate purpose for the place would be for the use of the Country Club, as it is with that understanding only that I am making concessions in the price.

Letter from C. L. Post to Stephen Rathbun offering to sell the property to the Country Club.

According to the negotiations, C. L. Post got to take down and keep the greenhouse where I found all the old bottles, as well as keep three acres of an adjacent lakefront lot. A price of $57,000 was agreed upon for the Calmary farm with a down payment of $7,000.

One of the sale requirements was that the property must be used as a country club. Post sent letters further defining the sale to "exclude any farm or garden tools, nor any furnishings of the house, nor the rectifier in the garage which is used for charging my electric car." Interestingly this same garage was later filled with chargers for the club's golf carts and, became our gang hangout as mentioned earlier. Work began on the course that fall, but the negotiations grew into arguments and a flurry of letters that continued well into the next year.

Crops harvested on the property that fall were to be retained by Mr. Post. With his sharp business eye for the bottom line, Post had his secretary Mrs. Cooper send letters asking that he be credited the $11.41 club employees had collected selling apples and vegetables.

CIDER APPLES
For Sale at Country, Club,
LAKE GOGUAC
Apply to Nelson Richards on Premises

Later she wrote asking that the remaining coal be measured and credited. She later sent invoices for items sold to the club including oats, hay, a wagon, scrapers, a plow team and a horse named "Bobby." The Club in response claimed Post owed them for property removed, along with pro-rated taxes. C. L. Post was livid, he retorted, "…it's a pretty small thing for you to undertake to split hairs on growing crops," and "…the smallness on your part…is enough to prevent me from further contributions…and improvements." Post finished his tirade by saying, "Now if this is not acceptable, all that is necessary is for you to say so, and we can go to the mat a settle it." The details were finally settled by the summer of 1920, with C. L. Post angry enough at the club to sell off the adjacent three acres he had earlier retained from the sale.

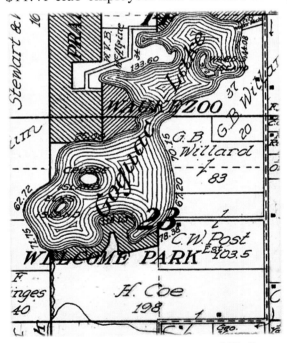

Plot map showing C. W. Post and H. Coe properties that became the golf course

83

One-hundred acres of the adjacent Henry Coe farm was also purchased by the group with 50 acres set aside for the golf course. Coe had been selling off lots along the lake for $1000 to build log cottages on (seen on page 108), which were reached by an access road that ran by what is now #4 Green and 15th Tee. Those lots along the lakefront were also purchased by a consortium of club members, in what was called Welcome Park, now called Mustard's Point, where the 65-foot excursion steamer named *The Welcome* was once docked and later sank when it was destroyed in a fire.

The steamer Welcome wintered at Welcome Park off #8 Fairway.

The purchase money was raised by using a loan from the Old National Bank. In a few days, the group sold $40,000 in bonds. Another $98,000 was soon raised through stock, and the process of dissolving the old club and building a new club organization was completed. The original Post family estate home served as the original clubhouse and was expanded to add a ballroom and more apartments. The sale of the old Country Club site for $35,000 to Mrs. Leila Post Montgomery, along with proceeds from the sale of the adjacent lake lots, paid for the necessary improvements and initial investment.

Over 200 members purchased 25 shares of stock, including W. K. Kellogg.

Back then, selling off adjacent lots was a relatively new way to fund golf courses. Finally, in October 1919, on the southeast shore of Goguac Lake, the new Battle Creek Country Club was founded.

Interestingly, the only specific mention of our home was in an August 30th, 1919 *Enquirer & News* newspaper article describing the sale, where the property is explained: "Calmary Farm is one of the most beautiful and commodious country places in southern Michigan, and its possession will give the prospective country club a home second-to-none in the country for a community of this size. Mr. Post

Herman Verdine and "Nelse" Richards are at the gardens during first year(s) of the Country Club.

has spared no pains or expense to make the place a model of beauty and convenience in every respect… There are barns and other buildings, all modern on the place. The present building equipment includes extensive greenhouses…There is a modern heating plant and power plant, with a water system. The place is connected to the city electrical system but has its own generating plant for use if desired…and

the property also includes *the six-room cottage fronting on the Lake Avenue road*, at the entrance to the drive." To get persnickety, Lake Avenue road is now called Capital Avenue and our house had more than six rooms!

This photo on the previous page shows the extensive gardens of the estate, it was probably taken the first year the club was in operation. It shows Herman Verdine and Nelson (Nelse) Richards (right), who by then were working on the course for Andy Peck. Our Country Club Drive home (insert) can barely be seen along the distant treeline just to the right of Richard's head. The tent is likely the first 'starter house.'

In my search for the beginnings of our home, I found that Richards was a caretaker of Post's Calmary Farm and likely an early resident of our house. Because he had a different address in 1914, the house was probably built between then and 1919. That helped narrow down the question of when it was erected.

Building the Course...

The club's founding fathers reached out to the most famous and available, golf course designer of the time, Scottish architect, Willie Park, Jr. Park was also an accomplished player, equipment maker and publisher of two instructional golf books, and furthermore had won the British Open in 1887 and 1889. He had designed numerous courses in England and the US and was known for carving golf holes into the landscape rather than onto it.

NOTED GOLF EXPERT HERE TO LAY OUT A MODERN GOLF LINKS

His Name Is Willie Parks, and He Comes from Scotland And Is Proud of It.

Says the Grounds of the New Location Are Among the Very Best in the Country.

Hoot, mon! Did ye ken Wullie Par-rr-k was he-rr-re? Aye, mon, Wullie Par-rr-k himsel. Nane ither. Wullie Par-rr-k, o Musselburgh, Scautland—just a wee bit oot o' Edinborough. And he's nane ither than the mon that hae laid oot more golf cour-rr-ses than ony ither mon living. Aye, and mony o' the most famous cour-rr-ses on baith sides o' the herring pond. Wullie is e'en in Battle Creek the day, and sleepit the nicht gane at the Post Tav-er-rr-n.

And, hear-rr this, mon! What's mair, Wullie has ganged oot to Goguac lake the morn, and is e'now planning oot a muckle cour-rr-se o' 18 holes anent the lake, that he says wull be ane o' the verry finest in a' the land.

86

Park took the job! His design and supervision fees were $1,800, and the original design length was a Par 72, 6,574 yards. The local paper announced his hire with a play on Park's Scottish accent:

"Hoot, mon! Did ye ken Willie Par-rr-k was he-rr-re? Aye, mon, Wullie Par-rr-k himsel. Nane ither. Wullie Par-rr-k, o Musselburgh, Scautland - just a wee bit oot o' Edinborough. And he's nane ither that the mon thath hae laid oot more golf cour-rr-ses on baith sides o' the herring pond. Wullie is e'en in Battle Creek the day, and sleepit the nicht gane at the Post Tav-rr-rr-n."

"And, hear-rr this, mon! What's mair, Wullie has ganged oot to Goguac Lake the morn, and is e'now planning oot a muckle cour-rr-se o' 18 holes anent the lake, that he says wull be ane o' the verry finest in a' the land."

Agreement entered into this twenty-sixth day of September, between Willie Park, Jr., and the Battle Creek Country Club, of Battle Creek, Michigan, in which the Battle Creek Country Club, agrees to employ Willie Park, Jr., to plan and supervise the construction of an 18 hole Golf Course on their property.

Willie Park, Jr., to receive the sum of $1800 payable as follows:

$500 upon the acceptance of this agreement, $500 upon the completion of the laying out and trapping of all the Putting Greens, $500 upon the completion of the trapping and bunkering the fairways, and $300 upon the completion of the seeding the entire Course.

Mr. Willie Park, Jr. agrees to visit the Course as often as he deems necessary during the period of its Construction, and not less than once during a period of one year after the completion of the course.

Witness: _____ Jones
September 26, 1919.

Accepted for The Battle Creek Country Club
By _____ Washburn, Pres.

Accepted by _____ Willie Park

Contract for Willie Park, Jr to design the golf course.

Park first visited the course in the fall of 1919, immediately after the sale went through, to begin laying out the new golf course. It was reported that Park declared the site "...the finest piece of land for the purpose he has ever seen, and when finished it will be one of the best courses in the United States and Canada." Interestingly, he also offered the identical quote to several other of his over 100 other golf course clients. Having a long-standing relationship with Willie Park and experience at golf course construction, the New York firm of Peterson, Sinclaire & Miller was hired by the club to build the course, with a Mr. Frank James as foreman. Mr. James placed ads in the

Willis (Willie) Park, Jr. – Scottish Professional Golfer, Club Maker, Golf Writer and Course Architect...

BCCC connected to legendary Old Tom Morris of St Andrews? Yes, tenuously; Wee Willie Park, Jr.'s family of Musselburgh, Scotland enjoyed a fierce business and competition rivalry with the Morris family. Willie's father, winner of the first British Open plus three other titles, taught Willie how to make clubs, balls and play the beautiful game. Like his father, Willie won the British Open in 1897 and 1898; he was listed in the top ten golfers twelve times. As golf's popularity exploded, in his thirties Park became one of the first full-time course architects, designing one hundred seventy courses in the British Isles, Europe, Canada and the U.S. The Battle Creek Country Club is listed among his top ten U.S. projects. His book *The Game of Golf* (1896) was the first golf book by a professional; it is still in print. Willie died in 1925 at the age of 61.

local paper to hire manpower and horse teams, while C. L. Post placed other announcements at the same time to sell his horses and livestock.

> **WANTED**
> Men and teams to work on new golf course. Apply to Mr. James, Calmary farm, Lake Goguac. Bell Phone 390.

My dad had often wondered where all the topsoil came from to build the elevated, large greens and tee boxes, and especially how it got there. We discovered that the sand and topsoil were brought in by railcar from New Jersey, apparently due to the relationships that the construction firm had with suppliers there. The golf course construction firm even had their own brand of topsoil - *Rex Humus* - which must have been very good dirt indeed! It took 300 tons of topsoil to build just the greens. All of it carried in dozens of rail cars, not to mention topsoil for the tees and bunkers, plus 30 tons of fertilizer and 30 tons of limestone for drainage. The topsoil needed to be mixed with sand for proper drainage, plus more sand required filling the bunkers. All would require many dozens of railcars, plus hundreds of dump truck and wagon trips from a rail siding to the course. This is certainly plausible, but questionable due to the cost of rail transport - a distance of 700 miles over the Appalachians. With sand quarries a short 50 miles away at Lake Michigan, the wonder is why the contractor would not want to save money and at least use the same local sand that was used in later years.

Preconstruction Report for Country Club Land Co.

❖ Putting Greens - 150 bushels of Carter's Finest Putting Green Seed—$1,500

❖ We advocate fairways 60 yards wide at least. 600 bushels of Carter's Finest Fairway Seed - $5,400

❖ 100 yards of rough in front of each of the tees and 7 1/2 yards of rough on each side of the fairways. Carter's Special Rough Mixture - $1,115

❖ Putting Greens - Per Green $864. Each green = 4 teams / 12 days at $8 per day + 10 men for 12 days at $4. Total for 18 greens = $15,552

❖ Supervising Constructor - 8 months at $300 /month = $2,400

❖ Foremen - 3 foremen - 200 working days at $ 5 per day = $3,000

❖ 10% commission to be paid the Peterson Sinclaire Construction Co for supervising the entire operation - $3,541

❖ Grand Total —$55,818.20

❖ (Although not listed, the difference of $23,310 must have paid for labor and the "Rex Humus.")

This pre-construction report prepared by Peterson-Sinclaire outlines what was required to build the course.

The grass seed was supplied by the Carter Tested Seed Company, a London outfit with a long relationship to Willie Park and the construction company. That team had then completed almost 20 courses in the US. What is curious is that my father recalls they planted live sprigs of grass, called stolons, in the fairways and tees by hand: *"These guys would go in with long-handled spades and a potato sack of Bent stolons. Stick the spade in the ground and push it forward to open a slit, drop in the sprig and then step on it. Guys lined up across the fairway doing that."* This was a very labor-intensive process but more likely required for the first eight holes as they were quickly put into play the next midsummer of 1920. With only 3 months to grow in the turf that spring on the course, using the stolons apparently worked.

From fall through the spring, Mr. James hired local laborers and teamsters to shape the greens, tees and bunkers of the first nine. What was remarkable is that they did it mostly with horse-drawn earth movers and graders called Fresno scrapers, moving less than one cubic yard at a time. My dad's Uncle Lou said, *"If you caught a root or a rock while scraping and had a hard grip on the tiller bar, it would flip you right over and throw you up onto the horse team."*

One exception to the horse-drawn scrapers was a Cletrac tractor; manufactured by the Cleveland Tractor Company starting in 1916. It more closely resembled a small bulldozer without the blade than a tractor. The Cletrac was likely brought in by Peterson Sinclaire, and with so much earth yet to move to build the back nine; it was eventually purchased by the club. The nearest rail siding was over three miles away, but hundreds of yards of topsoil and sand needed to be hauled to the site. In 1919, motorized dump trucks were still somewhat of a rarity, so it is likely a lot of the hauling was done by horse, and some of that done by Andrew and his team. Trees were pulled, and the fairways tilled and graded out. Sand and topsoil had to be mixed, moved and shaped for the greens which are exceedingly large even by today's standards.

A Cletrac tractor was also used to build the course.

New 18 hole course under construction by

PETERSON, SINCLAIRE & MILLER, Inc.

ARCHITECT—WILLIE PARK

for

Country Club Land Co.

Battle Creek, Mich.

A Green Under Construction

Golf Course Construction

The initial cost of construction is a permanent investment.

Money expended for scientific construction at first will save thousands of dollars outlay in future years.

We handle every detail from the start and produce a finished course ready for play.

Consult us for Estimates, Plans or Advice. We are prepared to begin work now—or plan work for 1920.

Peterson, Sinclaire & Miller, Inc.

25 West 45th St.   New York City.

A large crew was needed to plant Washington Bent Grass stolons.

A New Job...

Luckily, Grandpa Andy was well-liked by the members, and sometime that fall or early winter he learned he'd be hired on as Greenskeeper of the new course to help with the transition and establish the new grass. With a great deal of relief, late that winter the newly married couple, Andy and Rena, moved into their comfortable new home, the former Post Estate

The horse-drawn Fresno Scraper was used by Andy Peck, but could only move about ½ cubic yard.

91

caretaker's house on the corner. At a very young age, my grandmother had a new household to set up, along with three very young children to raise, and my grandfather returned to farming of sorts...becoming a full-time grass farmer.

The first eight holes, known as the front nine, were roughed in on the Post estate farm that fall, with a short, temporary hole from the practice tee to the ninth green. That next spring Grandpa oversaw the seeding and sprigging, completed in time for nine holes of the course to open in July of 1920, but undoubtedly the turf was rather coarse at that time. The back nine was a much greater challenge to build as a large portion of the land was swampy muck; that nine took two years to finish. Parts of those holes had been shaped and roughed out during the initial construction, but Andrew oversaw the finishing and seeding. While peat is great for fertilizer, the muck was less than ideal for golf, and numerous drainage tiles had to be installed before these areas would be dry enough to work. A lot of fill was needed, and the Rex Humus that may have been brought in to cover the fairways would have soon mixed with the muck. Some portions of several fairways had wet spots, and the turfgrass planted on this muck always had an unusual bouncy or spongy feel to it.   Large portions of the 6th, 9th, 10th, 13th and 14th Fairways were often underwater after a rain.

This horse-drawn scraper was another machine used to build the course.

Early aerial photo of the front seven holes soon after construction. #1 Fairway is along the left, and the new Country Club Hills subdivision is along the top. One Country Club Drive is in the upper left.

An unusually wet spring in 1922 was a setback for the opening of the second nine. Several of those areas were submerged for weeks, killing the new grass. The high lake level made matters worse with the overflow from the lake being channeled through a county-owned overflow tile running across the 7th, 11th, 13th and 6th Fairways. Grandfather added a bit of fuel to the controversy by blocking the tile to prevent the lake runoff from flooding lower parts of the course. According to a May 9, 1922 newspaper article, there was a running dispute between the Township and the golf course, with Grandpa blocking the tile one day and the county opening it up the next. This went on for more than a week. The tiles and a dispute over tax assessment for the new Lakeview School led to a suit by the club against the Township. With the tile blocked the water finally receded to give the grass a chance to

grow in. The second nine finally opened in July of 1922, and the total construction cost was still pegged at $55,818.20.

Early Mowing...

A One-Horse-Power 3-Gang mower (Courtesy John Mascaro)

Maintaining the eighteen-hole course back then was a physical challenge. Motorized equipment was rare, so a lot of manual labor was required. Everybody walked to get anywhere while working on the course. Watering the course was done by hand, dragging the heavy hose and sprinklers everywhere. Sprinklers and hoses were not plentiful; they were both a new and somewhat expensive invention. Although three-unit reel mowers drawn by horse or tractor were used to cut fairways, the mowing of the tees and greens were cut solely by hand. The early manual push-type greens mowers were exhausting to use. Back then muscle-powered reel mowers were used because any gasoline engine would have been too heavy. The grass had to be short and smooth, so these reels were spaced very close together for a fine cut. The mower wheels were geared to rapidly spin the closely spaced cutting reels, which made them difficult to push. My dad, who loved to tell stories, told me about when as a kid about 1935, he tried to use the push greens-mowers:

"Early on when they went out mowing greens, they had the old push mowers. The reel was geared so fast on those mowers it took an awful lot to push it even if you weren't cutting grass. Sometimes they'd push one way across, and then they'd have somebody else there to push it back, or they would have a rope tied to it and one guy pushing and one guy pulling. Especially if the greens got a little too long, they pushed really hard. I know I was out here on 17th green one day and I tried it. And one of the guys says, "Here, you push," and I got a hold of it. I couldn't push it at all. Of course, I was just a kid at the time.

"But then in later years, why, Claire Morse wanted one because he put in a little bit of a putting green at his house. And I took one over to demonstrate to him. And by golly, I couldn't push it. I couldn't push it at all. He got a hold of it and he pushed it. But he didn't use it for very long; he gave up on it.

An early manual-push greens mower. (Courtesy John Mascaro)

"The greens used to be bigger than they are now. The greens used to be mowed by hand out to the edge of the banks. You take #18...one big green! If you had to push that mower, I don't know how in the world you'd ever get it up that hill. But of course, the men were stronger in those days.

Andy Peck on a smooth #1 Green. One Country Club Drive home can be seen nestled in the trees left of flag.

"Changing from the push mowers, I remember seeing the first Jacobsen power mower for Greens, and I think that was the first one ever built. My dad said, "you're going to put that heavy thing onto a green?" It was unheard of at the time, but it had a fine-looking engine on it. Double flywheels on the engine, one on each side, but it was the greatest thing. And one man could mow all 19 greens with it.

Early Jacobsen power greensmower,
shown without catcher basket

"But sometimes if they were in a hurry, they had a couple of guys still going around mowing by hand. That didn't last long after Jacobsen came out with that mower with a two-cycle engine on it. And, boy, that was a beautiful thing. It did a beautiful job. And of course, we used those for years. They had another mower that they used for tees and it was about 28 inches wide; a Jacobsen mower with a double flywheel on it. They called it a four-acre mower. They mowed tees with that, but it would take a guy all of a day to mow tees. And the funny part of it was, the tees were only a fraction of the size they are today.   *-H.P.*

Andy Peck with Ray Lampke at the wheel of the new Roseman Turf Tractor in 1925.

A view of #2 Fairway and our house from the new Country Club Hills subdivision. The building in the foreground was a sales office for the subdivision.

It's little wonder in those days the rough was mowed only twice a year, fairways and tees twice a week, and greens every other day at best. Needless to say, the person mowing had to be in really great shape to do it.

As a teamster, Grandpa must have had mixed feelings about switching over to modern powered tractors and not using his horses to mow. The Cletrac with its bulldozer-like tracks would have torn up the turf and been a relatively poor example of modernization, though. Nevertheless, that was the future. The club purchased a new Roseman Tractor in 1925, shown on the previous page with Ray Lampke at the wheel and Andy Peck enjoying the new ride in front of the club gardens. Even though tractors weren't as reliable, tractors didn't have to be fed, watered (as much) and rested, and didn't have to wear turf boots or leave manure to clean up. The tractor's metal wheels apparently didn't tear up the grass as much as horses, so after that first year of use there was no question the turf was more beautiful than ever, and compliments from the membership were growing. That may have led to Andy selling some of his horses.

FOR SALE—Good work horse, 1700 lbs. Kind and sound. Double or single. Call at Battle Creek Country Club. See Peck.

The practicality and success of that Roseman tractor led to Andy trading the Cletrac for a new Staude Golf Course Mak-A-Tractor to mow the fairways in January 1927. This machine was just a stripped-down Model T with big metal wheels. It came in a kit; you took your old beat-up Model T, stripped off the body and tires, and put on the big metal wheels. Sometimes the seats stayed, but usually they were replaced with a pan-shaped metal tractor seat. They were quite popular, since there were a lot of beat-up Model T's around, and the club eventually owned three. My dad recalls:

"I can vaguely remember watching some of the guys and how they were working the golf course. I remember one time as a kid watching a man mowing # 17 Fairway with the old Staude tractor, which was a tractor with a model T engine in it. Apparently, there was something in the fairway that he had to pick up. So without stopping, he jumps off the tractor, runs around in front, picks it up and goes back, and hops back on the tractor. And I thought at the time when I saw him doing that, 'Man, isn't that something. What if he'd fall. He could injure himself real good.' He could get hurt real bad, but I don't know if they ever worried about that much. It wasn't done very much, that's for sure.

"But when it come to mowing bunkers, every time when the bunkers need mowing, why, they had a guy that would walk around. He'd stick a whetstone in his pocket and carry a scythe with him, and he'd take off walking. He would cut the grass on the bunkers with that scythe all day. Of course, it got pretty high too.

E. G. STAUDE MAK-A-TRACTOR CO.

Golf Course Tractor Specialists
2670 UNIVERSITY AVE., ST. PAUL, MINN.

A GOLF COURSE MAINTENANCE MACHINE

That anybody can operate—
That any Ford dealer can service—
That can be turned in a short space—
That is low in first cost—
That is low in upkeep and maintenance cost—
That is in universal use on golf courses—

THAT IS THE STAUDE GOLF COURSE MAINTENANCE MACHINE

A Tractor—Hauling—Mowing Outfit
Fully Guaranteed

PRICE ONLY $695.00 F. O. B. ST. PAUL
Patented and Patents Pending

The cut below shows the Staude Golf Course Maintenance Machine complete, including Staude General Utility Golf Course Tractor, slip-on body, three unit mower hitch, three 30" cutting units, all complete and assembled, as shown.

Nothing Better at Any Price

Get our prices on Tractors—Mowers—Hitches. Write to-day for descriptive literature.

98

1928 Model A Dump Truck with 'Battle Creek Country Club' painted on the door.

"But he cut the grass on the bunkers. And as far as the sand traps itself were concerned, why, I guess they would go around and rake sand traps only once in a while. But everyone always walked around the golf course. And I started working for my dad and did a lot of walking around the golf course too. If you wanted to do anything, you want to get around the course, you'd walk. Once in a while, you'd get a chance to get on the old '28 Model A dump truck and drive around, but that was a case of we didn't do that very much. We consistently did a lot of walking on the golf course. -H.P.

Early Workers...

"Going back to some of the early days, I remember dad (Andrew Peck) telling me that when the Depression hit, they cut him down to five men in the summer, sometimes less. That's all they could afford. And they paid them at that time twenty-five cents an hour. And I thought, "Wow, that's something else." Of course, they worked fifty hours a week, and I'm thinking, "Well, these guys aren't getting much money." But what few guys they did have worked hard and they worked efficiently. You didn't see a guy at all goofing around. They didn't goof around at all. It was a case of they had to get the job done.

The "new" Roseman tractor with Ray Lampke driving in front of Maintenance Garages

100

And I don't know if my dad was really tough on them, but that's just the way you handled them. Why, he just got a lot of work out of them, cause they knew jobs were hard to come by.

"I remember one of the men that he had working for him was Leroy Jones, back in the early '30s. And Marshall Country Club needed a greenskeeper, so Dad recommended him to go over to Marshall Country Club. Then he went to the Country Club of Lansing which was a real good job. And another man that he had working for him was Wesley Watkins, who was the son of a farmer that lived out south there. Marywood needed a greenskeeper, so Dad recommended him, and he worked out at Marywood for a good thirty years anyway. But some of the other guys that worked for Dad, when the war broke out, of course, they were kind of compelled to go to work in factories which people did in those days. They had to go for the war effort. But it was all quite a deal. But the guys got a lot of work done at that time.

The Maintenance Crew weeding a green by hand, about 1928 judging by the trees. According to Harold, his dad hired quite a few women to pull weeds out of the greens, tees and fairways.

"One of the men that mowed fairways years ago, I used to ride with him once in a while on the old Staude tractor. I don't know how I was ever allowed to do that, but I was a kid and they let me ride with him. Today, I never would let anybody ride on the tractors like we did then because he was pulling a seven gang behind that old tractor. They mowed fairways with that old tractor, and I guess they did quite a lot with it. But [chuckles] it had to be something else to keep some of that old equipment running, because it was never as efficient as equipment today.

Grounds crew Herman Verdine (right) Dave Harper (middle) and Cal Stump remove the bunker by #1 Green, while Shirley's boy Russ Conklin looks on in 1941.

"One of the guys that Dad used to have during the '30s, who worked here for quite a while was Dave Harper (photo middle). He lived way out North Avenue, pretty near the Astoria Center. And he was kind of a heavy guy. He came to work every day. He came in about twenty minutes after 6:00 a.m. And he'd sit there having his coffee in the morning. Went to work on the course at 7 o'clock.

"And then there was two guys that lived out south of Battle Creek. Right out by Dubois Corners. They lived side by side out there and they worked for dad for quite a long time...Roy Harper and Roy Kissinger. They worked when I was a kid. They were working for dad so long it seemed like they were the golf course.

-H.P.

A Terrible Scandal...

While digging through my grandma's pile of newspaper articles, I was fascinated to discover a sensational national scandal that had its beginnings on the golf course. The 22-year-old son of one of the founding members was out on a date with a girl one night. At some point they went out on the golf course, and that was where he viciously beat her up! Arthur Rich had been club champion just the previous year, in 1924. According to later court testimony, he took Miss Louise King out on the golf course to "describe his record golf shots and get a drink of water," likely at the hand-pump or log shelter near #11 Green. They were out for the evening with another couple who stayed behind in their car. Rich returned carrying the girl's unconscious body, claiming she had fallen over an embankment. They drove around for an hour hoping she would wake up before finally taking her to the Sanitarium Hospital.

The 19-year-old girl had severe fractures of the upper jawbone and other internal injuries; it took her many weeks to recover. Rich, whose millionaire father owned a major manufacturing business in town, was arrested several days later and then freed on bond. The first trial in the city was deadlocked, as three of the jurors reportedly claimed the girl was a modern young flapper who rolled her stockings, drank wine, smoked cigarettes and went on automobile rides at night. To them, she deserved to be assaulted at the "ultra-modern petting party." There were also claims of jury tampering. A second trial was held in the state capital, with over 3,200 pages of testimony presented and there was extensive coverage of the sensational trial in newspapers across the nation. The defense made similar claims during this trial, by playing on her attire and the sipping of wine and suggested that the girl's failure to make an outcry somehow implied consent. After deliberating only twenty-four minutes, the jury returned a guilty verdict for the criminal assault charges. The judge immediately sentenced Rich to life imprisonment; he was led off to Jackson State Penitentiary. On March 11, 1926, *The Enquirer and Evening News* reported:

"The conduct of the young man and all of his family and friends who have tried to save him from punishment for the crime he was accused of committing and the militant attitude of his chief attorney, who drew the censure of all people following the case because of his nasty treatment of prosecution witnesses, materially aided in bringing to the young man before the bar the full force of the court and public's disfavor."

During a third civil trial, another jury awarded the girl $50,000 in damages, a record in the state at that time. An appeal for a retrial of the criminal assault charges eventually went all the way to the Supreme Court two years later, primarily based on the consent question due to her failure to make an outcry. That court barely affirmed the verdict by a 4-4 decision, a sign of the times. The Governor refused to pardon Rich, but after serving seven years in prison the next governor, possibly influenced by a rumored $250,000 in campaign donations, pardoned Arthur Rich. At his release in 1933, he escaped the press and went to live in California. A few years later he moved back to town with a new wife and apparently had a successful career and social life. My grandparents knew the Rich family well, and I wonder what they thought of the dreadful affair.

Supreme Court Affirms Life Sentence for Rich

LANSING, MICH., Feb. 4.—(A. P.)——The conviction of Arthur C. Rich, son of a Battle Creek millionaire manufacturer, sentenced to life imprisonment on a charge of criminally assaulting Louise King, Battle Creek co-ed, was affirmed by the Supreme Court today.

The assault, it was alleged, occurred on the links of the Battle Creek Country Club, following an automobile ride early in 1925. Rich's petition for a new trial was denied.

The eight justices of the court divided evenly on the appeal, four voting for affirming the conviction and four being for reversal. An even division means the lower court ruling stands.

Pittsburgh Post-Gazette, Feb 5th, 1927

Life at Home...

Cousin Martha Post (left), Rena Peck, and baby Harold being held by cousin Francis Peck at the Garden Trellis by the Clubhouse

Andrew and Rena didn't waste much time adding to their combined family of five. Roy came along in 1921, followed by Harold in 1922, Les in 1926, and Winifred in 1930. A cousin Francis was also living with them for many years. This assuredly necessitated quite a bit of juggling around in the four-bedroom home. The two older boys had one room, the three younger ones another, and the girls had the third. Shirley moved into the unfinished attic in the summer. Here is a very tolerant Harold being held by cousin Francis, mother Rena in the middle and cousin Martha Post at left. They are in front of the rose garden trellis at the clubhouse.

105

The exclusive Country Club Hills subdivision under construction across Lake Road (Capital Avenue), with the stone pillars at the entrance to Country Club Drive

A look through Andrew and Rena's diary in early 1927 shows a busy time for Andrew as both greenskeeper and teamster. He had many club duties that winter including fixing mowers, painting, keeping the furnace going in the clubhouse and a fire going in the pumphouse for water and fire protection. He was the only employee through the winter and during which time he needed to watch over the club and complete any repairs at the clubhouse or on the course equipment. He also plowed snow and later used his team to help with the grading at the exclusive development of Country Club Hills, across the street from the house. As a teamster, he also drew loads of gravel, cinders, etc. for various clients like the city of Battle Creek. This hardworking man needed to supplement the club's modest salary.

For over a month in the early weeks of 1927, Andy became a vagrant of sorts, living out of various places because the rest of his family was quarantined in the house. Scarlet Fever was an epidemic then, and after some of their children started getting sick, the Doctor advised putting everyone under temporary quarantine. Pretty soon everyone became sick except Andy, who had begun sleeping down at the clubhouse. The quarantine was quickly formalized with the official

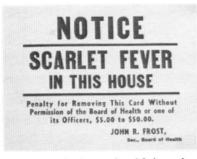

red card in the front window signifying that the house was off limits to all but doctors. The next few weeks must have been miserable with fever rash, ears popping and general malaise. Poor Rena had to take care of everyone. One diary entry said, "poor husband who doesn't have a home," and another entry said simply, "…got scared last night." Everyone recovered, although sadly 1-year-old Les retained a heart condition that years later likely caused a heart attack at a relatively young age.

This unknown couple were the first visitors photographed at One Country Club Drive.

Dad's Stories About Growing Up…

As anyone who knew him would recall, my dad was filled with stories about growing up on the golf course. I really enjoyed it when he described the history and evolution of the bunkers, tees and greens, gardens and outbuildings. One day I asked him about all the many odd bunker remnants near the tees around the course, and he explained, *"The architect put lots of small traps close to the tees to make the poor golfer improve his game. Some of them, like the two that were once on either side of #10 Fairway at the top of the hill, were there as a guide to direct the golfer toward the green that couldn't be seen."* -H.P.

Some of the big greens had been even bigger at one time, but both he and his father needed to use some of the grass from the front of those greens like #3 to make emergency repairs which shortened them up. Much later Harold built the nursery, where we grew and mowed sod used to repair the fairways, tees and greens.

Dad mentioned two small gazebo-like rain shelters with a white trellis, one at #7 Tee and another near #16 Green. I remember seeing those as a little kid. He also describes, *"a little toilet house – an octagonal-shaped outhouse on the south side of #6 Fairway with a peaked roof and having with a men's side and a women's side. There was always a peephole cut from one side to the other, and no matter what they did to cover it, someone always cut that hole again. One day someone burned it down."*

- H.P.

Cousins Wendell, Luella and Isabell Peck (right) at a log cabin at Welcome Park on Goguac Lake. The cabin was later moved between #7 & #11 Fairways as a shelter. Torn down in 1934, the wood flooring was reused in the kitchen of One Country Club Drive.

He also described a shelter between #7 and #11 Fairways that, "...*was an actual log cabin, about 12'x18' with a hardwood floor, that my dad (Andy) somehow moved from along #9 Fairway (where Holmes' house is now) all the way down there*". The photo on the previous page shows that cabin before it was moved with cousins Wendell, Luella (center) and Isabell Peck. What is particularly interesting is the picture is dated 1918, over a year before the country club bought the property, so that may have been their cabin. When that cabin-as-shelter was torn down, he related, his dad Andy took up the hardwood floor and put it down on the kitchen floor of our house.

I was also fascinated when my dad recalled the equipment stored in an old shed south of #5 Tee which ran alongside a dump. That dump had to be moved behind the tennis courts when the land south of the club along what is now Linwood Drive was developed by a group of club members along the lake. Dad mentioned his father was asked to invest in that development too, and I always wondered what it might have been like if Andy had bought property there and we ended up living over in that neighborhood.

At the end of 1928, the future was looking very promising. The Balance Sheet on the next page shows that the Battle Creek Country Club and the Country Club Land Company, which actually owned the property and leased it back to the club, was doing quite well. The Country Club operation had a profit for the year of over $11,550, with the golf course upkeep costing only $12,750. The Land Co. had a surplus of almost $8200.

Little did anyone know an economic disaster would soon happen and last for almost ten years, leading to foreclosure, salary cuts for my grandpa, and a drastic lessening in the course maintenance. But that comes later...

CONSOLIDATED PROFIT AND LOSS STATEMENT OF
Battle Creek Country Club and Country Club Land Co.
December 31, 1928

HOUSE ACCOUNT

	Receipts	Expenditures	Profit or Loss
Cafe	$28,813.11	$23,019.16	
Room Rent	3,117.76		
Entertainment	50.50	1,462.27	
House Expense	253.36	7,192.75	
Depreciation—Furniture and Fixtures, Etc.		1,451.52	
	32,234.73	33,125.70	
Loss			$ 890.97

GOLF COURSE

	Receipts	Expenditures	Profit or Loss
Golf Course Upkeep		$12,750.81	
Ground Tees	5,695.00		
Membership Fees	250.00		
Depreciation—Machinery and Tools Fairways and Piping		931.36	
	5,945.00	13,682.17	
Loss			$ 7,737.17

LOCKER ROOM

	Receipts	Expenditures	Profit or Loss
Men's Locker Rental	$ 1,365.00		
Ladies' Locker Rental	77.00		
Locker Room Concessions	2,556.11	1,904.00	
Men's Locker Room Expense		969.45	
Ladies' Locker Room Expense		208.87	
Locker Room Salaries		1,010.48	
	3,998.11	4,092.80	
Loss			$ 94.69

DUES

Profit	$31,588.32

GENERAL

	Receipts	Expenditures	Profit or Loss
Administrative Expense		$ 2,111.14	
Extraordinary Expense		279.05	
Garden and Lawn Upkeep		809.61	
Interest—Notes and Bonds		4,385.00	
Sports and Pastimes		516.37	
Taxes		2,007.32	
Insurance		1,087.11	
Depreciation on Buildings		1,968.83	
Discount on Purchases	37.44		
Garage Rent	65.00		
Interest Received— Certificate of Deposit	498.40		
Stock Transfer Fee	1,000.00		
Premium on Stock	250.00		
	1,850.84	13,164.43	
Loss			$11,313.59
Net Gain for Year			11,551.90

CLAUDE B. HALLADAY, Treas.

CONSOLIDATED BALANCE SHEET
OF
COUNTRY CLUB LAND COMPANY
AND BATTLE CREEK COUNTRY CLUB

DECEMBER 31, 1928

Stockholders and Members,
Country Club Land Company,
Battle Creek Country Club,
Battle Creek, Michigan.

GENTLEMEN: In accordance with instructions of the Board of Directors, I have prepared consolidated balance sheet of the Country Club Land Company and Battle Creek Country Club for the year ending Dec. 31, 1928, as follows:—

Deficit of C. C. Land Co., Dec. 31, 1927	$5,915.18	
Deduct Profit for Year 1928	2,514.54	
Deficit Dec. 31, 1928		$3,400.64
Surplus B. C. C. Club, Dec. 31, 1927	$2,559.51	
Profit for 1928	9,037.36	
Surplus Dec. 31, 1928		$11,596.87
Net Surplus Dec. 31, 1928		$ 8,196.23

In Spite of the Depression…

According to the 1930 census, ten people were living in the four-bedroom, single bath home; Andy (48) and Rena (35), Andrew Everett (15), Philip (13), Shirley (11), Roy (8), Harold (7), Leslie (4), Winifred (0), and a cousin Francis Post (24). With all those people, that single bathroom was the reason Grandpa built that crude shower in the basement which caused my childhood angst.

A pig sty and chicken coop are behind the garage at One Country Club Drive.

In addition to Grandpa's team of horses, they kept pigs, cows and chickens, and cultivated a large vegetable garden, essential to living back then with a big family. My Aunt Winifred told me they never went hungry, an unusual accomplishment during the depression. Everyone chipped in, but it was a lot of work as Harold describes it:

"In our childhood, we roamed around this place and it seemed like we had all kinds of fun. My dad would get the garden plowed. Usually, he would have us kids do it or sometimes hire somebody to come in and plow the garden. And the garden was the whole backyard from the back of the old garage. Dad would get it plowed and dragged, and then we'd go work out there, too. Us kids would have to work in the garden. Man, did we hate it! We just hated working in that garden. Pulling weeds and that sort of thing. We had to take care of our chickens and help dad milk the cows too, but we were told if we wanted to eat, we had to do it.

Harold plowing the backyard garden next to Lake Rd. (now Capital Ave.)

"And, of course, when it came fall – why, usually us kids were in school at the time - but before we'd go to school, we'd get a bunch of canning jars and stuff out of the basement and bring it up to mother, and she would can everything. My mother used to can an awful lot. We had big bins in the basement - not just shelves like we've got right now. And we used to put up an awful lot of stuff and

112

put it down there. In fact, we had a bunch of two-quart jars - to feed nine of us we needed that kind of food. But mother used to can an awful lot, and we'd get a lot out of that garden. She'd put up a lot of applesauce, because we had apples out of the orchard down at the club. We'd pick those apples up and store them in the basement of the cottage by the clubhouse where Ron used to live.

"That cottage was empty in the winter time, and we stored a bunch of apples down there and they wouldn't freeze. And one time, a couple of weeks before Christmas, we took some apples out to Yawger's Cider Mill out here by Minges Brook where the pumping station is now - the old cider mill - and we then ground them up and pressed them. And we brought home a keg of cider - about 10 gallons of cider - and we loved it. That was good stuff until it started to turn.

Yawger's Cider Mill on Mingus Brook was just south of the golf course, a short walk along Lake Road (Capital Ave)

"This reminds me of one-time mother put up a whole bunch of grape juice in cans. And, of course, it was in the basement. And one time my brother Roy says, "Hey, you taste this?" And he opened a can of it. It had a little tang to it. So between Roy and I - mainly just Roy and I - we drank quite a lot of that grape juice. It had started to turn just a little bit to where it had a tang to it, and of course it was real good- - but we knew what it was, and it surely had started to turn to wine.

"But as soon as mother found that out, all that was dumped, because my mother was definitely against drinking anything - even wine. But us kids got away with a lot of things like that. We'd go out in the garden, and we didn't eat much out of the garden raw like that, but we had three apple

113

trees out here in the backyard and we used to pick up those apples and eat them too. She'd can them, and through the winter we appreciated it, especially when-- well, through the winter we'd otherwise run out of a lot of things.

"I know one-time dad bought this steer and he raised it all winter. Down in the barn was a shop which we now called the maintenance shop, but we called it the barn at the time. We had a little place down there fenced in where he kept this little steer, and he raised it most of the winter. Well, in fact, he tended it all winter from a calf.

"And then in the spring it got to a pretty good size, so we butchered it. And I tell you, we had some real good eating then. We had good steaks, hamburgers. Of course, we had to take it and get some of it processed. Well, we did make hamburger out of some of it, because we'd go to the club and get the big mixers, we'd grind it, and we could make hamburger that way. But a lot of the meat, we took it to the food locker at the store. That was a real good deal. But we were getting to where we were teenagers at the time, and we were probably in junior high. But a lot of those things happened, and it was all part of growing up. Everybody goes through some of the things like this growing up.

-H.P.

Here's a picture of Les and Shirley's boy Russell taken about 1942, trying to ride the steer in the field between the house and #2 Tee. It sure seems funny to me to think of cows and horses out on the golf course, and pigs and chickens in the backyard.

They did everything possible to make ends meet during the depression. What was quite unusual for the time was that Grandma also raised grass seed and stolons (live sprigs) for sale to other golf courses, which

Les Peck introducing the new sport of "calf-riding" to the golf course with cousin Russel.

114

was apparently quite a useful and necessary side business. Her 1932 diary mentions many sales of stolons, plus picking and canning 312 quarts of strawberries! I remember how much work that was when my mom used to put up a few cans, but Grandma filled that large root cellar every year with hundreds of jars. She dilled a year's worth of pickles in a large 25-gallon crock, which is now a giant flower pot in our living room, and shucked bushels of walnuts each year from the two walnut trees after spreading them out on the basement floor all winter to dry. She also managed to keep a beautiful flower garden between the house and the #2 Tee.

Grandma Rena, with her camera, took many of the photos in this book.

1932 Diary…

Andy and Rena Peck kept a diary for many years, but the entries from 1932 have many interesting details and provide a remarkable snapshot of their life that year. One of the notable items in the diary was how often people were sick. Boils or carbuncles were frequent and painful with several mentions about them having to be lanced or a tube put in for drainage. Trips to the doctor frequently occurred, several times a month and in some cases daily. Colds were prevalent and ran through the tightly packed household affecting everyone. Andy was sick a lot and his bouts seemed to follow soon after applying various chemicals to the course, what they called "doping." Was

there a correlation between the application of the chemicals and Andrew's chronic illnesses?

In those depression years, most people had little money, and those with a paycheck knew it didn't go far. In January of that year, the diary mentions that the parents borrowed twice from nine-year-old Harold totaling $1.03 from his paper route money. He and his brothers Roy and Phil all had routes, but, being the youngest, Harold had the shortest route along the lakefront. Most of the residents in that

area had only summer cottages and moved into town for the winter, canceling their subscriptions. The upside of this is that every spring for many years, they renewed their papers, consistently giving young Harold the award for the most sign-ups. Harold enjoyed several all-expense-paid trips to Chicago and often told stories about his paper route days including winning the trip to attend the Indy 500 race.

Harold is holding pets Anne & Fanny about 1932.

"Mr. Frasier used to move into town in the wintertime. They lived at 20 Elizabeth Street downtown in the winter, and my buddy Dave Frasier and I would sleep out there once in a while. I'd sleep at his house, and he'd sleep at our house. So Dad took me down to his house and let us stay all night. On Friday and Saturday we'd stay all night-- and golly we had a great time. I remember going to Central Football Field, and there was this whole bunch of us kids that were just having a great old time, a great wrestling match, and just horsing around. We were probably ten years old at the time. And of course, when I went someplace like that to stay all night, I had somebody else take my paper route.

"Because when I was about five years old, why, I had an extension of my brother Phil's paper route, which I had five customers. From the club on down the drive to just the little house the other side of Lassen's, I had five customers. And it was only in the summertime I took care of those because the wintertime us little kids didn't go out in the snow delivering papers. Once in a while maybe two or three of us would go together, but actually, this was my paper route. And whatever profit I made, which was six cents on a customer a week, why, I'd get to keep. Which, okay, that wasn't too bad, until I got a little older and graduated to a paper route that took me from to Steadman's [grocery] way down to where Frasier's lived in back of 8 Tee.

"Then in the summertime, I'd have about 35 customers. This whole side of the lake, and every resident that lived on this side of the lake was my customer except two. There were two people that I could not get to pick the Enquirer & News. They took the Moon Journal, which was the other paper in town. But I made my own spending money. Pretty soon Roy graduated to the route on Country Club Hills and Old Mill Garden. And he had quite a paper route. He had a big route, but he didn't have to travel quite as far as I did. Both of us would go together to get our papers with Ted Anderson, who lived out here just not far from where Minges Brook school is now.

"And we used to go down on the corner of Foster and Bigelow, the little old building down there which was a substation for the paper. We'd go down there and get our papers. Roy, as soon as he

Harold (front left) at the newspaper substation with his Newsie buddies

3-year-old Harold posing by the backdoor at Halloween.

got back to Capital Avenue, he'd stick his thumb out and it didn't take long for him to get a ride. But Ted and I walked most of the way because I took the route that started right there at Steadman's, at Capital and Columbia. I can't tell you who lives there now, but some people that were in that route were Elliot and Barabou, and Vanderbert.

"There were four houses that were on the corner of Capital Avenue, and Columbia, and Ted and I would trade off. One day he'd take my papers and pedal them up there, and I'd pedal his down to Breezy Bluff, and then we'd meet down at the end of Willard Park. "Quite often, we'd get together and we'd help each other pedal papers. It worked out real good. We got to be pretty good buddies. And of course, we were both in the same class in school, too. But I was always grateful for the paper route. I made enough money pedaling papers, so I bought most of my own clothes, and if I wanted an ice cream cone, I had money to buy it. Once in a while I'd get clothes for Christmas or a birthday, but I bought most of my own clothes

"Then sometimes in a point in-between, my folks would buy me some clothes, but not very much because my folks didn't have any money to spend on us kids that wasn't absolutely necessary. My dad was making $62.50 (in 1927). He would draw out every two weeks, or twice a month, he'd draw a check, $62.50. And I tell you, that didn't go very far. But, for us kids having paper routes, that helped out, and that worked out real good.   - H.P.

Rena and Andy Peck

According to that 1932 diary, the Pecks were still wealthy enough to have a car, making payments of $30 per month, perhaps helped along by the club's need for occasional errands. They often helped out family and friends with rides. Interestingly visiting with friends or having folks over for dinner or cards happened very frequently back then, with several mentions in the diary every week. Attending a movie or concert was an exceptional event, and each was mentioned in the diary: "Jan 30, Phil and Harold went to see *Ben Hur*; Feb 7 Went to Show, *The Big Parade*". A special event that year was "motoring" to Detroit to attend a greenskeeper's meeting and visit with relatives.

The diary contains many entries about working on the course, mostly about purchases, repairs or "doping" the greens with chemicals against disease or worms. At that time, worms were considered vermin on par

Grandpa Andy is spraying around the clubhouse gardens. Ice house is behind the trees.

with gophers since they would leave slimy trails and dirt mounds. But in my dad's era, they were considered a valuable asset contributing vital soil aeriation and allowing moisture to get through the dense roots. My dad was an avid fisherman, and many nights he went out to catch night crawlers which might account for some of his fondness for the giant worm. As a young kid my first couple of outings with my dad were both scary – "hunting night crawlers" – and exciting – they were huge and really, really fast. My dad had a special way to sneak up on them since they could feel the vibrations, he said.

He held a rag over the flashlight to see them. Slowly he reached down then quickly grabbed them at their hole and pulled them out. They were quite often over a foot long. I never could catch them anywhere as good as he could.

The diary also mentions a few times in 1932, when Grampa and even Grandma, actually played golf on the course. One very curious entry, however, is on July 28th, when Grandma casually mentions that the notoriously famous touring golf professional Walter Hagen played golf that day. The diary lists the foursome as including [Argentine champion Jose'] Jurado, [club professional, E.W.] Harbert, and a "Mystery Man" [Frank Gottshaux of New Orleans]. The newspaper complained the next day that although Hagen and Jurado won the match, there were only three birdies by the foursome, and Gottshaux played particularly badly, watched by a modest gallery of 230. "The Haig" won the Michigan PGA tournament held at the club the previous year and walked away with the modest $250 first prize.

Walter Hagan

Walter Hagan – Extrovert, Golf Pioneer, First Pro Sports Millionaire…

When Walter Hagan was playing at the BCCC he didn't need to change his clothes in the driveway like he did winning the first British Open in 1920, when he famously parked a Pierce Arrow in the club's driveway to serve as his private dressing room. As a professional he was refused entrance to the clubhouse dressing room at a time when amateurs were favored, and golf pros were not even allowed to enter the clubhouse front door or use the facilities. He won the British Open three more times and was a crucial figure in the development of professional golf.

Hagan is still regarded as one of the top three all-time golfers, but he started at the bottom as a ten cents a round caddie, pro shop clerk, and teenage instructor. At his first U.S. Open in 1913, he was intimidated by the young swells but vowed to return and win the next year. He did just that at the age of twenty-one and again in 1919. He racked up forty-five PGA Tour wins including five PGA championships and captained the first six Ryder Cup teams. Hagan popularized golf with his dashing, assertive character and numerous exhibitions. Likely the first sportsman to earn a million dollars, Hagan quipped he "never wanted to be a millionaire, just live like one."

Apparently, there were still enough people around in the depression years who could afford $1 to watch the tournament, but it would have been a struggle for most. In 1932, Andy had only 5 workers in the summer, so the depression must have made it very challenging for the Country Club since club membership would have been one of the first luxuries members gave up. Although

Andy and Rena's July 28, 1932 diary entry mentioning Walter Hagan, Mystery Man

many of the members were wealthy, largesse was not their strong suit. It was probably all that Grandpa and his meager crew could do to keep the grass from getting too long.

That became painfully evident with the most poignant entry in the diary - the last line of the May 2nd, 1932 diary entry says merely, "Salary cut from $2750 – 2160". While losing $590 a year doesn't sound like much today, it was more than a 21% pay cut which must have been very challenging and scary to Andy and Rena. That reduced salary was not raised until the 1940s.

This 1920s postcard shows Golfers on #9 Fairway, with Country Club Drive and Goguac Lake in the background.

As the depression dragged on the club had its share of financial worries, and those would have significantly affected my grandparents. Membership fees were slashed in 1933 from $100 to $50 in the hopes

of attracting and retaining new members. Financial issues remained for the next seven years, with the club shortening its operating season and services, and again reducing greens fees and membership costs by one-third even as late as the 1938 season. These woes came to a complicated resolution in 1941, as the Country Club Land Co., owners of the club property, went into foreclosure. However, this allowed the bondholders to sell the property back to the club, although at a loss. But that maneuver did keep the club operating, with anticipated help from an increase in membership from officers at nearby Fort Custer. This was no doubt a huge relief to my family which depended on the club for both their income and their house.

At the end of their diary, there was another tiny but fascinating item…their phone number. Having a phone was probably unusual during the depression, but especially noteworthy was the number - 7796. This phone number, now with a 964 prefix on the front, is the same number that our family has always had at the house! For totally sentimental reasons that number still rings in my home today.

Ice Harvest…

Having ice and refrigeration is taken for granted today, but back in the 1920s and '30s ice had to be harvested and stored for use during warmer

Cutting ice out of Goguac Lake

months. The weather was always a serious concern because there might not be enough ice to harvest. On Feb 11, 1932, Andy writes that the "…ice went out of Lake, about 10 days of ice [only] got about 3 in. thick down here"; and later writes on Feb 17, "…ice went out of lake again." It must have been with considerable relief that on March 14th they finally began the harvest; "Andrew started [to] put up ice, Bert, Roy, Wesley put in 10 hrs., Cable 8; got 13 loads, 5-6" thick"; and on March 15th "Breakfast 6 AM, Put up ice, Bert & Mr. Wicks, L.D. and Leo helped, worked till 7 PM, Bert hit Bert with pike pole in nose, Wesley dropped ice on toe." On March 16th, "Still putting up ice, Leo Hall helped," and March 17th, "Finished ice at 3:30".

Ice was stored in the Ice House to the south of the clubhouse. It went four-feet below-ground and eighteen-feet above; it was shaded by the apple trees in the orchard. The walls were filled with sawdust and the roof covered with straw (harvested from the rough) to keep it frozen through the summer and into the fall. For harvesting, workers first marked off the ice with notches using ice plows pulled with horses. Then, using big saws, the ice had to be cut out of the frozen lake in blocks and floated over to a place where it could be hauled onto sleds and carried into the Ice House. Grandpa's horses were also used to pull the blocks out of the water and onto the sled. Harold retells the story of a time when one of the horses fell through the ice, and everyone thought the horse was done for. Grandpa Andy calmly threw a rope around the horse's neck and pulled it tight enough to choke the horse. It could inhale but not exhale, and the horse bloated up enough to float right on the surface. The men were then able to drag the animal safely to shore. Grandpa then released the noose; the horse stood up, took a deep breath and shook off the effects of its near drowning.

WILL CUT ICE FOR USE OF COUNTRY CLUB SOON

One Hundred and Fifty Tons Will Be Stored—May Have to Haul by Wagon.

Due to the thaw and warm weather of the last two weeks the cutting of ice in front of the country club was delayed. However Andrew Peck, who will have charge of the work said yesterday that they would go ahead with the cutting this week or the first of next week. The ice he said has reached a thickness of 12 inches and is just right for cutting. They will cut and store 150 tons of ice for the use of the Battle Creek Country club this year. If enough snow does not fall before the time they start cutting the workmen will be forced to use a wagon instead of a sled to draw the ice. This will slow up the work considerably.

123

Putting up the ice was very hard and dangerous work, but vital to the preservation of food in the family's icebox, and the clubhouse's much bigger one. Ice was also important for one of the household's favorite activities – a frequent Sunday night ice cream making event. For special occasions or just hot days, Andy and Rena invited the men to the house after lunch for a special ice cream treat. Everyone had to take turns hand cranking the machine. The lake ice also had another important use at the club that is taken for granted today – it was chipped at the bar to go in all the mixed drinks, microbes and all (yuck!). Harold recalls:

Winifred, Harold, Rena, Leslie, Andrew, and Roy, as Roy was leaving to join the Marines in 1943

"We had an icebox in the pantry in the back of the kitchen here. The way they handled that, we had a card that mother would put it in the window and she turned whatever number of the weight of the block of ice she wanted on that. And the ice man, he'd come around and he put that block of ice right in the icebox. It wasn't ideal because us kids could go get a little ice pick and pick off a little chunk

and chew on it. Our parents were very strict about wasting it because the ice melted. Sometimes we would get ice from the club and make ice cream, but we didn't get ice every other day. It was every two or three days whenever we needed some for the icebox; I guess the deal was there was that it was club's ice. It wasn't ours. Dad had to get permission from somebody at the club to get part of a block of ice to make ice cream with. I guess that was all part of growing up.   -H.P.

Growing Up…

Harold had a lot of tales about growing up in the '30s around the course and on One Country Club Drive. Like me, as a youngster Harold didn't play much golf but he played around on the golf course. He worked from age five delivering papers, so being a caddie wasn't an option. I'd like to share more of my dad's stories, especially some about his father Andy, just as he told them…

"As kids, we didn't really get into a lot of mischief; we'd just roam around back in the woods across the creek at the end of the drive. When I was the littlest it was a gravel road or cinder road, I should say. I can vaguely remember when they had a steam shovel and dug the road up. They used a lot of it to grade along the edge, and I guess they must've hauled some away. But they did change the route of the road down by number 7. The road used to go up pretty close to the lake - in fact, I would say probably 30, 40 feet from the lake - but when they paved they set it way out. They could've just as well set it out farther because the club doesn't need all that property. But anyway, that was part of the club's subdivision. And us kids used to play all through there.

Winifred (right), Shirley and children are driving Andrew's horse and wagon next to the house.

125

Golfers and a young Caddie on the course in the '20s

"As far as the golf course is concerned, why us kids had very little interest in golf. We hardly ever played golf. I do remember one time. It was either early spring or late fall. It must have been on a Saturday because I was home. My dad come and got me and said, "There's a man that wants to play golf and he wants a caddy." He says, "I want you to go caddy for him." "Well, okay." But I couldn't have been very old at the time. I was just a little shaver. This guy had a little bag and a few clubs in it, and he was interested in playing golf. So Dad took me over to where he was and he started talking to me. He never stopped talking until we got back to the clubhouse, but it was just a lot of fun. He played one, two, and three, and maybe four because that was a short hole. And then we just walked across back to the clubhouse. When we got back up to the locker room, the guy gave me a silver dollar and I thought, "Oh boy, this is really something."

Dr. Walter T. Bobo – Local Golf Pioneer, Medical Entrepreneur

Early golf pioneer Dr. W.T. Bobo helped organize Merritt Commons, the town's first golf course in 1900. Its nine holes bore catchy names like Punch Bowl, Long Game and Hard Luck. By 1909, he helped establish the new nine-hole course on the banks of the Kalamazoo River that became the first Country Club of Battle Creek. In 1919, he and five others organized the new Battle Creek Country Club at Goguac Lake. The BCCC members celebrated his special service during a Labor Day weekend in 1923.

Dr. Bobo never practiced medicine but used his medical degree to start the Dr. Peebles Institute of Health, selling medicines and medical appliances. Ever the entrepreneur, he owned or managed a variety of businesses including the Easy Truss Co., the Battle Creek Appliance Co., Phytamin Corp., the Physicians Treatment and Advisory Co. and Sanborn Laboratories. The FTC and US Postal Service dissolved these businesses for misleading medical claims shortly after Dr. Bobo's death in 1934.

126

"There might have been two or three other times in my lifetime that I caddied for somebody. Being right here, there was a chance to make money. But I never did much since all us kids had paper routes and we didn't have time to caddy. And then we didn't really play golf very much. We'd go out once in a while. My dad had a bunch of old golf clubs from one of the members by the name of Doctor Bobo. W.T. Bobo instigated building the golf course here. In fact, he was chairman of Green's Committee for the first 11 years the course was here. A lot of these clubs used to belong to him. They're wooden shaft clubs. We didn't call them 8 or 9 irons. We called them a niblick or a mashie [chuckles]. We had those up in the attic for years, and to this day I have no idea what happened to them.

"When I was a little kid us kids used to go roam around the golf course, and we rigged up a small bamboo pole and put a little minnow net or something on the end of it. And we would go down on the creek - across 6 and 13 Fairways - and we'd fish out golf balls. And of course, we hunted for golf balls all over the course, but we would go up to (the members) and they'd give us a nickel or a dime for a golf ball, and we'd sell them back to the members. Of course, a lot of them probably belonged to members that lost them. But in those days, when you lost a golf ball, you lost it. -H.P.

Andy's Testimonial Dinner for his 20 Years of Service

After 20 years of service as Greenskeeper, the Club honored Andy with "a testimonial dinner, marked by speeches lauding his long tenure and his craftsmanship." The clubhouse manager, Miss Anne Brainard, fashioned "a golf course down the center of the tables, complete with sand traps, trees, tractors at work, men playing golf and all the trimmings." Among others, two former pros, Arthur Kennett and E. W. (Pops) Harbert gave talks complimenting Andy, and the new Club Pro, Chick Harbert credited him with making the club "one of

the finest in the country." In the photo on the previous page, Andy (second from right) is shaking Steve Rathbun's hand, seen with founders George Rich (left) and Dr. R.D. Sleight. Rathbun, who was the first President of the club, gave Andy this engraved gold watch from the membership.

Dog n Slide...

"As young kids we wandered around the golf course... and used to go swimming a lot down at the club, and I remember one time I rode my bike down to Dave Frasier's. He lived in the house that's right off of 8 Tee. I rode my bike down there and I stayed all night. And in the morning after we had breakfast - of course, we always had to wait an hour before we could go swimming - we got in his boat. We had a pretty good sized 14-foot boat with about a 4-foot beam, and it had a little Elto engine outboard motor that was the cutest little thing. And we would roam around the lake...

"I remember one particular time when I stayed all night, and we got in the boat and we were heading over to the club to go swimming. We liked to swim at the club, well, because in front of their house it was a muck area. And they had a Springer spaniel dog that was pert'inear a buddy of ours. It was a buddy of Dave's, but we always had a lot of fun with that dog. But we took off without the dog, and pretty soon the dog jumps in the water, and he followed us from their house way over to the club. He swam all the way, and then we'd go swimming over there with him.

"And one time, Dave and I-- we'd go up the steps to the big slide. We'd go up the slide and down the slide and just having a great time. And pretty soon, here comes the dog, and he climbed up the steps, and then he'd sit down. He stood up there in the top for a little bit - he needed a little coaxing

- but finally, he slid down. And once he slid down, gee, he thought it was fun, so he went back up, and he did it three or four times. The dog was really having a great time. But when we went back, we did put him in the boat because he was growing tired. But he was a great dog. He used to do everything with us.

-H.P.

Fishing and Camping...

"But getting back to running around on the lake, why, us kids would go out fishing. In fact, we went out fishing a lot of times. And we had our spots we'd go fishing at, and we'd catch a bunch of bluegills, clean them, and every once in a while, the girl that worked for Frasier's would cook them, and we'd eat them there. Quite often, why I'd bring them home, and we'd have David come up here and mother would cook them. Quite often we had enough fish for the whole family. Not always from one catch, but from a couple days. But most days, we didn't keep them more than a couple days, because we did not have an electric refrigerator where we could freeze them.

"A number of years ago, young Dave Fraser and I, on June 24th, we used to take a pup tent and we'd take our gear and we'd go off down near 7 Fairway along the edge of the lake south of where they lived. We'd pitch the tent and build a fire and we'd cook our supper, and we'd just sit around and chat and have a good time. At 12:00 in the morning when fishing season opened, we'd go right out

A lanky Harold showing off his catch.

fishing. In those days, fishing season opened on June 25th. One night we were down there, and we had the tent all set up with a little campfire there, and pretty soon crashing through the willow brush there came a Model A Ford. And here were my brothers Phil and Roy, and they come crashing right through all these saplings. They wanted to scare us,

"We had such great times! A couple of times we did go out fishing at midnight. I remember one time we went out fishing and we couldn't see. Couldn't see a thing. Couldn't see the sky, couldn't see the shore, couldn't see anything. So we didn't get very far out, and eventually we came back in. We had a little campfire there, and we could see that to guide us back to camp. But that was quite an ordeal [chuckles]. But it was fun.

We used to wander off down through the woods or across the city ditch where the end of the road is now. There was a ditch between the lake and Minges Brook. If the lake got high, they could drain it down. If it got too low, they could run water in from Minges Brook. But we used to wander up and down through there and go off through those Minges woods, and we just wandered around, didn't really do anything but be kids. But it did take us through a few Cowslips and we always brought Mother home a bouquet of Cowslips. Off in this area (behind the course) with all this camping, why it was just a lot of fun. For about five more years, we went out camping down there.

Harold motoring in his home-built boat on Goguac Lake

"And one time Dave and I decided we were going over on Wards Island at the other end of the lake. We pitched our tent and camped out, and we dug a little fire pit, cooked our supper. Then we sat around the fire talking and we decided to go to bed, so we crawled in the tent -- we had no sleeping bags at the time. We just had blankets. We crawled in, and it clouded up, and it rained. The wind blew, and it rained. It blew our tent down and we got soaking wet. I'll tell you; we got wet, did we ever. Actually, what we did is we just huddled up and pulled the tent over us and kind of huddled up and stayed there until the storm was over and it let up. We didn't even get up and

130

put the tent back up. We sat around and waited for daylight. And as soon as it got daylight, we loaded our gear in the boat and went back home. That was enough of that because we were soaking wet. Everything, our clothes, our blankets, everything was soaking wet.

"But, that's all part of growing up, I guess. And we used to go to a place over near in front of our house that we used to call 'the log' which was over on what was then Club property but back behind about where Pres Kool's house is. Pretty near to the property line, there was a big log from an Oak tree laying there. We used to go over there every once in a while, and build a bonfire, roast marshmallows, or cook hot dogs. Every once in a while, we'd go there, pitch our tent and stay all night. We never ran into rain some of those times; not like Dave and I did down on the island, but as a kid, we used to have a great time.

-H.P.

At some point, I realized that was the same old tent my dad lent to the three of us to camp in our backyard that I'd mentioned earlier in this story. I remembered when I'd talked him into letting us leave the tent up, which became our base for several escapades one summer…like father like son. And then I remembered too that I had left it out all summer without taking care of it, and by the end of the summer, it had rotted so that it had to be thrown out. It was special to my dad, and sadly I'd let him down through my youthful foolishness.

More Growing Up…

As a teenager Harold worked on the course for his dad, Andy, and he also worked for club members, Doctor and Mrs. Mustard. The Mustards lived in a grand home between the golf course and lake on a peninsula aptly named Mustard's Point. The opulent castle-like home had a beach house, tennis courts and many rooms. Harold was a babysitter, houseboy, errand runner, and landscaper. In other words, he did just about everything for them.

After graduating from Lakeview High School, he continued to work for his dad on the course. But his primary job during the war was working nights as a machinist for Clark Equipment Company because of a wartime deferment for his hernia. Here he talks about some of his early memories of the course:

"I don't remember hearing too much about the construction of the course. But I do remember one time when the club decided to build a ditch. They didn't really want the ditch, but there was a tile from Goguac Lake into Minges Brook that went across 7, 11, 13, and 6 Fairways and over to the brook. And of course, when they built the course, I assume that some of this was open, but they put a 12-inch tile in and covered it up. The tile was there, but it would get filled up and water would run from the lake, and the course would flood. If the lake got pretty high, it would flood some of that area down there where 6, 13 and 11 is.

At 17, a spiffy Harold poses along Country Club Drive

"So the club went to the county because it was a county drain and complained about it. The county says, 'Well if you don't like it, we'll just dig an open ditch.' They did it. I remember going down there one time with my folks, and I saw - they called it a steam shovel at the time - digging this ditch, and it was across 6 and 13. Of course, they took the tile out and they curved the ditch. The ditch didn't go straight like the tile did, but they curved the channel. And therefore, the club now has the ditch, or creek, curving across 6 and 13 Fairways.

"But it was all through a muck area, which was quite a deal. We always had trouble maintaining it and had to clean it out a lot. I remember when I worked for my dad, every once in a while, we'd go down and clean that out. It would get weeds in it, and we'd go down there and we'd rake. It was just a muck ditch. We pulled out a whole lot of golf balls because people would hit a golf ball in it and the balls would go right down in the muck; you couldn't find them. When we raked it, why, we'd find a bunch of them. And some of them had been in there long enough to be waterlogged and discolored, that you'd go to hit them with a golf club and they'd go kind of thud. They didn't go very far. -H.P.

Early Equipment...

"I can vaguely remember, years ago, that my dad had an old model T pickup truck. I think it was a convertible thing since it had a canvas top on it. I think that burned up in the fire when the Maintenance barn burned down. They had a barn, right where the center maintenance shop is now, two-story barn with a haymow up above, and all the regular stuff. That barn burned down one night. I remember mother carrying me to watch it burn. She had me in her arms - I was that little. That little old pickup truck got burned up in that fire along with the old Staude tractors that they used to mow fairways. I don't know whether they had two tractors or one, but I do think the tractor they got to replace those was about a '31 or a '32 Model B tractor, or Toro tractor with a Model D Ford engine in it. We used that for years and years. In fact, I think I got rid of it about '52 or '53.   *-H.P.*

BATTLE CREEK COUNTRY CLUB BUILDING BURNS

Special to The Free Press.

Battle Creek, July 29.—An equipment storage building at the Battle Creek Country club burned to the ground early today. The damage was estimated at $10,000, partially covered by insurance. The origin of the fire is undetermined. Equipment lost in the fire included electrically operated lawn mowers, tractor and two automobiles.

Detroit Free Press 1927 article about the fire

Old maintenance shed rebuilt from the original barn

Rumors were rampant in town the next morning that the clubhouse had burned down, as the fire could be seen from the city. The July 29, 1927 article in the *Enquirer and News* mentions the fire being discovered by caretaker Asa Littlefield, "...who was watering the eighth green with a tank wagon and team of horses." Asa was burned trying to put out the fire before waking my grandpa. Two fire companies could not save anything. Over seven tons of hay, three tractors, the Ford truck, several power mowers and a Chevy Coupe were destroyed, although the horses the club (or Andy) owned were out to pasture for the night and weren't harmed. The article went on to say, "This morning the country club employes' (sic) force practically without means of tending one of the finest and splendidly maintained courses in the state of Michigan..." The old maintenance

shed in the photo on the previous page was built up from the foundation of the Post era barn but has since been torn down after my dad's retirement.

"Then in 1940, they bought a Toro Bullit tractor, which was a beautiful thing - orange, short wheelbase, had a six-cylinder Hercules engine in it, and plenty of power. I remember coming home from lunch from school one day when that tractor came in, and I went down to the shop with my dad, and I got to drive it off the truck. It had a sickle bar mower on the side of it, which ran off a belt system - power take off and belts. We had that tractor until pretty near 1980. I had it for a long time, but that Hercules engine was a good engine. It worked beautifully. In fact, we never had anything done with that engine.

"But I guess it was around 1950, I bought another Toro tractor. It had the six-cylinder engine in it. But that was way, way too much of an engine. It wasn't right because when we would mow with the 1940 tractor, we would mow in third gear all the time. In this Toro that I bought later, we had to mow with that second gear, but we had to rev the engine up pretty high, because third gear was too fast to mow fairways.

Glen Eggleston on Ford 8N with Harold and Toro Bullit Tractor; Curiously, they are planting trees in the winter.

"During the war we mowed the fairways once a week. After the war, we started in mowing them twice a week. Then we were mowing the greens four times a week. Well, it wasn't too long after I took over that I found out that the proper way to mow greens was to mow them every day. So I started mowing them five days a week, and eventually six days a week. Didn't mow them on Sunday though. Years later we decided that we should mow them on Sunday for the Sunday golfers. For quite a while, we mowed seven days a week. But the greens weren't small, so if we had pressure from extra projects, we'd skip mowing Monday unless there was an event going on or something.

-H.P.

War Time...

During the war there were many restrictions, although surprisingly fuel and oil were not rationed for maintenance of the golf course. Members though were challenged to keep up any semblance of the country club lifestyle. The clubhouse wasn't open for dining, and most of the club parties were pot-luck. When members had time to golf, they often car-pooled. Of all things, golf balls were rationed; to get a new one, an old one had to be turned in. No records can be found whether or not handicaps dropped! The club helped its members conserve balls by mowing the rough shorter and by stretching wire fencing over the water hazards. Dad couldn't enlist due to his hernia, but after working nights as a machinist to help the war effort he worked days on the golf course as he describes here. A war hardship of too few personnel taught my dad something that helped the course for years after...

"We had to mow in a hurry, but that got the fairways looking like a washboard. And I remember when Uncle Lou was mowing fairways, and he had that seven-gang fairway mower, pulling it behind that tractor. Why he'd go right up

Harold & Les (right front) with war-time buddies at home

over the tees and mow the tees with it. We had some little mushroom-type tee markers, and he'd run right over them because he was crippled up. He couldn't get on and off the tractor very much. But he always mowed fairways on that little Bullit tractor. In order to get the job done, we'd go quite fast because he'd get the fairways mowed and then he'd switch over and hook on to a set of Toro rough mowers, which were five gang but also were only five-bladed mowers. The fairway mowers were all seven blades. And then he'd mowed rough.

135

"One time during the war, I was out there working, and I took that little Toro Bullit tractor - and I cut the five gangs down. I took two units off of it, so I'm down to three units. And I'm out mowing the bunkers. I'd go up the bunker and down the inside and right across the sand. But the sand was all settled out and weeded over. I could drive right across it. We never maintained sand traps at all during the war. Those war days were something else.

"I found out that driving so fast on the fairways, like we did during the war, made the turf corrugated like a roof. The cause was from the mowers bouncing up and down - we were going so fast. Well, to correct that, when we found out what was doing it – was I started mowing fairways crossways, and it did help a lot. In fact, eventually, it smoothed them right up. It was quite a discovery to find out what was doing that.

"Like I said, during the war, Uncle Lou came and worked for Dad. Mostly he did fairways and rough on the tractor. When I went out and mowed, it was when he didn't show up. Every once in a while, some of dad's help would get drunk and not show up, and he needed somebody to take their place. Not mentioning any names...

"About the middle of the war, we had a guy named Claude Hyatt came to work. He lived out south in Factoryville, south of Athens. He would ride to work with some neighbors that were working in downtown Battle Creek. He mowed greens and he raked traps, and he did a lot of puttering around, but he would not drive a tractor, or the old Model A pickup or the Model A dump truck. But he was quite a guy. He'd do anything except drive the equipment. He'd run the putting green mowers, but when he mowed greens, he had an alarm clock that was probably eight inches high and six inches wide, a couple inches thick. And one time, when his watch wouldn't work, he'd take a piece of string and he'd tie that alarm clock to his putting green mower. I said, "What are you doing that for?" He always timed himself when he was mowing a green. It took him just so long to mow a green, he wanted to make sure he wasn't behind time. Because at that time, it was more or less of an honor for the first guy to get in. Because right after the war, I had three guys mowing greens. They'd go out on the course and mow and then the first ones in would start in on 18 and the practice green, then 9 as they came in. It was not a case of you go out and you mow certain greens and then you come in. If somebody else is not in, you go ahead and do one of the three greens that were out by the club. That worked out real good.

"Later on, Claude Hyatt had started boarding with my folks because Roy had gotten married. Roy and Les were in the service, and I was living at home, and Winifred was living at home, but we had a spare bedroom. So they rented that spare bedroom out to Claude Hyatt. He was right here handy and didn't have to come up from Factoryville anymore.

So he got started watering greens at night, but like I said he would not drive a tractor or anything.

This is likely the 1946 Michigan Open PGA tournament, won by ex-club pro and golf great Chick Harbert, who was a good family friend. He was known as the longest driver in golf, winning six Michigan Opens.

So he walked around all night dragging those sprinklers on the greens to make four settings on them, which took him five rounds. He'd make the four settings then when he got done, he'd set the sprinkler on the tee and leave it. We'd take care of it in the morning. But it must have been quite a deal with all that walking.

-H.P.

A Rescue...

One summer in 1943, Harold was motoring around Goguac Lake with his friends Craig Stover and Dick Weller in Dick's classic Chris Craft inboard. They came across two girls, Jayne Hosimer and her friend Mary Jean Pavlsak, who were struggling to get around with a rowboat. Seeing an opportunity, the boys came to the rescue and helped the girls get back to shore. It wasn't love at first sight though, since Jayne ended up going out with Craig that night. Nevertheless, the five became lifelong friends.

However, the next night Jayne went on her first date with Harold; she remembered being very unimpressed that his passenger car door had to be held closed with a rope. Later, on the front porch swing, when Jayne was talking to Mary Jean about her date with Harold, her mom Wini was eavesdropping. When the girls stopped talking Jayne's mom asked, "Well...what happened next?"

Harold and Jayne on a beach date

During wartime, people tended to be a little more spontaneous, and Harold and Jayne soon knew they were right for each other. Asking, "Why wait?" they wanted to get married soon, but the war left them few choices for a wedding and reception. Harold and Jayne decided to get married when their friends were home on leave, which happened to be on New Year's Eve 1944. The ceremony was at the home of my mom's aunt and uncle

Florence and Harry Bird. Afterward, they went out and did up the town at a ready-made reception on New Year's Eve.

After they were married, Harold worked for his father Andrew, becoming his Assistant after the war for two years. For that short time after they were married my parents and newborn sister, Andrea lived in the very same cottage down by the lake next to the clubhouse that my best friend Bobby grew up in. Harold remembers living in that house and working for his dad on a project in the clubhouse…

Newlyweds Harold and Jayne are out on the town at New York's Rainbow Room.

"Going back a-ways, I can remember that time when I first started working for my dad. We had to do a lot of maintenance in the clubhouse. I remember one time; they had just bought four fans to put in the ballroom. They had four wall sconces in the ballroom, so what they wanted was to take those wall sconces down and put little shelves up for the fans, and, of course, there was electricity right there. So, I was assigned the job, and the day I started-- why, I had been out the night before [drinking] with the gang that worked in the clubhouse, and my wife, of course, and various people.

"I wasn't feeling too well that day, so what happened was, I got started at this, but it took me pretty near all day to put the first fan in. Well, okay, I thought, "Oh, boy. Why did it take me so long on this simple job?" The next day, I went back to the same job, and before noon, I had the other three in, no problem, and took a coffee break in between, too. But that goes to show you. If you don't feel good, you can't get much done.

-H.P.

The End of an Era...

My grandpa had been told by his doctor fifteen years earlier that his heart was weak, would not hold up, and he should quit working. Grandpa could not leave his job though as they had no other house to move into and no pension. He had walked the course every day for years and was in otherwise good shape. His only indulgence was the family's Sunday night ice-cream binge. My grandparents had been packing and getting ready to leave for their second annual winter getaway in Sarasota; their clothes had already been shipped down. Wintering in Florida was a welcome bonus from the country club started the year before by members and PGA Pro Chick Harbert. The Pecks were given two months lodging in a beautiful apartment paid by the members for a job well done. After twenty-eight years of maintaining the course and clubhouse as well as raising seven kids, they were undoubtedly looking forward to a warm, relaxing vacation. While they were in Florida, my dad would keep an eye on the clubhouse and the fire going in the pump house while working as Assistant Greenskeeper.

Harold, Jayne & Andrea in 1946

My parents were having a last night out for a while by going to the Bijou Theater, as they could leave their young daughter Andrea with her grandma and grandpa. The movie was interrupted with an announcement asking my parents to immediately call home. All they got though was a busy signal...

Racing back to the house they had no idea what the emergency was and, of course, feared for their daughter. When they got back to One Country Club Drive, there were many cars; my dad rushed in to find his mom in tears. The doctor was already there and had declared Andy dead of a heart attack at the relatively young age of 67. The club president took Harold upstairs to see his dad's body.

Andy & Rena enjoying their first winter vacation in 1946 on the beach in Sarasota, Florida, courtesy of the club and Chick Harbert.

My father numbly returned to work right away as Assistant Greenskeeper, and he was soon offered the position of Greenskeeper at the same salary he was told his father had been getting for 15 years - $2400/year; he quickly accepted. Everything changed at One Country Club Drive - my mom and dad moved in, and my Grandmother was no longer the matriarch of the house. She never got back to Florida... and I never got to meet my Grandfather.

A SECOND GENERATION TAKES OVER

Some Big Shoes to Fill...

That fall of 1947 and the following winter were somber and challenging times for the entire family. My grandmother Rena had just lost her husband of twenty-eight years and was no longer in charge of the house. Everyone had to shift responsibilities, roles, and even bedrooms. Harold's wife Jayne, at the young age of 21, had the daunting task of taking over the household from her mother-in-law, and had more than a few changes to make it her own. The house was pretty old-fashioned, so she had a pretty long honey-do list. It needed modern conveniences like wall switches and electric outlets, a laundry room, a new electric stove, and a real shower. Jayne also had to fit into the country club lifestyle which included attending the many social events; luckily she already had the poise and elegance required for that situation. With her movie-star good looks and outgoing personality, she had no trouble meeting the challenge; quickly she became a favorite dance partner at club events. Until I came along seven years later, she was also busy as club secretary and sometimes bartender. Jayne's worries about appearances, for both herself and Harold, were a concern that always came up whenever they went anywhere together.

At the relatively young age of 25, Harold found himself in charge of maintaining and running the golf course. He quit his second shift machinist work at Clark Equipment and, over the following winter did everything he could to learn the detailed responsibilities of being a Greenskeeper. He and his father hadn't yet had the opportunity to share them all. He had to learn quickly while also doing all of the winter equipment maintenance and painting by himself. Perhaps a more important task that winter and spring was to get to know the membership – all of his bosses. A key aspect of his new job was developing friendly relationships with the club members. I always admired that about him when I was older and could appreciate the complexity of country club politics. That process was surely a new challenge for him. He had to balance the needs of the golfers with keeping up the course and the equipment; all with the constant pressure of doing things on a tight budget and keeping the Greens Committee happy. Trying to get the job done on a shoestring budget was a task he accomplished very successfully during his entire tenure. As Harold relates…

"It wasn't long after I started as Greenskeeper that I had a man mowing fairways, and I had him mowing continually. He'd get the fairways mowed and the driving range too, and around the practice green and practice tee. But he'd get through and he'd start right in mowing fairways again. And the deal was we wanted to do them three times a week. Then we got the new Turf King so that he'd do them three times a week and still have some time left so he'd start in again, which made

Harold mowing with his new Jacobsen Turf King on #8 Fairway in front of the waterhole

them real nice. I thought the fairways were perfect at that time. Most of this happened after we put the underground water system in. I thought that was quite a deal to mow fairways three and a half times a week. Eventually we were mowing greens six and seven days a week and we were mowing tees three days a week. To me, the tees couldn't make all that much difference in time, but later on, I think they figured the tees wanted to be closer. So after I left, they had them mowed pretty near every day. But now they only do them, I think, twice a week.

"But anyhow, through the years, I've seen a lot of things happen. We've changed our practices. We even bought a spray rig that we could set up in one minute and go out and spray greens. Then when we started using the Trucksters, we had a tank and spray nozzle that would shoot the water both ways up in the air. We'd spray greens by driving the Truckster right across the greens.

"Which, in my father's day to have even a power mower on the greens was a lot of weight. During the war, I'd mow the aprons with a gang mower and a tractor. That was against all the principals that my dad had, but we had to get the job done. We mowed when we could. We got everything done. We mowed a lot higher than we do now.

"I remember when I first started in 1947, we had a gauge that we set to 9/32" to mow greens, and then later we'd go down a little bit, and we got it to a quarter inch and we thought that was great. Everybody was really commenting, 'Boy, the course was beautiful,' and they liked the greens. They putted well. They all putted true, and I had a lot of compliments on how true the greens putted. They were green and looked good. They were beautiful.

"Pretty soon somebody come along and wanted them a little faster, just a little faster. So, we finally got down to 3/16". We kept them at 3/16" for many years. But after a while, well, at one of the golf tournaments they found out the greens were mowed at about an eighth of an inch. And by golly, I was told we got to get our mowers down to mow that close and of course, my argument was, 'Yeah, they mow that close but only for those tournaments. But then after the tournament, they raise the mowers back up.' Of course, my bosses at the club said, "No, no, no. We want them to go fast like they had at those tournaments. We want it all the time." But when I set them down to an eighth of an inch, I found that the golfers were complaining. The greens putted rough; they didn't put true. What's the matter? Well, come to find out, I set the mowers closer than the thickness of the bed knife and that sure didn't work too well.

"So we had to buy special bed knives. They were just regular bed knives but they had been ground down. In other words, I probably had some on hand in the junk pile that could have been machined and still used. But anyhow, we got by with it and we got it going where the greens got pretty smooth.

"But by the time we started doing that, we had just gotten the riding mowers, which was a great thing. The Jacobsen salesmen come along with a three-unit riding mower they called the Greens King. And he says, 'I want to demonstrate this.' I got pretty interested and called the chairman of the greens committee, and he come over and agreed, 'Let's just mow greens with that three-unit mower.' And then his remark was, Hey, leave that mower here and how soon can you get another one?' This was into September and a little late in the season, but the guy said that was his demonstrator and he couldn't leave that, but he could deliver one within a week. Well, what about two? He says, 'We've got to have two.' The guy says, 'Well, I'll see what I can do.' Well, he couldn't get two that fall, but he brought another one around in a week. Boy, that was quite a difference in mowing the greens. Made a big difference in the guys getting their exercise in the morning because you sat on your fanny mowing instead of walking.

-H.P.

Workers - and a Legacy...

"I'd mentioned that after the war when my father passed away, Claude Hyatt had moved back in to live with Mother, Jayne, Andrea and me. We had a built-in babysitter, but that wasn't the total reason because it was very convenient to have him there. He helped a lot in the garden and he helped in the house. He used to wipe dishes for my mother and then wipe dishes for Jayne. He was quite a guy. One morning, he couldn't get out of bed, and he'd had a stroke. That was it for him. But, very fortunate for him at the time, Mr. Thompson was the chairman of the greens committee. He says, "Well, we hope the man's going to get well so I want you to give him half wages. Pay him for half a wage every week." We paid every week at that time.

Tenant and course worker Claude Hyatt

"So we did and this went on for about eight months, until he finally decided he had to go back home. He lived out in Factoryville and he had a house all by himself so he went back out there. Then he got a trailer and lived all alone for a while. Even after he had that stroke and he couldn't do a thing. It was too bad, too. Because he was a good man and was a lot of fun to have around.

"My brother Roy was hired as Greenskeeper over at Kalamazoo Country Club after he returned from the war. After Dad passed away; he came over to help me on the golf course, which was very fine. Then that winter, he went to the University of Massachusetts and took their 10-week course in golf course maintenance. My brother Les also took that course, which was a real nice deal, and he came back and worked for me a while too.

"But that next summer when Les was working for me why, I had a man named Merton Nye come wanting to apply for a job. He had never been on a golf course in his life, but he needed a job. So, I hired him because my requirement was not that somebody had to have been on a golf course in order to go to work. He came to work, and he turned out to be a real good man. In fact, one day we got to talking, and we sat down in the back of the 6th Green for pretty near an hour talking about golf course maintenance, about the future, and he got real interested. He also talked to Les quite a bit about that course at University of Massachusetts.

"That winter, he got into the University course, which was a pretty good deal for him as far as that goes. It was a good deal for me too because he was a very good man. He was good help. He worked for me for I think about another three years or so. And then Roy Jones at Lansing Country Club got sick, and they hired Mert as an assistant to him. But when Roy Jones passed away, they wouldn't promote Mert, because the job was promised to a man that had returned from the service.

"So Mert stayed on and worked for him as assistant for a little while, then he went back home. But he kept in touch with the association, and there was a job come open at a golf course that was under construction in the Detroit area. So he came back to Michigan and took that job at Loch-moor, and he worked till they got the course built. Then he got a Superintendent job at Boyne Highlands up in northern Michigan, which was a pretty nice place. He worked there constructing a golf course, and then he worked there for quite a while after it was constructed. Then they built another 18-hole course at Boyne Highlands. He stayed there for quite a while and ran both of them, but then he

bought a golf course up by Mackinaw City. I got a Christmas card from him for many years, but I kind of lost touch with him after that.

"There were quite a few other people that worked for me that became Superintendents. There was the Dull family that lived down at the north end of Goguac Lake. And the older son Leo came to work for me one time, and then his father came to work for me. His father Guy worked for me for five or six years. Most of what he did was mow fairways. He had two other sons that came to work for me, but not all at the same time. But one of them left, and he had gone up to California and gotten a job as superintendent at a golf course out there. So, I can kind of feel a little proud about a background of having so many guys that worked for me that went on to [work as Superintendents in] other places. There were a lot of guys that worked for my dad that went on to other places too and been successful in most of them. Yep, that was quite a deal.

"I don't know if I mentioned Glen Eggleston before. Glen came to work for my dad in the spring of '47, and he ended up working here pretty near until the time he passed away in about 1975. He got to be my mechanic. He kept the equipment running, as well as he mowed the tees and aprons. He enjoyed working here, and I enjoyed having him here. He was a great fisherman, and once in a while he'd bring me a mess of fish. Once in a great while I'd go fishing with him, and so he got me back into fishing. I kept my fishing tackle right in the pump house down by the lake. Whenever I felt the urge, I'd go get that fishing tackle, and I had the bait right there in a pit, and I'd just go down, and get in the boat, and take off.

Hubert Dull

"Hubert Dull was another one that worked for me for quite a while. He was Guy Dull's brother, and he came to work for me after Guy passed away, and I put him on mowing fairways. He mowed fairways for quite a long time. And after Glen Eggleston died, Hubert became my mechanic. He had a stepson that came to work for me watering greens nights. He was my night manager. He lived in Nashville, which worked out pretty good. Then later on he quit, and his grandson Lee came to work for me. Lee was kind of a wild kid. Well, he'd get picked up for this, and that, and the other thing,

147

and I really don't know why I put up with him for as long as I did. I don't know whatever happened to him.

"Through the years, I had quite a few people working for me, and most of them were very good workers, some of them not so good. I think there was only about two guys that I caught sleeping on the job. I caught a couple more that would just go off and do something that I didn't want them to do and had to get rid of them, but I never really had to fire very many people. Got along with most of them and encouraged them to do what I wanted them to do. I had a pretty good relationship with all my help on the golf course.

"I retired 11 years ago. And there's one man still working there that worked for me, and that's Rick Johnson. He was the son of a man that used to be my greens chairman, Glen Johnson. Well, it's one of those deals where it worked out great for him. He became a mechanic. Nowadays, they've got so much equipment it takes a mechanic full time to keep it going. It doesn't seem like they have that much more equipment, but nowadays I guess it's more complicated, or maybe the guys are more reckless with it. But that's the way it goes. I guess that's progress.

-H.P.

Maintenance Man, and Jack-of-all-Trades…

Most of Harold's many stories are about the course, but several are about his maintenance of the clubhouse and the general responsibilities around the club that he assumed or were assigned. Like his father before him, my dad was a jack of all trades: plowing snow, fixing the plumbing in the clubhouse and locker rooms, painting everything, building and installing the dock at the beach. Their duties even included keeping the furnace going all winter in the clubhouse and a fire in the pump house down at the lake to prevent the pipes from freezing and provide necessary fire protection.

"We did quite a bit of maintenance in the clubhouse. I can vividly remember some of those projects. Why, there was one time when they had just done some remodeling in the clubhouse, and they took all the wicker furniture out and put in new furniture. That was kind of cheap stuff, but they wanted a change. So we had all that beautiful wicker furniture leftover. We took it up in the garages, and it was there for a couple years, and then I finally had a big bonfire and burned it all up.

148

"But during all the remodeling of the clubhouse, they wanted to tile the floor of the porch that was going to be the bar and lounge. And it was all windows - 16-inch square glass that was all put together to make up the outside of the clubhouse. Where the club ever got those things from, I don't know. But that was what the front of the clubhouse was.

The old Clubhouse looking South

"The deal was you had to put plywood down on the floor, and use six-penny nails, and drive the nails every six to eight inches apart in squares.

This was the carpet-laying people's recommendation, so we had to do it. I got elected to do the job, and I kind of frowned -- this was after Dad had passed away and I was in charge. But I frowned a little and thought, 'Oh my God. That's going to take me quite a while, and I've got all that equipment to go over.' They didn't let me have anybody else working in the shop at the time, so they said: 'Well, get somebody to help you.' So I mentioned to brother Roy about it, and he said he'd come over and help me, so he'd come over every day for about a week and help me pound nails in that floor.

"What a job that was. But we got that job done, and they redecorated the clubhouse. Took the porch, the main part at the north end of the building. They put in two huge double-paned picture windows, it was beautiful. And they put all new furniture in the lounge and rebuilt the bar. I don't think I had much to do with rebuilding the bar itself at that time, but they had quite a bar in there, and that bar was used quite a bit, too.

"There were a lot of things that came up that we had to fix. I actually did a lot of things throughout the buildings that they now have hired a man there to do them. Through most of the years in my tenure, they did not have a maintenance man in the clubhouse, and that kept bothering me. They had a janitor come early in the morning to sweep the floor. But they didn't have anybody regularly that would wash the windows, the glass, the floors, that sort of thing. As far as windows were concerned, you know right there on the lake all summer, when the sun comes down in the evenings, boy what a mess. I couldn't believe it. That was not one of my responsibilities. If a window got broke, I was called in to fix it. Then I would wash it, but that made the rest of it look worse because it was the only clean one around. But those things happened.

"We used to do a lot of things in that old clubhouse. One time they decided to paint the kitchen. The deal was Glen and I would paint it, but they would get the dishes out. They closed up for the winter and they paid a person to come in to get the dishes out of the kitchen, but they got only half of them

Club House with Ballroom at left behind garden; Country Club Drive about 1925

150

out of there and that was it. We had to take the rest of them out. Then we had to wash the shelves, the ceilings and the walls with a sponge mop. We put lye in the water, but the grease was so thick we had to wash it a couple times and we finally got the grease off.

"After we got the walls cleaned up, we took rollers and brushes and we put two coats on the walls and ceiling with semi-gloss enamel, bright yellow. And that really brightened that kitchen up. And all of the dishes, the pots and pans and plates and cups and saucers, are out in the ballroom. And we left it out there. And when the manager came back, he was out of his mind, and yelled, 'What about all of this stuff.' He said, 'Put it back where it came from in the kitchen! Well, I thought you guys would put it back.' I said. 'No way. Be thankful we got it painted. Because we did a hell of a lot of work to get that kitchen painted."

-H.P.

As a jack-of-all-trades, Harold was also in charge of maintenance of the old Men's Locker Room. It was built around 1925 at the cost of $15,000 and included the Pro Shop, bar and patio, a large locker room, club storage and caddie shack. The building was torn down in the mid-'70s when the new locker room was built.

"We had to take care of the men's locker room too. That was a pretty good-sized building. In the bar in the men's locker room they had a wet spot on the floor. And I said, "Uh oh." That was something we really had to find out what was happening. So I busted up the floor at the place and found where the water pipe went right across a conduit. And electrolysis had eaten a hole right through the water pipe. It was leaking, so we busted up some more floor and we ran some new galvanized pipe. I got into some of that sort of thing every once in a while.

"Another time when they were complaining they couldn't get any pressure for the showers, the plumber came by there and said, 'These need to be re-plumbed because these pipes are all getting eroded.' Well, then he told me that fixing it would cost a lot of money, and I said, 'Hey, why don't we do it?' So I saved them quite a bit of money, and we cut pipe and holes through the floor to come up with the piping, put the piping up overhead in each shower. We got the thing all done and we had people saying, 'Wow, this is really a difference. Now we got pressure.'

"Then I reminded them that we've still only got that little pump down in the basement. And I said, 'But you still can't run the showers more than one at a time since the pressure would drop down

pretty good.' Even if somebody was taking a shower and somebody flushes one of the toilets, the shower would get a little hot. But then we corrected that with the new pipes and pump. Glen Eggleston and I did most of the work, and we got that problem pretty well fixed up too.

"While the pump was down in the basement, the well was outside - way out near the middle of the parking lot. I had one hell of a time if that pump lost its prime. That pumped the fresh water for everything - the men's locker room, the clubhouse, and the lady's locker room. And it had a little two-horse pump on it. And I'll tell you [chuckles], that seemed like it never was going to work out.

"For the showers in the summertime, I would always switch over to lake water so we'd have plenty of pressure for the showers. But as far as the health department was concerned, I think they'd frown on that today, but then the club used to get only lake water for years. For the drain for the showers in the men's locker room there was a tile going out to the septic tank, which was out under the parking lot. They never did really know where it went until they pulled the parking lot up. But anyway, the overflow for the septic was a tile that ran past the shop down behind the tennis courts, and it just emptied down there, so a lot of the water from the showers in the men's locker room and the toilets too usually ended up down there in a man-made swamp.

Old Pro Shop & Men's Locker Room with the Caddy Shack behind the fence

"The well had a pit out in the parking lot, and it had the manhole to get into it. When we shut the clubhouse down for the winter, we'd have to drain everything including that well. Boy, I'll tell you that was something else. Shut that pump off and go through the clubhouse and go all through there with a little pump, pumping out all the toilets, and the traps in the drains, all the toilets for the apartments upstairs, downstairs, the kitchen, in back of the kitchen, the men's room, and oh boy. We had one hell of a time draining all those pipes.

"But then the well went bad out to the parking lot. They drove a new well right in the back of the men's locker room. I remember they had two guys that drilled a two inch well that went 150 some feet. It took them pretty near two weeks to drill that well with the rig. Boy, they had good water! They should have put a well in for the clubhouse too, but they didn't. The water in the clubhouse still came from the men's locker room. Going back many years ago before they built the men's locker room, the Post family and the other people got their water out of the lake. At one time that used to be permissible, getting water out of the lake to drink and everything else. That was something!

"I know we had lake water to the lady's locker room. But if that pump went bad in the men's locker room, the whole place was without water. What a deal that was. If that pump lost its prime or quit working, man I would get the calls. We had a meeting, mainly house committee members, and the manager of the club wanted to get walkie-talkies so that they could get ahold of me right away. So if I was out on the golf course and got a signal, I'd come a-running to the clubhouse and find out what's going on. And we had a meeting one night, and we discussed that to quite an extent, and I finally said, 'Well, wait a minute. Where does it say that my responsibility is to keep all this stuff running? My responsibility as far as I'm concerned is on the golf course.' We didn't get the walkie-talkies; still it was quite a few years before they got a maintenance man, but, you know, these things happen.
                                                                                                    -H.P.

Tending Bar and Other Good Times…

In the '40s and '50s, working at the club was a family affair. My dad Harold sometimes helped out by tending bar at night, and my mom, Jayne, was working in the office as a secretary. Sometimes they

worked together at the bigger parties. My mom recalls that the phone booth next to the men's room got a lot of use on stag nights, Thursday nights, and she suspected it was for making unscrupulous dates. (I always thought it was strange to have a phone booth indoors.) If they weren't working at the parties, they were going to them. My mom loved to dance and was a great dancer; my dad had learned long ago that he couldn't keep up with her on the dance floor. She was a very popular dance partner at club social events.

Club Costume Party in Ballroom

Harold recalls the country club social life in its heyday…

"In fact, I remember Thursday nights, in particular, were always party nights. Why that bar was just chock-full of people. And there'd get two-and three-people-deep right at the bar. In fact, there were times when they would have the Thursday night buffet, and there would be a little contest just to see how many people were going to come to that buffet. And it was something past 60, 70, to sometimes even 80 people would come. And they also had those buffets on Sunday, and sometimes they had 80 to 100 people at those buffets. It was a lot of people, but they don't do anything like that anymore. They don't get that many people, and of course they don't have those regular buffets anymore. They have a buffet now, but that's just for special holidays.

"But anyway, I had to participate in some of that stuff. Sometimes I would have to tend bar in the clubhouse in the evenings. So I would go in and help Timmie Meyers. He was the bartender, and I was assigned to help him. And the deal was I'd say to Timmie, 'I don't really know how to mix too many of those drinks - some of the fancy drinks they want.' He says, 'Well, you just do the ones you know how,' and he says, 'I'll do the other ones.' I says, 'Okay.' So we worked our fannies off tending bar when they had a good-sized party. And when we get through at night, we'd split the tips, probably $15 to $18 apiece, which in those days, was a pretty good haul. And then sometimes when they had really big parties, Timmie and I

Jayne with a friend at Club Bar

worked the front bar, and Joe Zangaro would work a temporary bar in the ballroom, and Jayne would help him. She would take the cash, and they would split the tips. Of course, Joe had some pretty crafty ways of getting tips, which was something else. But they were to split tips with us. He would tell Jayne, he says, 'Here, put this in your shoe and don't declare this,' but she would tell me later, she'd say, 'It's yours too. But I'd say, 'That's the way Joe operates, so that's the way we do it.'

"I know at the time, years ago, when Chick Harbert was Pro, and when I was working with my dad, after the war when [Harbert] came up from Florida, he brought a man up with him for a bartender, Buddy Hall. They put Buddy up in one of the rooms in the clubhouse, and he was a bartender mainly in the men's locker room. He turned out to be a pretty good bartender, but he didn't have any transportation and he liked to go drinking and dancing. So he'd get through work and he'd call, 'Want to go to dinner?' Sometimes he'd even call before he got through with work, he'd say, 'Don't eat yet. I'm going to take you over to Schuler's for dinner.' And almost invariably he picked up the check because we had the transportation. I had my little '41 Plymouth Coupe. We'd go to Schuler's and have dinner and then we'd always have to stop by Mar Creek Inn on the way home and have

another couple drinks. Sometimes when that happened, I wasn't really too sharp the next morning. I look back at that and think, 'How'd I ever make it?' But I was young at the time. Hell, I was only 30.

"In fact, at the time, about the second year that he was here, Buddy was hired as a manager of the clubhouse; manager of the whole thing. The clubhouse and the bars and the whole thing. Nothing to do with me, but he was the manager. At that time, he'd say, 'Do you and Jayne want to come down to dinner with me. Come down to dinner and I'll take care of the check.' And he did. We didn't go very often because we didn't want to overdo that. But it all worked out pretty good.

"When Buddy was Manager, and it so happened that even before he was manager, we had a certain group of the club members that loved to party. And they didn't need much of an excuse to have a party. They'd just stop by, and then a bunch more of them would stop by and have a drink and then somebody else would stop and have a drink and it would go on into quite a while. For a couple summers, there was kind of a ritual. About once a month I think it was, they had a shrimp dinner in the men's locker room, in the laundry of the men's locker room. They would cook up a whole bunch of shrimp and they

Harold, standing at the old Locker Room Bar

had shrimp sauce, and I guess we had some salad too. There'd be a bunch of us get together and we'd go to these shrimp dinner parties. We just had a great time. Man, we loved shrimp too. I still like shrimp.

"But there was a lot of things happened in those days that you really wouldn't dream of them happening today. The funny thing about it, when Buddy Hall was the manager and then even Al Scheff after that, they'd never let me pay for a drink or food. And they said, 'Man, you do enough around here. You don't need to pay for any food or drinks.' And then one time something come up from the Board of Directors and they put a notice above the time clock that no employees were to have any free drinks or food. I went in and had a drink one day and I went to pay for it, and the manager's right there, and he says, 'What are you doing?' And I told him-- this was Al Scheff. I told him, I said 'Well I saw the directive.' He says, 'You don't think that pertains to you do you?' He says, 'That sure doesn't pertain to you.' He says, 'Your drinks are free.' So that made me feel pretty good, but the whole deal wasn't too bad. If I'd had to pay for a drink, they were only 75 cents a drink anyway. Or 50 cents. Yeah, Seven Crown was 50 cents, which wasn't too bad. But, of course, they're a lot more than that now. But I didn't drink too much anyway, so it was no big deal.

"It was quite a deal working with Timmie Myers.

Vaudevillian Timmie Meyers (left), Buddy Hall and Freddy Taylor work the bar in 1948.

Before he came here Timmie was a vaudeville actor; he played the circuit for quite a few years. How many, I don't know, but he'd been all over the country playing different theaters and doing different, mainly comedy skits. Every once in a while, he would get to spewing off on some of his jokes and some of his skits and do these little things. He was quite an entertainer. Everybody loved him. At a slow time when there weren't very many customers, somebody might ask him a question. He would elaborate on it as a joke or humor like he was a comedian. He'd been onstage for years and he just loved to talk. And he talked an awful lot [chuckles], but it was kind of fun to listen to him. Old Timmie was something else.

Timmie Myers – Club Bartender, Vaudeville Actor, Dancer, Singer and Comedian…

Timmie went from crooner to chicken rancher and back again for a spotlight moment at BCCC. In 1947, Chicago's Midnight Four was singing for the annual Rotarian's bash at the clubhouse. Their manager had known Timmie previously on the Vaudeville circuit. Timmie grew up in Battle Creek, winning Amateur Night prizes as a youngster at the local Bijou Theater with a song and dance act. His career was launched at Marshal's Eagle Theater run by Albert Schuler (father of local restaurateur Win Schuler). He played Detroit's vaudeville houses at night and bell-hopped by day. He continued at dozens of upscale hotels and theaters in the Midwest including bell captain and *Maître' d* at Milwaukee's Pfister, Chicago's Palmer House and Detroit's Pontchartrain. He was fired from the latter after informing the Dodge brothers (those car guys) they couldn't dine without dinner jackets.

In 1921, he had married performer Betty Krause. They toured twelve years from coast to coast with the "Betty and Chappie" act on the Lowes, Pantages, Keith and Orpheum circuits. With $15,000 earnings, they started a chicken ranch that at its apex had 3300 hens and 33 greyhound dogs. The depression forced its closure. Timmie divorced Betty, remarried then separated from his second wife. He went back on the circuit with a variety of singing groups and wrote numerous songs and acts including *The Three Gay Blades* He returned home to manage the Wee-Nippy Club at the Post Tavern, and then arrived at the BCCC in 1946 at age fifty-five - just in time to stand in with the Midnight Four.

"He used to come out and tend bar. He might close the bar up at – what – midnight? When everybody left and quite often two-o'clock. After they got the television set, he'd stay open till two-o'clock anyway. He would have no customers, but he'd still keep the bar open that late. Some nights he might close up the bar and go to number one fairway and pick up a bunch of night crawlers and he'd go down and get in my boat. Because I had two boats down there and he had the right to go fishing any time he wanted to use one of my boats. He'd go down, get in my boat and go out fishing. He loved to fish. And what night crawlers he would have left over, he'd bring them back in the clubhouse and put them in the room in back of the bar.

"One time I talked to him about it. I said, 'Timmie, you want me to get you some crawlers to go fishing tonight?' 'No,' he says, 'I got some,' He took me back of the bar and he showed me-- he just reached in and showed me a whole handful of night crawlers. After that, he comes back out in the bar and, of course, he turned the water on and just rinsed his hands off and then that was it [chuckles]. The next time somebody comes in, he had to mix them drinks, picking up the ice cubes with his hands. You could do those things at that time. I don't think anybody ever got sick from any of that anyway, because a lot of the ice – not so much the when Timmie was here - but before that, the ice that they mixed drinks with was right out of the lake, and we chopped it up and put it in drinks.

"But little old Timmie. He was kind of devoted to the club for tending bar, and he did a good job. And it went on until one time when they got a new president at the club. I had no idea who it was. But we got a new president in the club, and he kind of had it in for Timmie Myers. It went along and he kept riding Timmie, and so finally Timmie quit. There was a lot of opposition amongst the club members because everybody liked Timmie. But the way the word come out, Timmie had decided to quit all on his own, but there was some of us that had a pretty good idea what was happening. In fact, we knew what was happening, because Timmie'd been an actor and all that, and the president didn't like those sorts of people. I can't even remember who it was, but I remember I don't think I thought too much of that president of the club either. But that's all water over the dam now. Anyhow, we still used to have quite a time.

"And we had a place there in the kitchen where Hattie, (hostess) Evelyn (Ellerton's) mother, used to work. She was the salad girl and pastry cook. I rigged her up a bakery table with a two-and-a-half-inch thick maple top, which I now have in my basement as a workbench. After that, I made a bench for her to make salads on. And I did a really good job of laying some maple flooring on this tabletop and shelf, sanded it and made a very beautiful wood bench for her.

Jayne and Evelyn Ellerton, who was a close family friend and beloved club waitress and hostess for 54 years, are playing with Tinkerbell and Schatzi in the dining room at One Country Club Drive.

Also I made a table out of it, and the nice thing about that was, I remember many, many times, that I'd go down in the morning for coffee. I'd sit down at this table for coffee, and whoever would come down, Hattie would make them some breakfast, which was great. We used to sit around chewing the fat and have coffee at that table pretty near every morning.

"I'd eat breakfast at home in the morning before I'd go to work, but I'd go up there to the clubhouse about 8:30 and have coffee. And quite often somebody, or the manager, Buddy Hall, would come for coffee or breakfast. And some mornings the man living upstairs would come down and Hattie'd fix him bacon and eggs. We had a lot of fun in that old kitchen. But for quite a long time I'd go in, have coffee every morning with Hattie. She had the bakery counter back there, which was a big table that she had to roll out her pies and cakes on. When they remodeled the clubhouse, they threw that table out. It was a big heavy thing with flour and sugar bins in it and drawers in it. But I saved it and brought it home to my basement for a workbench. Many times, I'd see her rolling out biscuits and pie dough, making great stuff on that maple-topped table.

"Then they threw that one out when they remodeled the kitchen, I'll be darned if they didn't put another one in just like it. When they remodeled that kitchen again, why they ordered up another table. That second old table I picked up and took it up to Marty's house. So we both have heavy workbenches like that.

"But we used to have a lot of fun back then in the kitchen. Quite often we'd have parties and maybe Jayne and I'd be down there working the bar with Timmie the bartender and Buddy Hall.   With Freddie and another bartender named Freddy, we'd sit down there and get pretty well looped up after the party at night. Usually it was on a Saturday night [chuckles] when I didn't have

Harold, Jayne and friends are having late-night drinks in the old Kitchen.

to go to work the next day. In those days, you never did anything on the golf course on Sunday. Years later, we did more things on Sunday. Up until I retired, we never did any more than mow greens on Sunday, unless there was something special going on, then we'd change cups. But we used to have some great times in that old building.
-H.P.

"You Don't Mess Around with any Club Members"…

"Outside of tending bar, I never waited tables. I never washed dishes, but I understand years and years ago my dad used to go in and help wash dishes in that old kitchen. That old kitchen was something else. It had a little hallway back to the kitchen. The walls of that hallway had shelves on it where all the dishes like the plates and cups and saucers and glasses and all that stuff were stacked up. They had gas ranges in the kitchen. Down below the kitchen, they had a laundry room, and they had two great big soapstone laundry tubs. I guess they were from the original days of the old Post home and even when the place belonged to the people before them. There was apartments upstairs,

and they did laundry for the apartments, but the people that had it before Post bought it, probably used the laundry too.

Windows all along the Clubhouse Ballroom faced Goguac Lake

"They had a little old room up half a flight off the kitchen that was kind of a porch. One of my first jobs in the kitchen was to enclose that room, because I was kind of a half-assed carpenter, so they had me enclosing that room and putting shelves in. I never will forget one time I got a little worked up, because I had a key to that room and they had some of their merchandise and food stored in there. One day the manager come to me, and he said, 'Did you take that such and such?' And I said, 'What are you talking about?' Well, he said, 'Somebody run off with some food.' I don't know now what it was, but I said, 'No. I had nothing to do with it.' He says, 'Well, in as much as you got a key to the place, so I had to ask you,' and I says, 'I'll tell you what, and I took the key out of my pocket and give it to him. And I said, 'I no longer want a key to anything here in this kitchen. I got to have a key to the clubhouse, yes, but I don't want a key to anything in the kitchen [chuckles].'*

"That kind of got me out of a little work in the kitchen, but I do remember another time we had a broken pipe down in this little laundry room that serviced the lavatory and one of the bedrooms upstairs. And my dad got the plumber out here to fix that pipe, but pretty soon my dad come and got*

me, and he says, 'The plumber needs help.' So I went up there, and there was a crawl space up in the ceiling, about a two-foot crawl space, but the plumber was too big to get in there, so he got me to go in and I fixed the pipe. I guess they paid the plumber a plumber's fee, but I wouldn't get anything extra for anything like that. Of course, that was all part of my job, but that did seem kind of funny to me.

"Another time – and this happened when I was superintendent - they had done a bunch of redecorating in the clubhouse one winter, and they wanted to paint all the windows along the front of the clubhouse towards the lake. There're over 500 windows, and they're all about 16 inches square - like French doors. They wanted these painted on the inside. And they talked about hiring some painters to paint them, and I said, 'Now wait a minute.' I said, 'I got a man working on the golf course. He's a real good man, and he can't stand to be laid off in the winter time because he's not a rich man. He's got to work.' And I said, 'How about we give him the job to come in and paint those windows?' And they thought, 'Well hey, that's not a bad deal.' So, I got Glen Eggleston to stay over [the winter] and paint the windows. By the time he got started at it, I had talked the chairman of the greens committee into him doing more work. I said, 'Hey, when he gets done up there' I said, 'we got some things in the shop that I'm going to need help with.' I said, 'I can't do it all.' So that was fine.

"From then on, I kept him on every

Classic view of Goguac Lake seen from clubhouse windows

163

winter. *Glen started painting those windows, and it was hard to see, especially as he had only one eye. They all faced the lake with the snow out there; he'd got a reflection from the sunlight. And you're trying to paint white against white, and it's amazing how hard it is to actually see what you're doing. So he got the floor lamps out of the lobby, and he set two or three-floor lamps behind him to really light up these window casings so he could paint them. He had that all set up one morning, and the manager who lived upstairs at the time came downstairs and right away when he saw that he said, 'Man, you're using up a lot of electricity,' and he went around and turned the lamps off. Glen dropped his paintbrush in the can of paint and walked right out of the clubhouse and come down to the shop. I was in the shop. He told me what he'd done. And by that time, the manager had left. He was the manager at the Athelstan Club at the same time, and he had left. So, I waited a few minutes and called the Athelstan Club, and I talked to him, 'Now listen.' I said, 'He had to have those lamps on so he could see what he was doing, and you come around and interrupted him. I said, 'If you want those windows painted, you better leave us alone because we got to have the lamps on in order to see it.' Well, he apologized all over the place and I said, 'Well, okay.' Glen went back up there and kept on painting and pretty soon when the manager came in that afternoon, he come over and he apologized all over the place to him and said he didn't realize how the light was there and he needed the lamps on.*

"These are all little things that happened through the years. I'd had times when there'd been little things that would go wrong in the clubhouse and I'd get called up. If the drain was plugged up, I'd get called. See, they didn't have a maintenance man. I'd get called, and I'd grab a plunger, and I'd go upstairs to whichever room, and sometimes I'd have to get a wrench and a bucket and take the traps off and clean them out because people would drop everything in these sinks and the toilets. I did a couple times have to take a toilet out and clean it out because it had rags in it. That was quite a job because the first one I ever did leaked on the floor afterward, before I ever found out that you had to replace that wax seal. But you learned those things.

"There was one time we had a tenant upstairs, Mrs. MacDonald. She had more things go wrong... They had redecorated the number one and two rooms upstairs. They were regular apartments. Both of them had bathrooms, but she was always having trouble with the drapes. The lines on the traverse rods would get all tangled up. So, she'd call, want me to come up. And I'm out on the golf course one day doing something, and somebody from the Pro shop come out and says, 'There's an emergency call for you up in the MacDonald's apartment.' I said, 'Oh God, not again. Not again.' I went up there, and she had just turned the traverse rod loose. Didn't break it down, but it was loose, so I had to get up there and fix it. There was many times I went just to fix the traverse rods. And, of course, there were a few other things...

I need to interrupt Dad's story to explain that apparently there was

Bill "Mr. Mac" MacDonald – Clubhouse Resident, Bus Driver, Fight Promoter and Multimillionaire...

Mr. Mac was a clubhouse summer resident in the '50s and a flamboyant multi-millionaire. As a self-proclaimed promotion man, a lengthy *Sports Illustrated* article detailed his exploits prior to the infamous Sonny Liston – Cassius Clay fight in February 1964. He and his wife Victoria were owners of a company then worth $52 million, including a stud farm, race track, golf course and a baseball team. Mr. Mac came from humble beginnings starting at eighteen as a Chicago bus conductor, working in the trucking industry, then inventing mobile homes and eventually becoming the world's largest manufacturer of them. They owned a yacht and mansion in Florida but returned to Battle Creek each summer for his company. He sold that company in 1960.

MacDonald promoted golf tournaments and one of the biggest boxing matches ever. As he said, "I dropped about $200,000 promoting golf tournaments but I made a million friends." He sponsored three Los Angeles Opens, two international tournaments in Miami, the LPGA Battle Creek Open in 1955, bankrolled Dick Mayer when he won the 1957 U.S. Open, accompanied two Ryder Cup Teams to Europe and chaired the PGA Advisory Committed.

And the Clay – Liston fight? Mr. Mac spent $625,000 on live promotion, but made a mere $250,000 because the fight got caught up in lawsuits. In the article Mr. Mac did predict he'd lose money on the deal, and contrary to most writers and bettors, he correctly predicted Clay as the winner.

quite a bit of prestige with having an address at *The* Country Club, although I don't think the apartments would have been considered special. Many tenants as my dad called them were wealthy business leaders who resided down south in the winter, including Ezra Clark who ran Clark Equipment, a local manufacturer of heavy equipment. Chick Harbert also roomed upstairs with his parents, and Ezra took him to the school on Highland every morning. Another summer tenant was Bill "Mac" MacDonald and his Polish wife, Victoria. Mac was a millionaire who ran a manufacturing firm in town and promoted sports ventures and donated the giant 100 foot-tall flagpole that used to be next to the club entrance. Mrs. MacDonald, who my dad talks about here, probably had the right to be a little spoiled.

A young Andi golfing. Harold's favorite car, the '47 Pontiac Coupe, is in the driveway.

"This was the lady that one time she wanted (our daughter) Andrea to go play golf, so she called Andi up to go play golf with her. Andi had a piano lesson or a doctor's appointment or something in the afternoon, but these two women went out-- Andi and Mrs. MacDonald went out in the morning, they went out and played golf. So along about an hour before Andi is supposed to go to this appointment or whatever it was, Jayne called me and said, 'Go find Andi. She's not home yet, and she's got to go to this lesson.' I went out and found both of them on the seventh fairway. They had been three hours or more going from one tee to the seventh fairway, about the middle of the seventh fairway. I said, 'Oh my Lord.' I think that kind of discouraged Andi from taking up the game. But that's some of the things that happened with interesting people around the club.

"And one-time Mrs. MacDonald called up wanting me to come up, and here she's got just a real thin negligee on. You could see right through, and I thought, 'Oops, this is something else.' And I went in and I said, 'Well, I got to go get some tools. I'll be back after a while. It'll take me a while. So I walked right on out [chuckles]. You don't mess around with any club members. That's for sure. But a lot of those things happened...

-H.P.

A Painting Bee...

"I never got into painting the men's locker room except one time we had a painting bee at the lounge in the men's locker room. They had a bunch of club members out there to paint that. And it worked out pretty good. But another time, we decided to have a painting bee to paint the ballroom and clubhouse. Glen and I got the walls ready for the paint. I got the paint, and they come in with a cooler filled with beer. I got a whole bunch of brushes, and people brought more brushes. The whole gang of people out there started painting. We got a lot of the painting done. And we brought in dinner from the Leon Gardens, a chop suey dinner. I sat down and started eating dinner along with the rest of them.

"After we got through, I went back with a paintbrush and it wasn't very long before I just sat down on the floor. I darn near passed out. So I walked right out and I went home. As soon as I got upstairs, I tossed my cookies in good shape, and then went to bed. But I'll tell you, the next morning when I went over to the club, Glen and I had to clean up paint after all these people. We looked at each other and I said, 'Man, this is more work than it would've been to go ahead and paint the room ourselves, just the two of us painting the room rather than have all these people here.' There was paint all on the floor. We didn't even paint the ceiling. But we had to scrape paint off the floor and clean up and scrape the windows, and good Lord it was a mess. In fact, some of it we even had to do over again. Anyhow, I think that came after we did the lounge in the old, men's locker room. Luckily that was the last time they decided to have the members paint and eat.

"Another painting project that I got into was when they wanted the (old) ladies' locker room painted. They had no heat in the ladies' locker room so we couldn't do it in the wintertime. After we started to work on the golf course, the weather started to warm up, and now we can paint the ladies' locker room. I sent a couple guys up and they got the windows painted. And then the weather got nice and we went outside to work. And I got a call, 'When are you guys going to paint the ladies' locker room?' 'Hey, my job is working on the golf course.' 'Well, it was supposed to rain, but, I said, 'Yeah, but I'm standing out here in the shop and it's not raining, and I got the crew out there on the golf course.' I said, 'When it starts raining, we'll be up there.'

"Pretty soon it started raining, so I called her. I said, 'I got the crew ready now to go to work.' And I said, 'Where's the paint?' 'Oh, right there,' she said, 'I'll be right over.' This was about ten o'clock in the morning. She came over and said, 'Well, we got to change the paint. We got to change the color a little bit.' So I started dumping this in and dumping that in and stirred and pretty soon I had no idea what I'd put in and what I didn't put it. We spent just about the whole rest of the day arriving at the color of the paint - getting the right mixture. By the time I got it, she said, 'That's what I want.' Well by now, I didn't know what was in it, so I didn't know how to make any more. She says, 'Well, this is what we want. Okay, go ahead.' And I said, 'No. Mrs. So-and-so', I said, 'My crew has to quit work in about a half an hour.' And I said, 'And that's a day's work.' I had sent the rest of them out someplace else to work in the shop. 'Well, they've got to get this job done.' 'Well, I know, but the crew only works so long.' I said, 'If you want a bunch of these guys to work overtime, we have to pay time and a half. You'll have to pay it. 'No, no, no, no, no. We can't do that. 'But

The old Clubhouse, entry and Gazebo seen from Country Club Drive

lady,' I said, 'Now, our time here is charged to the ladies' locker room. Well that's just the way it goes.' She said, 'We can't have that! Well, I will see about that!' And I said, 'We can't get anything accomplished yet today. If you don't want to pay time and a half overtime, we will wait until tomorrow.' The next day it was raining a lot and I had four guys go up there. They painted the ceiling and walls in one day. And she said, 'Okay that's fine.'

When I made out my payroll, I charged just so much time to the ladies' locker room. Of course, my personal time is not charged to a particular place. And it so happened that this lady's husband was chairman then, and he found out about what I had charged to them and he came to me and he said, 'You charged only this much time for getting that ladies' locker room painted.' And I said, 'Yeah.' He said, 'The only thing I can't figure out is how in the hell did you get it done so fast.' He said, 'It had to take you guys a lot longer than that to do it.' And I said, 'Well, after all,' I said, 'The guys were just standing around there half the day while we were trying to mix the paint up and they're not doing anything.' I said, 'I didn't charge that time off to the ladies' locker room.' And I said, 'None of my time is on there.' And he said, 'That's why it's so low. My wife complained that all this time was charged off to the ladies' locker room', and he said, 'and I can't for the life of me figure out how in the world you got the job done for that little amount.' He shook hands with me, 'We have to get along with these women, don't we?' And I said, 'Yeah, I guess so.'   -H.P.

Who's the Boss…

My dad had 300 bosses he had to please; imagine that! Sometimes it seemed every member had an opinion about the way the course played, or where the pins were cut in, or the trees or bunkers. But his big boss (besides my mom) was the Greens Chairman, a man elected or re-elected every year; he was the one who gave Dad his marching orders. Sometimes he'd get additional requests from the Pro, the clubhouse manager, other chairmen, or the club President. It had to be pretty confusing…

"I remember one time that they were doing some redecorating. They took through the wintertime to decide just what they were going to do. In the spring, they suddenly decided what they were going to do. They had things they wanted to do to the ladies' restroom upstairs but ran out of money. The president of the club came to me and said, 'We want you to put up the partitions.' They wanted to

partition the new toilets and put a swinging door on each one. "Well, okay. I can do that." I don't know what the deal was, but there was another holdup on it, and finally I got started at it when we had some bad weather. Then when the weather cleared up and it was nice outside, I went off and got my crew on the golf course started to work.

"The next thing I know, I'm on the golf course and the president came along, and he says, 'Hey, we got to get that job done up there in the ladies' restroom.' And I says, 'No. I need time to get my crew going on the golf course here.' I said, 'I understand that my job here is the golf course.' And this guy says, 'Now, listen.' He says, "If you want to keep your job here at the country club, you get your fanny right up there and you finish that job in that ladies' room because we want to get it open.' So I said, 'Well, okay. But I said, 'If I get any complaints about the golf course, I'm going to steer them to you.' Well, fortunately nobody came and complained to me, so I didn't have to steer anybody to him, but that kind of teed me off that time. And that was the only time in my 40 some years that I was ever threatened about my job. Of course, after that one time, I got along pretty good with the guy anyway.

"Another time when they first started rebuilding the clubhouse, they had to dig up the fuel oil tank. We used to shovel many tons of coal in that boiler down in the clubhouse. When the oil went in, that was the greatest thing. Then a few years later when they went to build the new clubhouse, they switched to gas, so we didn't need that fuel oil tank. I was elected to get that out of the way so they could go ahead and build this clubhouse. So I just hooked the tractor up, hooked a chain onto this tank, which was at least

Clubhouse lawn as seen from the deck of the Beach House

170

1,000 gallon, maybe bigger than that. I picked it up, carried it down with the tractor to where we had a dump. I set it back there in the bushes. Well, we got that out of the way.

"It went along fine until the next summer. I got a call from the manager of the club one Thursday night, his name was Al Scheff, and he said, 'Did you sell that fuel oil tank we had here at the club?' And I said, 'No, I didn't sell it.' I said, 'It's back there by where we have our dump back of the shop back in there 'Why do you ask, Al?' He said, 'Well, I'll talk with you later. 'Okay, goodbye.' Then the next day he told me, he said, 'The president of the club questioned that.,' He thought that I had sold that tank and pocketed the money, and he wanted to know what happened to it, you know? And, of course, Al Scheff couldn't tell him because he didn't know what I'd done with it. So that's why Al called me. When I saw Al the next day, he told me about this, and I said, 'Well that guy doesn't need to talk to me anymore at all.'

"Al then says, 'You know,' he says, 'we've been paying King Seed company for all the fertilizer in here and it seemed like an exorbitant amount to this same president of the club, and he was questioning why it cost so much. King Seed had gotten a partner that was in the dog food business. They took loads of stuff that Kellogg and Post had from making cereal, the leftover, whatever they called it. He took it up somewhere in Wisconsin to make dog food out of it. Then he'd pick up a trailer load of Milorganite in Milwaukee, and he'd deliver it to us, which was great. We didn't have to go down to the railroad siding and unload the car. Before that, we'd drive down, load two tons of it at a time on the truck, come out here, unload it, go back, pick another load up, dozens of times, and that was quite a job by hand. But this deal was they'd just deliver it into the shop all at once. They'd bring it down to the shop, and we'd unload it. We handled it just once at that time.

"Then what happened? Well at that time this president of the club was questioning who was pocketing the money that the Club was paying to haul that Milorganite because it didn't cost that much before. The reason it didn't cost that much before was because the railroad freight was different. But then it saved us hiring extra men in the wintertime to go and unload it from boxcars and haul it out here. Actually, the club was saving money, but it didn't show up on the books, so he was questioning that, and Al Scheff told me about this at the same time. I said, 'You know, I don't think I think too much of that president of the club, because he never said anything to me, but I think

in the back of my mind I had an idea that here was some guy that thought I was trying to cheat and get away with something. But it wasn't true. It wasn't working out that way at all.

"But later, when King Seed was hauling the fertilizer, they ended up bringing it out and he'd set his semi-trailer up there on the hill in the back of 10 Tee, and it sat there until we got it unloaded. We'd unload it from the trailer right into the fertilizer spreader. Only handled it one time, rather than taking the truck and going down to the siding and handling it onto the truck, bringing it home, handling it into the shop, and then handling it from there onto the spreader. It just saved us an awful lot.

"But the way it worked out, that wasn't to be so. When the guy at King Seed come around, I found out later, he was questioned too about it. He and his partner - both of them came to me and they said, 'You are going to have to get your fertilizer brought in by some private trucking outfit or by rail like you've been doing because we are not going to haul it anymore, because we have been accused of pocketing extra money. They told me they had even been accused on suspicion that they had given me some money in order to let them do it. They said, 'We are no longer going to haul any more

Harold is **dog** tired after dealing with club politics.

Milorganite from Milwaukee Sewage for you.' I think from then on we had it come in by rail freight because that was the cheapest way to get it or they hired a trucking outfit to bring it. Overall it cost the club about twice as much for the fertilizer as it did the way we were doing it before. When I come up to the greens chairman and told him about it, he said, 'Well, I guess that's the way it is then. If somebody accuses somebody of something and it ends up costing more money than it did,

well, that's our tough luck.' he said. 'I guess we'll just pay this extra money to get it.' But that was one of those rare bad experiences I had with the president of the club. Otherwise, I didn't have any trouble with the club presidents.

"I do remember one time when the new president was elected. I got a letter from him telling me that they were going to have a board meeting at a certain time. They wanted me to come that night and give a dissertation on what I thought my duties were, and what I would like to do in the future at the Country Club. So, I made up a little speech and went to them and I told them, I said, 'I feel my main duties are as the golf course superintendent of the Country Club. My main duty is to maintain the golf course in such a manner that people could play golf at almost any time they want to under the best conditions and maintain it as nice as possible.' I said, 'That kind of boils down what I feel my duties are: to maintain the golf course well, but not the clubhouse.' Then I told them what I'd like to do in the future. And my speech was kind of short, and they all stood up and clapped when I got through, so I sat down, and the manager got up and he did his talk. He went on about what type of steaks we should serve and this and that. He talked for quite a while about the technical part of the food service part. My talk went over a lot better than the managers did, but it was all right.

"But anyhow, at that talk, I mentioned something about making the pond that we now have between 9, 10, and 14. I then asked them to come up with the money for these proposals to fix the fairways which I'd gone through before. But another time I went to the board meeting to ask the president of the club a question, 'I know the board doesn't seem too interested in this,' but I said, 'Our dock is getting pretty well worn-out,' and I said, 'I'd like to propose for us to build a new dock.' Right away he said, 'Have you got this written up to come to a board meeting and let us know what it's going to cost to do it and how are you going to do it?' So, I drew up some diagrams of supports for a dock and took these diagrams to Morse Brothers. Then I drew up the diagram with what would make the sections of the dock and then I figured how much it would cost to build the dock. I said we'd build the dock right here in the ballroom of the clubhouse, in the wintertime. I had figured out kind of a ballpark figure of what it would cost. This was the only other time I went to a board meeting, but they okayed it. They said, 'Okay, go ahead and do it,' because we needed the dock. Okay.

"That was only the second time I ever went to a board meeting. But now, I guess, the superintendent goes to all the board meetings. He's usually a part of every one of them, but I never had to give

another report. In fact, the only report I ever had to give, was to just jot down the different accomplishments that we had done through that fiscal year, and the approximate cost of some of it, the different projects and so forth and the chairman would make it up into his report. I feel pretty lucky because I never had to do any of those reports.   *-H.P.*

My dad kept a lot of these things to himself when I was young. Now that I'm older I can really appreciate all the things he had to deal with; budget, weather, politics, keeping the grass mowed and the members happy. Back then the work he did just seemed like a lot of fun because my dad didn't share any of those worries or problems with me. I was so anxious to work on the course that none of that would matter to me anyway.

A New Clubhouse...Finally

With all the ongoing maintenance my dad got saddled with at the old clubhouse, it's no surprise that for many years the members had been talking about building a new clubhouse. With the upturn in the economy, replacing the clubhouse was first talked about in earnest in 1940, but the war delayed any progress.

This 1946 proposed Clubhouse rendering was the first of many.

After the end of the war, this clubhouse rendering was the first of many proposed plans shown to the members in a 1946 edition of *The 19th Hole*. In it, architect Lew Sarvis described the existing clubhouse

as: "originally an old farmhouse (that) was moved to this site for a summer residence. It was adapted to a summer house and was never intended as a year-around building...with several different floor levels. Some of the old additions have even the eavestrough sticking through the inside of the building. There is evidence of dry rot in the frame." He further mentions that a new roof was needed, all new plumbing and electrical was needed, and closes with, "Further money should not be spent trying to make major improvements to this building, as it will be a continuous job." It turned out he was right, as there were many more years my dad was stuck with the somewhat traditional job of maintaining that old clubhouse, in addition to his regular duties of running the golf course.

It wasn't until 1959 that the club finally began the first phase of construction of a new clubhouse; it would take over ten years to finally complete it. The $100,000 cost of this first phase had been raised by selling lots along the north side of Country Club Drive (what used to be my grandpa's hay field). One wing of the old clubhouse was demolished, and a modern new stone building housing a new kitchen, entrance, office space and restrooms were added onto the existing white clapboard clubhouse. The result was this somewhat unusual hybrid of old and new shown here. Also in the photo is the start of my dad's renowned "Rose Circle" to the right that was the source of table flowers for many years.

The Old Clubhouse (rear) met the New (front) for a few short months in 1960.

This rendering for a new Locker Room was barely voted down in 1968. It would have been located where the practice green is now.

The next year the second phase of construction began with the razing of the remainder of the old clubhouse. My dad remembers just before they tore it down there was a raucous demolition party: *"we got the pitching wedges and 9 irons out and we were knocking golf balls out through the windows along the lake."* Then construction began of the new Ballroom, South Grill Room and (not old) Ladies' Locker Room. The big emphasis in all the newspaper articles and promotions was that it was of fireproof construction, and the main floor was all on one level. One unfortunate result was that the service entrance which was used by delivery and garbage trucks faced the putting green and 1st tee, just to the left of the photo on the previous page. That was a frequent annoyance to my father as doors hiding the unsightly entrance and garbage dumpsters were often left open.

By 1968 a plan was put forth to the membership to build a new Men's Locker Room, Pro Shop, Grill Room and cart storage. There was an elaborate special presentation meeting that included brochures with attached photographs showing several views like this rendering and plan. Surprisingly, this addition added a new Ladies Locker Room (once again there would be an *old, ladies'* locker room). The proposal asked for $550,000 in member assessments to build this separate building across Country Club Drive on what was (and is) the site of the Practice Green. At the time, members were used to having to walk between the Clubhouse and the Locker Room and Pro Shop, so perhaps this arrangement

seemed natural. The rendering is looking east from the Drive and new Clubhouse toward the 1st Tee. The plan of this version had shown a second tiny kitchen serving this Grill Room; it would now seem quite inconvenient to have duplicate kitchens and to have to walk across Country Club Drive to go between separate buildings.

APPROACH FROM COUNTRY CLUB DRIVE

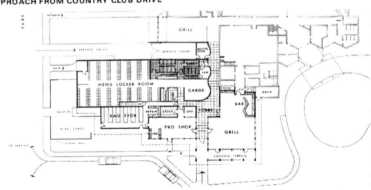

FLOOR PLAN

BATTLE CREEK COUNTRY CLUB ADDITION

SARVIS ASSOCIATES • ARCHITECTS & ENGINEERS

This rendering and plan show the Pro Shop, Locker and Grill Room addition that was finally built onto the Clubhouse in the late 60's.

My dad and, as it turns out, the majority of the members were against the version in the 1968 presentation on the previous page. Quite literally back to the drawing board, architect Lew Sarvis designed this striking 1968 version, and a new Locker Room and Pro Shop were finally built looking west with the lake behind it. It attached the Grill Room directly onto the kitchen where the service entrance was, and it didn't require rebuilding the Ladies' Locker Room. The old Men's Locker Room and Pro Shop were torn down and became more parking lot. This was the clubhouse building I remember and where I spent most of my teenage years hanging and working around.

Pros and Cons...

While Grandpa and Dad were the curators and sculptors of the golf course, the club's Golf Professionals were the coaches and mentors for the members. Over the years they all worked closely together and became very good friends, so it's only fitting to mention the Pros who worked with Andy and Harold.

Famed Golfer Chick Harbert shown here with his dad E. W. (Pops) Harbert; both were Golf Professionals at BCCC.

Walt Andrews came over from the old nine-hole course, and, according to a 1921 article, "...fifty lessons per day are being given," and "all the golf clubs are made to order," so maybe he left at the end of the club's second year due to exhaustion. Arthur "Art" Kennett was Pro from 1922 to 1925, when E. W. "Pops" Harbert became Pro. E.W. was Pro for the next nine years. His famous son Melvin "Chick" Harbert grew up at the Battle Creek Country Club to become a champion golfer and close family friend.

Chick Harbert receiving the Ryder Cup Trophy in 1955.

In 1933, Art Kennett returned to the golf club when E.W. took over at another local club, Marywood CC. Then, in 1940, at age 25, after winning numerous amateur titles, Chick Harbert turned Professional and became the Pro at the Battle Creek Country Club. When Chick enlisted as a pilot at the end of 1942, E.W. Harbert returned as Pro for the next four years, making this the only club around to have a Professional during the war.

As mentioned earlier, Chick and E.W. arranged a much-deserved winter retreat for my grandpa and grandma near the Harbert's winter lodgings in Sarasota in 1946, and planned the 1947 vacation my grandparents never got to enjoy.

While my dad Harold was Superintendent, Buck White was Pro in 1947 and '48. White was well known for throwing and breaking a lot of clubs. Near the end of 1948, Ron LaParl was named as Golf Professional; He enjoyed a long tenure and very close friendship with my dad. Harold and Ron worked, hunted and hung around together for almost 40

Melvin "Chick" Harbert – Clubhouse Sprog and Resident, Club Professional and Ryder Cup Captain…

At age 20, the youngest player ever to compete in the US Open was Melvin "Chick" Harbert. Ten years earlier, in 1925, he had moved into a clubhouse apartment when his dad became the Club Professional. He grew up at the club learning golf and was named Captain of Lakeview High School's golf team. He won the Michigan Open in 1937 with a record 268, shooting successive rounds of 63, 64, and 67. He won numerous other amateur titles through 1939, and the next year at age 25, Chick Harbert turned Professional and became the Pro at the Battle Creek Country Club. Club member Glen Johnson wrote an article for *Golf Digest* that details how Chick shot a 74 round on the couse in less than two hours, *using only a four iron.*

Chick won two national tournaments as a rookie, then after three years as Pro he enlisted in the army as a pilot in 1942 and was seriously injured in 1945. After returning from the war, Chick Harbert maintained an illustrious career as a golf professional, winning the Michigan PGA Championship six times. On the PGA Tour, he won seven times, was runner-up in the national PGA Championship in 1947 and 1952, and won that Championship in 1954. His team won the Ryder Cup in 1949 and again with him as Team Captain in 1955. In 1968, he was named to the PGA Hall of Fame. Long drive contests were his specialty; he won forty-two of them including one of 358 yards!

Ron LaParl – Bobby's Dad, Club Professional, and Good Friend...

Through hard work, Ron rose from being a caddy at the Country Club of Lansing to Assistant and then Golf Professional by 1943. The war interrupted, and he became a radar instructor with the Army Air Corp while managing a military golf facility. After the war he was Pro at Cadillac CC prior to coming to the Battle Creek CC in 1948, when he vowed to be a resident Pro rather than touring Pro. The caddy scholarship he began continues to this day, as does the Custer Greens golf facility he started at the Veterans Administration hospital. In 1968 he was named 'Professional of the Year' by his fellow PGA club pros, received the Horton Smith Award in 1979, named PGA 'Teacher of the Year' in 1989, and was inducted into to the Michigan PGA Hall of Fame in 2013. Ron retired in 1983, but along the way, he scored the course record of 63 in 1976.

years. The two of them, along with many other friends, continued to frequent LaParl's hunting lodge near Grayling, Michigan. That cabin is where I first heard Ron's favorite nickname for my dad – "*Hairy Pecker.*"

During golfing season, the golf Pros were furnished housing in the clubhouse or cottage next to the old ladies locker room; usually they moved south for the winter which is why my mom and dad lived there for a very short time right after they were married. My dad remembers doing work in that cottage and finding that it was built from old Postem (cereal) wooden crates. Ron, his wife Yvonne and children, (little) Yvonne, Ronnie and Bobby, lived there until the mid-'70s, when they bought a quaint log home on the lake just south of the clubhouse, and the cottage was taken down When Ron retired in 1983, Keith Mohan took over as Pro. Current (2019) PGA Professional Doug Kreis began his tenure in 2001.

Ron LaParl and Harold Peck spent their careers working together as best friends.

So, you might be wondering who the *cons* are, but first a little background is needed. The club's golf professionals earn their money from a variety of methods like lessons, Pro Shop sales, rentals and occasionally tournaments. In the club's early years, private clubs were permitted to have slot machines, and the one-armed bandits were owned and operated by the golf pros. My dad said, *"They were next to the door to the Locker Room and when you walked out, invariably you put in a nickel or a quarter in the doggone machine...went right into Pop Harbert's Pro Shop."* No one is saying the golf pros were cons, not at all (although they likely could adjust the payouts of the machines). But there were a couple of incidents where the term was appropriate.

In August 1936, three men wearing suits entered the locker room as the attendants were about to put the slot machines into lockers and close up for the night. Two of the men were armed with revolvers and ordered the attendants to: "Give us those machines and do it quick, no fooling!" One bandit stood guard while the other two moved the slots to a window, and an automobile drove up. The leader ordered the attendants to remain seated while the bandits loaded the machines containing about $75 each into the car. They later found the slots smashed up with no money. That armed robbery caused me to again wonder about how that bullet hole got to be in our leaded-glass window on the porch.

As almost a repeat, my dad said that in August 1938, *"right in the middle of the afternoon, two cars pulled up. You know, those old touring cars with the luggage rack on the back. Four well-dressed guys got out and one comes in and pulls out his wallet and here's a badge. The manager of the locker room, Charley Strawder, believed their claims and offered no protest. The men lugged the four slot machines of the half-dollar, quarter and nickel variety and put 'em onto these luggage racks on their waiting cars and took off. The manager then gets suspicious and calls the police and the sheriff and finds out nobody had anything to do with it, and so figured they were "conned" and told the sheriff to search for the car."* The men got away with over $100 and the slot machines.

ANOTHER GENERATION WORKING ON THE COURSE

My First Lessons...

It was the first week of summer vacation, and I was thirteen years old. After years of pestering my dad, he was finally going to let me work for him! I knew I was young for the job, but after all, I was mature for my age, and I had been driving the Cushman Trucksters by myself for several years, so I was filled with young confidence and anticipation. I didn't find out until later that I wasn't old enough to work legally, and Dad had worked out a deal to pay me a dollar an hour out of his pocket. He should know; an earlier precedent had been set by my dad and his brothers working for their dad at an early age. I was thrilled; the day had finally come when I would be working. I imagined myself running the tractors or the Truckster and doing all sorts of important work. But my dad had a couple of lessons to teach me first...

On my very first day, my dad took me into the shop and showed me bags of flower bulbs that had been dug up last fall. He said, "Here, you have to sort these out to get rid of the rotten ones and clean up the good ones." That was the smelliest, grossest job I could ever imagine! They were slimy, moldy and the smell did make me retch. I couldn't believe this was my first project! I probably did complain, but I went ahead and sorted them all over the next day or so.

A couple of days later he had me cleaning up trash on the lawn of the clubhouse and beach. Once again, this was not the glamorous work I had imagined. And I didn't even get to drive the Truckster to the beach. I had a bucket and was walking around picking up trash and cigarette butts and stuff...boy that lawn seemed much bigger than I'd ever known. Suddenly, I came across a five-dollar bill, just lying there! I couldn't believe my luck! As soon as I got back to the shop, I showed my dad. He said if no one reported it lost I could keep it. Years later, even though I asked him several times, he would never admit to planting that $5 bill for me to find. But I just know he did...at least I'm pretty sure.

The Maintenance Shop...

The maintenance shop always had this great, peculiar smell to it I will never forget. A mix of gasoline, chemicals and newly cut grass...now that was real perfume to me. I can almost smell it while I'm writing these words. There were two big overhead garage doors facing the clubhouse and lake, with the south (right) half of the shop including the workbench, tools, hoist and welder where all the equipment was repaired. The north half was storage for the tractors, greens mowers and chemicals. When I started working, the middle area

The "Shop" with Dad's office behind the center window was filled with memories.

between the doors was used to store the smaller walk-behind greens' mowers, and the bathroom was in the back that included lockers and my favorite thing in the whole shop – the Coke Machine!

Back then, my dad had a simple desk in the south part next to a window; it was out in the open with all the tools. After working a year or two for him, I thought he deserved something better and convinced him to build a real office. We put up a couple of walls and doors in the middle part of the shop and created a private space for my dad and a little lunch area for the men. We'd found an old window air-conditioner I put above the ceiling and tried to run ducts from that into the new spaces; it never worked well but sort of teased us with some cool air. I did build him a nice paneled office complete with rubber flooring left over from the pro shop, lockers that I antiqued red and black, and a built-in drawing board. It could only be my dad's shop; a heavenly place full of tools, machines and experiences. I loved it!

I also loved the people who worked in it. My dad already talked about one-eyed Glen Eggleston, who always knew how to fix anything and mowed tees with the Toro 76" Turf Pro mower; the driver had to twist his seat and hips to steer it. Glen was like an uncle and had worked for my dad since he first took over as superintendent in 1947. Hubert Dull was a quiet, gentle man who had always been there, too; he mowed fairways did all the spraying and took over the maintenance when Glen passed on. Harold Holmes was called "old man Holmes" by the younger guys because he was about 80 and moved and talked really slow but liked to work. Don Ballard was an even older fellow but always showed up to mow the rough every day. O.D. Nelson ran the Jacobsen fairway mower each day that steered from the rear. These guys were like a family and they always watched out for me.

I hung around the most with the younger guys, mainly because we worked on projects together. We did have a lot of fun. Pete Otis and John Wright were a couple of member's sons and avid golfers who really enjoyed working on the course; they helped me automate the water system. Bobby's older brother, Ronnie, also worked a while for my dad, and he had the nickname Pearl. The name had something to do with the way he blew his nose, and Ronnie was renowned for "laying a patch" of four rubber tire marks all across the parking lot with that ancient Toro tractor that was mostly all engine. Harvey Hansen was a quiet, laid-back guy who was Ronnie's age; he still has his long hippie-era hair and lives on Country Club Drive off #1 Fairway. The club manager's son, Steve Converse ("Spoon") and one of my best friends, Mark Radebaugh ("Rat-a-balls"), worked with me nights watering the course before automating the water system. We had way too much fun!

According to my dad's 1948 and 1952 *Weekly Time Book*, he had seven or eight people working in the summer, three to five in the fall and spring, and just himself in the winter. When I worked for my dad in the summer of 1977, he had eleven employees. By then I was officially his Assistant, and my earnings had skyrocketed up to $5/hour. He'd added additional staff that year: two working on the water system, plus the usual - one full-time maintenance man, one gardener, one man who always mowed fairways and another on rough, and four to mow greens, tee bunkers, plus rake traps, change cups and tee markers, trim trees and other general maintenance work. I was quite surprised to notice during a recent visit to the maintenance shop there were two dozen people on the course payroll now, compared to the usual ten when my dad was in charge. But times and expectations have changed, and I have to say the course did look beautiful and was immaculate.

Truckster Heaven...

I've already talked about the Trucksters too many times, but I really was obsessed with them. My dad let me steer them even before I could reach the pedals. As soon as my short legs could reach the pedals, I was driving solo, so my dad often brought one home for me to drive it in the backyard. Trucksters had a hi-lo transmission and a governor, so at first he set those so I couldn't go very fast, but by age ten I was driving at full speed any and every chance I got. I loved the freedom and the fun of driving, plus I got pretty good at it.

Marty driving around the house

By the time I started work I was an old hand at driving one. I loved zipping around the course, usually as fast as I could, but I learned to cool it around the clubhouse and members. Dad was always telling me to slow down over the bumps when he rode somewhere with me. If I were working on a hot day, a quick trip into the shop to get something/anything would cool me right off. The Trucksters accelerated fast, and, being three-wheeled, they could turn in a circle so tight one rear wheel would hardly move.

Speeding along on the golf course was simply magical. It was freedom; it was being grown up and in charge; it was being able to maneuver around and impress my friends, and it was exceptionally gratifying having the course to myself. Whether it was early in the morning, the evening or after dark, floating through the fog and flying over hills or dips was something very special. I just loved it!

One of our favorite Truckster tasks was knocking the dew off the grass in the morning; we called it "dragging the fairways." A couple times a week when the dew was heavy or if something was going on in the morning, two of us would each drive a Truckster out and hook a long hose between the two and across the fairway. We flew around all eighteen holes pulling the hose between us over the tees

and fairways. I had a fun technique of driving in a circle, pulling up and replacing tee markers and other obstacles without having to get off my butt. The most fun was doing it with my dad, even though he was slower.

My first wheelie on a Truckster was right in the middle of #1 Green! I was about nine or ten, and my dad was letting me drive along with him to spray greens. A big tank of chemicals was in the rear, and he was sitting back there on the fender. Because I was little, all the weight was in the back; the front

Harold is sitting on the Truckster by #18 Green.

wheel quickly lifted off the ground as I dropped the clutch. I was very surprised and apologetic, and I hoped I had set it down gently and without leaving a dent.

When I got older, I wasn't so shy about pulling wheelies or even going airborne. I knew when the balance was just right to execute the move, and occasionally lifted the front wheel up and gently set it down by accelerating, but only when nobody was looking. The sand trap bunkers were an ideal shape for speeding around a banked turn or, on rare occasions, for launching the Truckster through the air. I was careful but typically fearless as a teenager, and lucky I didn't cause damage or get someone hurt. Most of these antics I did at dusk when I was watering.

As I got older, full speed wasn't fast enough. I learned that the governor kept the RPM's on the engine down, and I devised an 'S' shaped clip out of coat hanger wire that I dubbed the LSD, for "Lightning Speed Device." By inserting it over the linkage, it bypassed the governor and let the engine rev up a lot faster than it was supposed to. They were so well built that, thankfully, I never blew an engine and had only one accident (more on that later). I didn't use it much, and only when no one was around or when I had to dodge an oncoming golf ball or rainstorm, but that change added 10-15MPH on top of the standard 22 MPH top speed. Again, someone was looking out for me.

Way to Mow…

My second year working on the course, I started mowing greens with the walk-behind greens mowers. They were tricky since they went really fast and I had to almost run with them but not quite. Approaching the apron, I pushed down on the handle to raise the reel off the grass and then with one hand spun the mower around 180 degrees, gently dropping the reels down again right on the edge of the playing surface. If the handle slipped out of my hands or the mower got away from me, it would likely dig into the taller apron and leave a scallop mark in the grass which would then often die. Very bad! I had to keep the lines perfectly straight, and it seemed like I was always trying to catch up with the mower. We got to "rest" by picking up the trap rakes and raking all the sand traps by hand. With those hand mowers, I really did trot between greens, which was a lot of exercise, and I was always tired afterward. Working on the golf course turned out to be real work!

So, I was especially grateful to Jacobsen for inventing the Greens King Triplex riding greens-mower! I was there when the "Jake" salesman brought one by to demonstrate, and the Greens Chairman and my dad quickly said, "We'll take two!" It made mowing greens in the morning almost fun if you didn't mind the gnats buzzing around your head, or getting up really early.

That was one thing I didn't like about working on the course; getting up early. Even at 6 AM, if it was humid, I could always tell it was going to be a scorching day. Everywhere I drove the Triplex it left three dark green lines in the silvery dew, but the sun got there before me and was burning the heavy wet droplets off the grass. Those tiny gnats were usually out in full force swarming around my head. I could briefly leave them behind by driving into the wind, but they were really hiding out just behind my head. At least they were out of my eyes part of the time. But, as soon as I raised the mowers at the edge of the green and turned, they caught up with me…in between my glasses and my eyes, up my nose and even buzzing in my ears. I'd try going fast enough to get away from them, but the Greens King riding mowers weren't fast enough to beat the bugs.

I still loved the early mornings on the golf course before the golfers came out. I had the place to myself, and it was magical with the wisps of mysterious fog trailing away with the sunrise.

Glen Eggleston mowing around #10 Green with the original Jacobsen Greens King mower, which was converted for a second life of mowing borders.

Getting up early to go to work was hard because I was a typical teenager. My dad and I had developed a ritual every morning; he got up around 5 AM, went down and opened up the maintenance shop, then the clubhouse where he'd start the coffee. After that, he'd come home and start breakfast. He'd get out the special grill that sat over two burners of the huge old white stove and start the bacon using his special invention to keep the bacon flat – a flat plywood weight with a handle on it. About then he'd go into the living room and bang on the wall beneath my bedroom – a tune I woke to every morning. After a healthy breakfast of bacon and eggs, or sometimes pancakes, we'd make it to the shop in time for everyone to punch in at 6:30 AM weekdays or 6 AM on weekends.

Usually, my first job in the morning was to rake traps or mow greens. If today was Tuesday, for example, according to the chart my dad invented, we were to mow them in the 2 o'clock to 8 o'clock direction. He'd made this chart years ago when he first got the big riding greens mowers, and it became essential to mow in all different directions because of their weight, even with the big tires. We mowed six days a week from May through September; Wednesday took the longest to finish because we mowed from 3 o'clock to 9 o'clock, across the shorter width; Thursday was 4 to 10, Friday was 5 to 11, Saturday was 6 to 12, and of course Sunday was 1 to 7. I think the different direction broke up the monotony too.

Don't get me wrong, mowing was fun. The hydraulically-powered Triplex greens mower was brand new technology that we sat on to drive. Before the Triplex, it took three times longer and five men to mow greens, now it took only two men riding these new mowers. My dad saw the advantages right away and didn't need to convince the greens chairman to spend money on the two mowers. But driving around the course on precision equipment wasn't easy. They steered in the rear and maneuvering was tricky, plus the mow-er had to keep a straight line down each row to make the greens pretty. And just like Dad said about Claude Hyatt, we always competed to see how fast we could get done. Usually, we weren't in a hurry unless there was a tournament or a shotgun start. Rushing to finish was kind of dumb really, because finishing quickly meant the harder work would start sooner, and we risked screwing something up.

And when something got screwed up, it was a huge deal. I mean, missing a spot always made the green look sloppy as golfers approached it. Golfers would rather blame a bad putt on the grass than on the putt-er. A ball taking a little jog or bump where the slightly taller grass stood was a sure giveaway. With the Triplex the goofs were three-times bigger than with the hand mower. If the machine got raised too late, it left a gash in the apron of the green since it had to be timed perfectly within the width of the mower. If you slipped off the smooth edge of the putting surface when mowing around the perimeter, a yellow scalp mark would be left in the longer grass. Those mistakes showed up right away to ruin the perfect look of the enormous greens the course was known for. Worse yet, they often bleached or died out, leaving marks for a week or more or until the grass had been patched.

So everyone was always careful not to screw up, especially me, the boss's son! Not screwing up was sometimes difficult when swatting gnats or feeling them get in your eyes. Daydreaming was easy, with the repetitive driving going back and forth so early in the morning - back and forth, back and forth, and then back and forth some more. Sometimes I'd think about being a little kid growing up on the golf course. Sometimes I'd think of my dad's stories about what it was like when he grew up at the same place and in the same house. Sometimes it was about crazy things at school, girls, friends, wanting to be popular, or just wondering what I was going to do with the rest of my life as a grown-up. There was always plenty to think about besides what I was supposed to be doing.

Sand Traps vs. Bunkers...

"So a lot of things have happened to simplify the way we do things around the golf course. You rake traps now with a machine with a rake on the back of it that you drive around, when before we used to have to do it all by hand. And when I first started, we did it with regular garden rakes. Then we started using those wooden hay rakes, but the teeth were pretty far apart. Then they made special rakes for sand traps with the teeth closer together, which made a big difference for the sand traps.

"Now they got a little bit of a rake that they carry around along with the gasoline-powered sand trap rake. They drive around the trap a few times and take that little hand rake and go trim around the edges. They don't have any banks to do anymore because I sodded in the banks that were on those traps. But that's made a big difference on the golf course and on the maintenance of the golf course. It's maintained entirely different than it used to be.   -H.P.

I quickly became good at driving those sand trap rakes. Like my dad mentioned, it wasn't long after the riding greens mower was invented that someone invented a motorized sand trap rake (Yay, engineers!), and my dad saw the benefits right away and got one. The first ones were a relatively simple floating rake behind a Cub Cadet garden tractor. But man, did that save a lot of time and work!

Driving it was also a blast! I flew around the traps (We never called them bunkers – those were the hills and mounds *around* the sand traps), going as fast as I could. Again, that was kind of dumb unless golfers were coming because then I'd end up starting on a harder job that much sooner. There was something about getting done fast, kind of a race against the clock that was appealing. If I could have made the tractor go faster, I probably would have. For each long sand trap, I passed back and forth, or for a circular trap, I'd go around in smaller circles, and finally once around the outside to make it pretty. At the edge, I often pulled a little wheelie getting out of the trap. One morning that really backfired.

An early mechanized trap rake

190

I was finishing up one of the fairway traps along #2, when I hit the edge of the lip, which caused me to jam the hydrostatic transmission lever up faster than I'd intended and pull a nice wheelie up out of the trap. I kept that going for a couple seconds with the front wheels way off the ground. Then I realized that a turn would be needed pretty quickly because of an impending collision with a tree. One problem with that…it was hard to steer with the front wheels not touching the ground. I pulled back on the lever, but much too fast. The front end of the tractor came down with a whump and a crack! In my carelessness, I'd just broken the front axle of the sand trap rake. I had a long walk back to the shop, thinking about how to explain this to my dad.

In the end, I told him the truth, that I'd pulled a wheelie and broke the axle. He'd probably seen me do it before, but it was still hard to admit that I'd screwed up big time. Making the work worse was that for the next couple of weeks we all had to rake the traps again by hand. I didn't win the appreciation of my co-workers at all.

Two years later, Toro improved on that Cub Cadet tractor rake by coming out with their "Sand Pro" motorized rake. It was essentially a three-wheeled ATV with a rake on the back, and it was zero-turn in order to maneuver around inside the traps without having to go in and out nearly so much. That made raking even faster, and my dad eventually had two of them. Nowadays, those custom tractors also come with blades to push sand around and pumps to get rid of standing water; manufacturers sometimes call them "bunker rakes." Now raking a bunker doesn't make any sense to me, because we always mowed the bunkers and raked the traps. I guess it depends on where you come from, or maybe how refined you are.

Other Lessons Learned…

Like my dad before me, I had been driving Trucksters and other equipment for many years before getting my driver's license. Driver's Ed was, not surprisingly, a breeze for me; I was an excellent driver and very confident as I practiced with my learner's permit. I knew my driver's test would be easy and couldn't wait to finally be able to drive a car on my own. The day came for my test, and I blew it… literally…at one of the stop signs! I didn't quite come to a full stop and was penalized for "blowing" the stop sign. I think the instructor could sense my arrogance and wanted to teach me a

good lesson. He did, and I had to practice both driving and eating some humble pie for another two weeks before finally getting my license.

Not too long after I got my driver's license, I learned another good lesson. I was practicing driving in snow and ice and approached the turnaround at the end of the Country Club Drive; it was lined with metal posts. No, I didn't wreck my folks '67 Delmont 88, but I did have a scare. Creeping along as I approached those posts, I put on the brakes only to find that they made no difference – I was on black ice. I slid for hundreds of feet, it seemed, as the posts got closer and closer. Until finally…thunk! I got out of the car, promptly fell on my butt, then made my way around to the front to the car. With a small sigh of relief, the only damage was a notch in the bezel around a headlight. Still, the "perfect" driver ego was knocked down another notch, and what was soon to be my car always carried a reminder around the headlight.

This reminds me of another valuable lesson involving my dad. I was still trying to impress and get noticed around school, when I heard about a stash of surplus army coats in one of the ancient Quonset hut buildings near the airport not far from the school. There used to be a big army installation, Fort Custer, nearby, so that sort of made sense. For some idiotic reason (which still baffles me today) I drove over there in broad daylight, reached through a broken window and grabbed an old army coat. I proudly wore it to band practice that night.

During practice, my drummer buddies thought the coat was very cool, and I boasted at how easy it was to grab one. I guess I didn't think it was really stealing because I told myself it was some old government building. Soon the rest of them had cajoled me into taking them there after practice, and one of them drove over and dropped us off. We ran to the building and began to scope it out, when I saw a car come around the corner with its lights off. I yelled, and everybody scattered. With heart pounding, I ran all the way back to school, drove home and was, finally, safe in bed when the phone rang. My dad answered it and after a couple minutes hollered that it was for me! On the phone was a sergeant from the police department. He wanted me to meet with him the next afternoon. I was totally busted!

Apparently, we weren't the only ones grabbing stuff. The police had asked the airport control tower to keep an eye on the hut, which turned out to be kind of an army surplus store although it didn't have a sign. Of course, they saw us and called it in. The police pulled over our getaway driver who gave them

the rest of our names. I was understandably terrified, and my dad grilled me about the details. I did not sleep that night, and the next day at school I was convinced I'd be going to jail or worse. My dad took me over the next afternoon, and both he and the police gave me a good scolding, but I avoided all my worst fears. I did learn a huge lesson that day!

A Silent Spring…

My interest in chemistry had diminished considerably after almost melting the skin off my hand. However, now that I was working, I became intrigued by all the chemicals in my dad's shop. As is typical with most early high-schoolers, I was also still trying to get noticed. When it became time to pick a topic for a major school report, I thought of talking about Rachel Carson's book *Silent Spring*, and the damage pesticides were doing. I had no idea how contentious this would be or just how much notice I would get.

The book was very controversial in the '60s, and the topic still reminds us how easily technological advancements can backfire and harm our environment. Carson accused the chemical industry of intentionally spreading false information and public officials like the USDA of accepting these claims.

The book mostly describes pesticides' effects on natural ecosystems such as killing off birds, but it also details poisoning, cancer, and other human illnesses attributed to pesticides. To some extent, I was involved in this world of chemical spraying. My dad and his men were spreading some of these chemicals on the turfgrass that people and animals would play on.

At that time there was a major war being waged to combat Dutch Elm Disease which was killing hundreds of huge beautiful elm trees on the course. I had some personal experience with that when the giant sprayer from a tree company backed down our driveway like an army tank. A man sat up on the truck bed next to a huge turbofan in a barrel,

DDT was sprayed by a turbine to kill the beetle carrying Dutch Elm disease, and unfortunately everything else.

spinning around and aiming the barrel up into the trees to blast a smelly mist of DDT through the leaves and on the birds and squirrels. It was a futile attempt to save the seven majestic elms that completely enveloped our house, and the hundreds of others on the course from the disease carried by the Elm Bark Beetle. Science hadn't yet figured out the treatment, but killing the beetle was thought to be a good solution. I recall many dead birds soon after each spraying and the lack of birdsong did have an impact on me. As a youngster, I spent many summers trying to feed and raise orphaned baby Robins and squirrels. I will never forget that DDT smell.

I will also never forget the losing battle my dad fought against the disease. For years we tried to cut down the infected trees as soon as possible to keep the disease from spreading to nearby trees, but to no avail. Every few days the chainsaws would be started up, and more wood added to the massive burn pile that was continuously smoking. I remember using the two-man chain saw to cut through the seven-foot diameter trunk of one of those great elms around our house. Grandpa Andy had planted those elms when the course was built, and seeing those eight hundred huge trees die off was very hard on my father. Although the worst of the epidemic spanned a couple years, the course quickly became barren and naked. It was the worst disaster to befall the golf course. Losing hundreds of beautiful mature trees was the greatest disappointment of my dad's career. He spent years planting new trees to make up for the emptiness.

So it seemed like a good idea when I asked my dad if I could do a report on the controversy surrounding Carson's book and the battle against Dutch Elm Disease. My dad was his usual supportive self, but I don't think he really knew what it would stir up. I prepared a summary of the issues in the book; the tests, the genuine problems about killing off the birds, the impact on all wildlife, the cancer dangers to humans, and the cover-ups by the industry and the politicians. My dad found out just how contentious this topic could be when I tried to interview my dad's salesmen friends from the chemical companies. They were anxious and defensive and would not help me at all. These salesmen brought up the prevailing opinion at the time that the author was a radical just trying to sell a book, when our government said the chemicals were okay. I know they tried to convince my dad to make me stop. He didn't try, but that pressure made me realize that I was on to something interesting.

I was a particularly shy kid, not at all comfortable with speaking in front of the class. This wasn't a science project with all the props, but the teacher said I needed something to make it more visual and

thought-provoking, so the focus was not just on me. I had a few pictures of dead birds and thought about bringing some actual birds but decided against it. Instead, an idea struck home…there was all my chemistry stuff! I could bring the actual chemicals to class and show them the real thing. That would surely make an impact!

Gathering some test tubes and stoppers, I went to the shop and poured a small amount of chemicals into each tube, including insecticides like DDT, Chlordane and Parathion, and herbicides like 2-4-D, Cadmium and Arsenic of Lead. The labels and stoppers got a little sticky, and a little bit soaked into the paper lunch bag I was carrying them in, but I had the goods. Of course, they smelled horrible and there were many odd looks as I brought my smelly lunch to school that day. My locker probably needed to be decontaminated.

My report began with Rachel Carson's research describing all the environmental impacts, and then I went into the controversy and cover-ups. I was genuinely surprised that everyone's attention was glued to me as I showed a few photos of dead birds and described my first-hand experience with spraying DDT, and the soupy chemical swamp behind the shop where the drain emptied from cleaning out the spray tanks. As my report finished by describing the hazards to human beings, I rather theatrically got out my test tubes and beakers and poured out a bit of each chemical as I described it. The teacher looked horrified, and a few kids cringed and backed away as the noxious smell filled the room. The teacher asked me if it was safe. My dramatic moment had arrived when I replied, "…that depends on who you believe!"

Of course, I got the attention I wanted, but not necessarily the result. I had a potentially noxious mess to clean up, which today would have resulted in a hazmat team being called in. My dad got a call asking if the chemicals were real, and he had to assure the Principal that everything was safe. I don't know what he told them, but I did get an A.

With all those nasty chemicals being applied and many of them outlawed today, it was a wonder that my dad and my grandpa lived cancer-free lives.

The Tournaments...

Every year there was at least one really big tournament that hundreds of spectators came to see. This was in the sixties and seventies when touring pros actually toured to local clubs for Pro-Am and exhibition games. The club had to be in top shape, and if there was dry or wet weather, we had even more work to get it in perfect condition. On top of that, all the trees had to be trimmed up and around. The gardens had to be pristine. Everything picked up and spruced up. Then we had to put up ropes everywhere to keep the spectators and their cars where they were supposed to be. Finally, at the last minute, out-of-bounds markers and special signs and scoreboards had to be placed.

From July 8, 1948

The morning of the tournaments we'd be up early with all-hands-on-deck, so to speak. If there were a lot of players, then the competition might start early, so the maintenance crew needed to be scarce by then. All the greens had to be mowed, traps raked, the dew removed, and everything checked out by tee-off. Those days my dad went around with the pro or tournament committee and set cups (the flag locations) on the greens. The greens were so large, and some had multiple levels and slopes, so the pin placement for the flags was quite strategic. It was a hectic time!

Several hundred, or, in some cases, a few thousand people came to see the course, and the golf pros. My dad always got tons of compliments about the shape of the course. I mentioned earlier being introduced to some of the big-name Pros: Gene Littler, Gary Player, Fuzzy Zoeller (I liked his name), Chi Chi Rodriguez (he was hilarious and loved kids), and, of course, Arnie Palmer. At the time, meeting them was not as big a deal as it should have been; what I really enjoyed seeing was all the people flock to the course. The most impressive shot I remember was the guy who could shoot a ball through a couple of phone books. A few other big names who played on my dad's course were Ben Hogan, Sam Snead, Cary Middlecoff, Jimmy Demaret, Byron Nelson, Roberto DeVicenzo, Larry Nelson, Dustin Johnson, Jonathon Vegas, and, of course, Walter Hagan.

In 1968, the club hosted the Trans-Miss Women's Amateur Championship. I'd never heard of it, but the tournament ran for a whole week. The LPGA had just started a few years earlier and wasn't a big deal yet, so this amateur event was a huge affair with lots of extra details. I had to put out fifty big American Flags every morning that lined the drive down to the clubhouse, and then carefully roll them up every night. We had put in special flower beds on many of the tees, and the committee made a real totem pole we had to put up along with lots of other decorations.

The 1968 Trans Miss Women's Championship had a unique Native theme.

I had other special odd jobs during and after those big tournaments, like picking up the ropes, stakes and trash, but one in particular was especially fun. At the member-guest tournaments, they had kegs of beer at a couple of the short holes because play tended to back up a little. I got to go out and pick up those leftover beer kegs at the tees right after play was finished and load them in the back of the Truckster. Usually there was some left, and it was still cold. I'd drive up to my friends in my very own beer wagon calling "Beer here!" and draw them a free beer. I became very popular, even if it was just for a short time.

The member-guest first prize in the early 70s was the use of a fancy, new 30-foot-long GMC

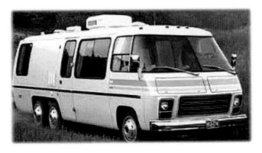

motorhome. The dealer, Orson Coe, brought it to the club, and I was asked to drive it out and park it on the Practice Tee so everyone would see it. It was really futuristic looking with air-conditioning, a sound system and a self-leveling suspension that was fun to play with. It was so cool; I decided to hang on to the keys until somebody asked for their return.

Michigan PGA Tournament at BCCC. That's probably Chick Harbert winning in the 1940's on #18 Green.

By that evening I had told a few friends about the keys and I was happy to show the motorhome to them. Pretty soon a couple more friends stopped by, and the tour turned into a regular party bus out on the course. That night we had the blinds drawn and were trying to be quiet, when someone noticed the rent-a-cop security guard driving out to check on the RV. He came out to make sure the doors were locked, while we were inside snickering, trying desperately to keep from laughing out loud. Some of my friends were the neighborhood kids who had a running cat and mouse game with the rent-a-cops, and I usually played the middle. After everybody went home later that night, perhaps to show I wasn't a prude, I took the RV out for a late-night road trip down to the end of the drive. Thinking back, it's hard to believe I actually did some of these crazy things, and I was especially lucky that nothing bad resulted.

The annual Jamboree Days were by far the most fun I had working on any of the tournaments. The first time I saw the normally well-dressed members and their guests playing in costumes was hilarious. The course was also included in the fun. When I was working for my dad, someone had the idea to put a box spring on one of the tees for everyone to tee off from; from then it was game on as I started thinking of all sorts of crazy gags. The next year, I convinced Dad to let me loose with all kinds of pranks. I'd place the pin on the slope of a green with a giant eight-inch size cup; on another green, we'd put out props that golfers needed to putt through like miniature golf. On one hole they had to tee

off standing on a step-ladder, but the odds were improved with three flags on the green. Then there was the time we lined one of the cups with fur and made it extra deep so they'd have to reach down almost up to their elbow to get the ball.

Every year the gags got more inventive and elaborate. The 8th Fairway had a waterhole next to the green, so I put a high-pressure nozzle on a hose and let it swirl around inside the pond. It would unexpectedly jump out of the pond, arcing out of the water like a giant sea serpent, surprising and spraying golfers. We had a telephone sitting on the betting table at the tee for the closest to the pin competition, and we rang it during the backswing to even the odds. At another, we drilled a hole in a tee marker and ran a tube from it through the ground to where I was standing behind a tree. I'd step on a foot-valve during the backswing, so the tee marker squirted people in the butt in the middle of their swing. During another hot summer tournament, we ran the tubing through a sand trap and a slit through the green to the cup; I squirted the players as they retrieved their balls. Another flagpole cup had a speaker hidden down inside, and we talked to the players as they putted in, saying things like "ouch," "that tickles" or "you just put your ball in my hole!" Then there was the custom oversize

Erie Sounds at Goguac Which Have Been Mystery Traced to Blethersm

The peace and quiet of the Battle Creek Country club has been disturbed for many days by eerie noises and weird cries.

The disturbances seemed to start about 4 o'clock and cease abruptly at t—ilight.

After this had happened for several days, those club members who had been bothered by the disturbances "arose in arms" and decided that no longer should they continue. They met in executive session, and by the course of parliamentary proceedings elected Arthur Kennett, club professional, as chief of the detective squad.

With a corps of assistants Mr. Kennett searched each nook and corner of the clubhouse, then the grounds, and finally extended his activities to the links.

About dusk on Monday, after searching each bunker and hazard, the committee suddenly came upon the object of their search. In a far corner of the course they found a well known club member emitting yells, cries and laughs, and putting himself through many contortions. It was decided that it would be pol-i-y to question the miscreant before banishing him from the club domains, and, upon doing so, they were informed that he was practicing for the "blethering" match to be played July 4.

For the information of those unfamiliar with bletheritis, or its symptom, bletherism, a blethering match is one wherein all may enter. The group starts from the first tee in a body, and the player with the most strokes drops off at each hole, but is not eliminated from conversation or other efforts to distract the remaining players. Thus the peculiar antics of the aforementioned player. A report has it that he was none other than an electrical man, whose name is frequently mispronounced.

That corner of the world near the south end of Goguac lake is again quiet and peaceful.

A curious Enquirer & News article from the 21st of June in 1922

199

flagpole cup we made that held water – along with a bunch of goldfish. I usually had the most fun operating the squirter, or speaker or whatever, but the golfers eventually wised up whenever they saw me standing nearby and knew something was up.

Mert Radebaugh costumed as Scissorhands, even before the movie.

But I don't think you could top one of the games they played back in 1922, called a Blethering Match. According to the article, apparently everyone playing started by teeing off from the same hole (which must have been remarkable in itself). Those with the most strokes dropped off but continued to follow along on the next holes, creatively gyrating and blathering to distract the remaining players until the only player left at the end was declared a winner.

A Few More Fringe Benefits...

Working on a golf course had its advantages to a youngster, but to be honest, the disadvantages should also be mentioned. Let's start with the heat, bugs, and rain. Becoming very good at watching out for golf balls is a priority. I could track them coming at me even if I didn't see the tee and surprised many a member by waving off their excited "Fore" and having the ball land next to me. Luckily, I never got hit. Being the boss's son meant I had to work hard and couldn't goof off in front of members or co-workers (or shouldn't anyway). My dad had this uncanny and well-known knack for driving up precisely at the instant any of us stopped working - even just for a moment to get a drink or catch your breath. But "HP," as the younger guys called him, always gave us that trademark "OK" sign with his thumb and forefinger. *Every single time!*

The benefits really did far outweigh these annoyances. The food was one great benefit, especially eating in the kitchen at the chef's table. The chef, most of the years when I was young, was Sam

Burleson, a generous (in spirit and size), happy soul who always made my dad and me welcome. Sam obviously enjoyed sampling his own art. My mom always had a nice lunch on the table when we came home, but I think Dad never minded an excuse to eat lunch in the club kitchen, which was at least once a week. Sam always whipped up something delicious, and quite often it was something he was trying out. I had many firsts there; escargot, brie, calamari, octopus...

Bobby LaParl and I had collected a lot of keys. He had keys to the clubhouse and his dad's pro shop, and I had keys to just about everything else. When I was young working on the course with my dad, he sometimes took me to the Beach or Halfway House for a candy bar or ice cream. When I was older working on my own, friends often helped me water at night, and if they worked late with me, I'd sometimes treat them to the same luxury of free munchies. Watering late at night if I got hungry, I occasionally made a hot dog at the Halfway House. I think Bobby was jealous because he always pestered me to make him copies of the keys. Instead, he would go into the clubhouse kitchen and make French fries because it was something he could do and I couldn't. I could have copied my dad's keys, but a sixth sense told me not to – I didn't want to be blamed if something happened.

Even though I was kind of shy and nerdy, driving up to a girl on a Truckster was a great way to break the ice. My dad always made talking to women look easy, but it was still hard for me to talk to girls. They didn't hesitate to ask for a ride from shy me though, and that was quite all right. I got a lot of ribbing from the other guys and my dad, but I didn't mind a bit. One memorable afternoon one of the cutest girls in the neighborhood asked me for a ride. Thinking it would be fun to go on a drive with her, I said sure; then, suddenly, three of her girlfriends appeared and they all piled in the back. I was not too disappointed though and took them for an exciting tour of the course. Later my dad kidded me a bit that I was showing off my harem.

In the summer before my high school freshman year, I almost got in trouble with one girl. We weren't precisely girlfriend – boyfriend, but she was adventuresome, and I was pretty naive. "Sharon" was attractive and comfortable to be with as I think she liked nerdy guys like me. We hung around together a few times on the golf course and did a fair amount of exploratory kissing. Bobby was often hanging around, which was annoying but looking back was probably a good thing. Somehow, she ended up at our house when no one else was home, and she had me sort of tie her up to my bed. Luckily, it was Bobby who discovered us and not my parents and nothing happened. A year after the incident, she

mysteriously dropped out of school; I learned she was hurt in a fire. I ran into her later and was so embarrassed that I just laughed, which was terribly rude and something I always regretted.

Why was I so shy growing up? Maybe because we lived on an isolated corner and one of the streets was very busy and I wasn't allowed to cross. Starting kindergarten late because of my late birthday when everybody else knew each other surely didn't help my awkwardness. Whatever the cause I was basically just shy, especially around girls. One particularly embarrassing time happened on a band trip when a family friend named Julie started egging me on to kiss another girl. Soon it escalated to everyone on the whole bus chanting "Kiss her; Kiss her." I finally relented and kissed her, but I didn't feel anything but total embarrassment. I'm sure she, too, was mortified.

A couple years later when I was fifteen or sixteen, I still hadn't overcome my ineptness with girls (and remain a poor student of the fairer sex to this day). There was one girl I'd become a particularly infatuated with. She was in the class behind me, so we never shared a course. Fortunately, she lived a couple houses right off the golf course, so I fancied impressing her by picking her up on the Truckster someday. After much childhood angst and a few practice speeches, I got up the nerve to call her for a date. It was classic me! When I asked if she was doing anything that particular night, all I heard was, "Well I have some plans…" Expecting to be turned down, I quickly interrupted with, "Oh well thanks anyway" or something dumb like that and then hung up. Just at that moment, I realized that when I'd interrupted her, she was saying "But"! I was so embarrassed and mortified I couldn't speak to her at school and ended up ignoring her completely. Totally stupid…

Another fringe benefit I should have taken advantage of was getting to know the waitresses. That was exactly how my grandfather met my grandmother, except instead of Trucksters he had horses. Anyway, the waitresses all knew me and waved when they were coming or going from work to their car. Finally, I got up enough nerve to occasionally stop and chat, and one afternoon a girl told me about a party her friend was having that night. They lived in a different rural school district, so I didn't know anyone or know what to expect, but I called a friend and we went to the party. When we got there it was four girls and three guys plus the two of us; I knew right away this party would be something different. The girls were overtly coming on to the guys like I'd never seen before. It didn't seem like they were girlfriend – boyfriend, but just all mixed together. Two girls climbed onto the back of the couch and put their legs around the guy's necks, and were rubbing up and down. After a while, as things got

hotter and hotter, I was getting really nervous not sure where this was going. My friend and I looked at each other and decided to scoot out of there. But I always wondered what would have happened if we had stayed.

There was a tradition at the country club of letting young members' sons run the valet service for club events. Today, it seems curious that back then no girls were allowed to do this, but I guess the membership felt more comfortable letting a boy they knew in their cars than an unknown kid or a girl. After getting my driver's license I, too, was allowed to park cars, which mostly involved a lot of running and trying to remember whose car was whose and where it was. This turned out to be a surprisingly lucrative benefit, as most of the members knew me and were great tippers. One night my tips totaled over $50, which led me to believe I was doing something right. A little maturity has taught me the truth of this tale. I've realized they really gave to show their appreciation for my dad.

There were challenges when everyone arrived at once, as in the case of a wedding reception. Cars would get very backed up, and we couldn't drive through the waiting cars to get to the parking lot, so we'd just leave them piled around in the street for a few minutes. In those days, we always left all the keys in the cars unless someone specifically asked us to lock them, something no one would think of doing today. Many times, we brought up the wrong car. At least one time a member went home driving the wrong car, too inebriated to notice the difference, and we had to swap cars to make it right. Unforgettable nights happened when someone arrived with an exotic sports car like a Corvette or Ferrari, and even the Rolls Royce that I got to drive. Now that was a fringe benefit...

During January, the club was closed, and the old Men's locker room made a great practice hall for the band that Bobby's older brother Ronnie, Harvey Hansen and others occasionally played in. Because we had keys to almost everything, and the locker room had tall ceilings and a big card room at the end it was a perfect rehearsal hall. They left their instruments there throughout January, and Bobby, Lon and I often joined them to hang out and be annoying as we were a few years younger.

At age 15, I had just finished building this light show rig shown on the next page for another rock band and brought it into the locker room to add a real rock show ambiance. It consisted of two rows of nine lights each in a long box that sat in front of the band as footlights. The control box I built had everything I could possibly think of: seventy-five knobs and switches, dimmers, keys to play the lights manually,

The Light Show project for a rock band resulted in a new career direction.

and a sound-to-light color organ. I'd even taken an old golf cart throttle with dozens of switches on a cam and hooked it up to a variable-speed sewing machine motor to make the lights flash with the music's energy; and when the band stopped playing it sounded exactly like my mom's sewing machine.

As a side note, a year later I took that light show on the road for the band it was built for. They had a gig at the club where my folks used to dance, the Mar Creek Inn. My mom asked me where my show was, and then said, "Oh, that's a nice place." My dad just grinned, since he knew that the club was now a strip joint. I worked there for almost a week getting an education on female anatomy before one of the girls asked me how old I was. Being 16 and much too truthful, I was immediately asked to leave.

The inflatable "date" was a gift from my sister.

On Becoming a Thespian…

I need to diverge from the golf course for a bit to explain why that crazy light show project would later become instrumental in future endeavors. That summer, at sixteen, I was looking toward my junior year in high school when my friend Dave Couch asked if I would be interested in helping him on a civic project. He'd seen the light show rig, and the project had something to do with lighting rather than grass. Up for something different, we went downtown to look over an old movie theater which was being converted into a new home for stage performances for the local Civic Theater. I quickly became intrigued by the old building, its movie history and old gadgets, plus the idea of working with electricity and lighting. I started volunteering my time and became one of the key volunteer "coolies," obsessed with the project and the comradery of working with other local adult volunteers like Dick Jones, Dr. Norm Lemaire and Judge Creighton Coleman.

After working there almost every weekend and many evenings, I soon had the trust of everyone and carried even more keys for the theater building. I found an ancient charm to the building and its haunted nooks and crannies. I was captivated and soon explored everywhere from the attic with its dust and dead pigeons to the basement with its musty corners and tunnels. While I was ripping out miles of old conduit and wiring, my dad told me the old copper had salvage value, so I burned the insulation off and turned it in to pay for my gas and fast food expenses. Previously, he had taught me about bending conduit and wiring, so I knew the basics and began installing new lighting fixtures and outlets. But I didn't count on getting into trouble one day while installing recessed lights in the ceiling of the new orchestra pit. A stranger walked up and asked, "What the hell are you doing!" I stammered a bit and said something obvious. He then asked me who authorized this and that, and it dawned on me that he was some sort of building inspector. My dad forgot to teach me about inspectors, so I got in a bit of a mess for being a 16-year-old unlicensed kid playing electrician in a public building.

That predicament got straightened out when Woody Bowers and his Vo-Ed students volunteered to do the electrical work. Under his direction, I learned a lot more and was able to concentrate on the stage lighting design and installation with Dave Couch. Woody and his students came to the rescue again when the schedule for opening night was threatened by the late delivery of the critical "patch panel," which allows grouping stage lighting fixtures to various dimmers. We ended up building the panel of cords and sockets from scratch and keeping the opening night schedule.

As the theater took shape and the lighting system was turned on, I invited friends to have their band practice on stage. This was the same group that included Ronnie LaParl who had previously practiced in the locker room. It was a chance for me to play with the lighting system and impress these much older friends. Word got out, and several people came to watch who were not invited. I realized this could seriously backfire when I caught one uninvited couple trying to sneak out the back door with an armload of costumes. Being much younger, I uncharacteristically grew a pair and kicked them out with considerable uproar. The impromptu party ended quickly.

A view of the original theater balcony and projection booth behind that became our stage lighting control room.

I was a freshman at college by the time the theater opened early in 1973. My dorm buddies were eager to help when I was asked to find limousine drivers for the grand opening night, a premiere of *Private Lives*. They got to drive fancy new cars carrying local dignitaries, including the Governor, up to the front door, complete with searchlights, red carpet and champagne. Through my activities at the theater, I'd even become friends with Wizard of Oz scarecrow Ray Bolger when he held an impromptu performance on stage.

This was my first grown-up project off the golf course. I stayed on to design and run stage lighting for all of the productions over the theater's first couple of years, learning as things went along. I will never forget the look on my dad's face when he came downstairs very early one morning and found me already in the kitchen making breakfast. I had just returned from one of my first all-night theater

206

parties; he was quite alright with me hanging out with that crowd. With some humility, I remember my first mention in a review sometime later said something like, "...the lighting was well done – finally." This building project set me on an alternate path that I am still involved in today, and I will always be grateful to my friend Dave.

Nocturnal Adventures...

"Even when it comes to watering, that's changed so much. When we originally put in the cast-iron water system in '62, we put sod cups in the middle of the greens. You'd have to hunt for and pull that sod cup to plug the sprinkler in. Now everything is automatic. Later we put the sprinklers in all around the greens and got them running automatically. Since I left, they changed that all around too. We had beautiful sprinklers covering all the greens.
                                                                                          -H.P.

For three summers I manually watered the golf course at night, a job known as the "night waterman." What an incredibly fun job with lots of freedom, and some escapades that when I look back were a little crazy. In the quote above, my dad was describing the installation of a brand-new cast iron pipe watering system he supervised in the '60s. It replaced the original system of buried hose boxes and crawler sprinklers, which wound up a cable when they rotated to pull themselves down the fairway. The new system had state-of-the-art quick-coupling valves running down the fairway center. Dad mentioned the valves in the middle of the greens under sod-cups, which were often very hard to find in the dark. My job was to drive the Truckster around, loaded with a rack of sprinklers, then plug or unplug these large sprinklers into the coupling valves. When those sprinklers came on, a ¾ inch round blast of water would spray over 100 feet out of the nozzle, with 125psi of pressure behind it. It could easily put out an eye, but I never told my mom nor worried about it for myself.

I'd start by setting out about thirty sprinklers along three or four fairways in about twenty minutes, wait twenty minutes, and then start a new run by moving the sprinklers to the next group of valves down the fairways for the next forty minutes, and so on. It would usually take about 6-7 hours, but Dad always put down eight because it was night work. Many nights I had a friend or two ride along with me for the first half of the night, which helped things go quickly. The last half of the night would get long, especially if you were wet and cold.

I knew the course intimately, every tree, trap, bump and blade of grass. I never used my headlight at night to see where I was going unless I wanted to chase someone off. Between moonlight, the city lights reflected in the clouds, or even lights from the street and houses around the club, I always knew right where I was. I was lucky though that nobody was ever laying in the grass out on the course where they might get run over.

Early sprinklers on #2 Fairway behind our house, looking south on the newly paved Lake Road (now Capital Ave.)

I absolutely loved being out on the course at night and having it to myself. The darkened course was mysterious and serene then, especially when there was moonlight and a little fog. The fog was usually in distinct layers, and those layers always drifted mysteriously in response to the sprinklers, so each run was like driving in a new land. Often there was a layer on the ground and another fog layer above my head; Driving through it was like flying in between the clouds in the moonlight.

The twenty-minute gaps between runs gave me time to get warmed up or have a snack, and sometimes talk with friends. Many nights somebody was around the shop hanging out, and, as I recall, some of them smoked a little pot, which was almost as routine as eating back then. I had to be careful I didn't smoke much or the night would get very long, and overwatering or underwatering could be a disaster for the grass. There was only one time I had anything to drink before the end of work. Ronnie brought a bottle of rum over; I knew it would be gone if I waited till after work and I didn't want to be thought

of as a prude. That was a mistake; the course got a little extra water that night, but luckily nothing terrible came as a result.

A Slalom Run…

I confess I liked showing off a bit when people rode with me around dusk to start watering the course. Thinking back, I realize now what a liability risk that was if someone had gotten hurt, but back then liability wasn't as much a concern, and we were all typically invincible teenagers. I always drove very fast, sometimes bouncing the sprinklers around when flying over a bump or hill. One of my tricks was to go "bunker banking" really fast around the inside of the banked sand trap bunker, and because my headlights were off no one riding along would expect the almost instantaneous change of direction. After flattening a few trap rakes, I realized even though I knew where the bunker was, I didn't always know everything and stopped that maneuver.

There was a narrow winding deer trail off through the woods by #3 Tee; it traveled into a long, wooded lot that went almost a quarter mile to a residential street, called Area RA when I was younger. It seemed a good time to branch out a bit and drive the Truckster on some new ground, and, besides, I saw kids running in there that might have been up to mischief, so one evening I drove down this trail. I went really fast, almost full speed, whipping around the narrowly-spaced trees, getting close but not quite hitting them. My friend Mark was riding along; he was amazed that we didn't hit anything. We got through the trail and down to a road that ran parallel to the course when I decided that since we were this far, why not go a little farther. We blasted down this new road in getaway mode; trying to think of a good excuse if we were seen because I really didn't have a good reason to be there. After about a half mile we found a way back to the course and, luckily, nobody saw us.

Water skiing was popular on the lake, and some of the friends who rode with me wanted to try it out behind a Truckster. Charlie Burnham, a club member's son who worked watering for my dad a couple of years before me, along with his brothers were the ones who started this "Truckster Skiing"; I think they even used a tow rope. The grass was very wet, so my friends hung on to the tailgate and slid on their shoes in the wet grass. They would eventually fall and get soaked which is why I never tried the

stunt. That wet grass was similarly hazardous when driving and stopping the Trucksters, as it was as slippery as snow or mud and the front tires were usually kind of bald.

One occupational hazard that occurred while watering at night was when, during the rush to get the rounds done in time, one of us would approach the sprinkler too fast, sliding the Truckster on the wet grass and running over the sprinkler, breaking it off. That was a real mess, kind of like having a broken fire hydrant shooting up in the air only a little less so. The brass stem broke off right at the ground, creating a 1-1/2-inch diameter gusher of water shooting up over a hundred feet. It quickly flooded the grass and dropped the pressure to the other sprinklers. Once or twice I had to go home and get my dad up to help, and he showed me the trick of sliding a sharp-edged screwdriver down right into the rushing water stream, catching it on the bottom lip and top edge of the broken brass shaft. With great difficulty, I could rotate the screwdriver and the brass stem out of the valve and stop the gusher, but it was tricky working with my hands in a powerful stream of water, getting sprayed up the nose and in the eyes. I'd be totally soaked. Sometimes the trick didn't work, and I had to shut off the main valve, or worse yet the pumps. I only clipped off the sprinkler a couple of times but became good at getting the valve stem out. When Mark or Spoon ran over the sprinkler, my skills were always in demand, plus I could always also go home afterward and change out of wet clothes.

Ode Of The Night Waterman...

The sprinklers are on the truckster
The last rays of sun fade fast
The caddies are picking up the range
The golfers on eighteen are the last
Someone has to protect the emerald jewel
That members pay good money to play
All alone I head out into the night
To labor in quiet darkness until the light of day
I thank you for the opportunity
To see her while she sleeps
Your giving me a chance to work at night
Is a memory I will always keep
Congratulations to you (Harold) and Lady
    Jayne for fifty beautiful years
May the good lord always be with you and
Green your course with his tears

- **Charlie Burnham**

Truckster Polo...

A couple of summers I had help; two of us were watering at night. My dad said it was because he wanted less water on the grass, but I sometimes wonder if it was more like he wanted us to watch out for each other. With two of us we usually had at least twenty minutes between rounds to kill. During those idle stretches, Spoon and I invented the game of Truckster Polo, where we tried to hit a tennis ball into each other's "goal," which we determined was the curb at either end of the big parking lot. And of course, we used golf clubs as mallets. This had to be a late-night game when the lot was empty and no one was around, because there was a fair amount of tire screeching and quick accelerating that accompanied the game.

With each of us driving a Truckster, we'd try to hit the tennis ball past each other, scoring a goal if the ball hit the opponent's curb. We each raced full speed to get to the ball, then stomped on the brakes and swung the club to hit the ball just like polo mallets. Like checking in regular polo, the Trucksters sometimes bumped into each other, and we made noise with the accelerations and screeches. Some neighbors lived close enough to hear us, and after a couple of nights, my dad got complaints and asked us to quit. We tried one more night to play quietly, but that didn't work and my dad got a little mad at us. It sure was fun while it lasted!

Night Watchman...

I really enjoyed having the golf course to myself at night. It was kind of my territory, so I chased people off who weren't supposed to be there, unless they were my friends. I bought a small searchlight and mounted it on to the front of the Truckster where it could be easily aimed and I equipped it with the same high-power light bulb used for aircraft landing lights. It was incredibly bright. I could see halfway across the course with it and occasionally chased someone off the golf course. That was fun, but then I added something more.

I built another gadget that turned out to be significant... As a drummer in my high school, I went on a lot of road trips with the band. Except for little transistor radios, back then no one had any portable music and no one had heard of boom boxes, Walkman's or anything similar. But I had an idea... The Pro shop had an extra, broken, battery-powered PA amp used for announcing golfers off the 1st Tee,

which I commandeered and repaired. I also had a twelve-inch speaker and a horn speaker; I built a box to mount them in and put that amp inside along with a simple cassette recorder. I think I created the very first portable boom box, five years before they were invented! It was a big hit on long bus rides, and I'd sometimes play sound effects I'd recorded.

So, my crazy idea was to use it on the golf course to scare people off. I recorded the sound effect of an oncoming freight train and strapped the boom box onto the Truckster, and for a few days I pretended to be – you guessed it – a train! I played the gag on some of my friends by driving toward them full speed with the blinding landing light and blaring sound effects, and they thought it was great. It caught them completely by surprise. I was then on the prowl for intruders and found a couple different groups of kids walking on the course. I had a fiendish, juvenile thrill watching them run for their lives as my approaching train chased them off the course.

It was part of my responsibility to keep watch over the course at night. It's not like there was a lot of mischief going on, but I felt it was my dad's course; both he and I took any vandalism personally. A couple times a year someone would steal a flag or throw tee markers around, but, occasionally, there was severe vandalism like the incident with the car and tow truck driving on #3 Green. There had been a couple break-ins of the Halfway House and Beach House, and the beach was a favorite hangout for local teens in the evening. The club manager, Fred Converse, hired off-duty local, township cops to patrol and chase them away. We called them the Rent-a-Cop, and Bobby's brother Ronnie started calling them Rent-a-Pig in the vernacular of the day. They were a running joke as the cops mostly sat in their cars and snoozed and then left after midnight. They rarely went out on the course, and, then, only to drive out to the Halfway house and check the door. Anyone who was doing anything bad would see them coming a long way off and hightail it or would just wait till they left.

> **– NOTICE –**
>
> TRESPASSERS on any of the Battle Creek Country Club Grounds will be prosecuted. This includes the golf course, tennis courts, swimming beach, and surrounding club property.
>
> Signed
>
> BOARD OF DIRECTORS,
>
> B. C. COUNTRY CLUB

The Club had tried many ways to stop trespassers, like this 1946 notice.

The rent-a-cop did give the neighborhood kids hours of amusement though, as there was always that cat-and-mouse game. One of the kids might shoot off fireworks at one end of the beach, and while the

cop went off to check it out, someone else shot off more at the other end. They might hoot and holler or sometimes egg the cop's car. I was always friendly with the cops, but I also mostly knew what was going on. Occasionally I sent the watchman in the wrong direction, so no one got caught, but it was always in fun with the kids I knew and nothing serious ever happened.

Occasionally, I caught someone riding their bikes out on the course and politely told them to walk their bikes across the grass because it would otherwise leave marks. But there was one night I did catch sight of some headlights out on the golf course, and I was quickly in high pursuit mode. Here was a real criminal – a malicious vandal! Flying across the golf course with the benefit of the LSD and without any headlights, I quickly caught up with the offender's vehicle near the back end of the course. I had them now! I pulled up next to the car as it traveled along a car path, and zapped them with my aircraft landing light… And I was shocked! Here was a car full of club members, including Lon's parents. Hugh Wright was driving, along with his wife Sally, Dale and Ruthanne Cumming, and Bob and Lois McNally were in the car. I'd scared the crap out of them, and my pulse was racing, too. They'd been socializing (polite-speak for drinking) at the clubhouse and had decided to see what the course was like at night by going for a drive and stopped at the ladies room at the Halfway House. After calming down, I politely but firmly, as adult-like as I could be, told them they shouldn't be on the course. I asked them to get right back to the street. Lon's folks were very apologetic, but we all had a good nervous laugh at me "busting" them. My dad complimented me the next day after he heard about it. He said I had acted "very appropriately."

Dancing with Lightning…

My primary responsibility at night was to make sure the right amount of water got on the grass. Too little and the Bent and Poa Annua grass mixture would dry out and turn crisp and blue in the hot sun the next day, and it would be toast when driven or walked on. Too much and the roots would shorten, meaning the grass would be all that much more susceptible to drying out in the hot afternoon sun. So, leaving the sprinklers on the right amount of time was important. When rain was forecast, we still had to make sure the grass got watered, especially because forecasts weren't that accurate in the '70s, and weather radar wasn't around yet. We had to keep at it even when there was lightning off in the distance

because no one could be sure it was going to rain until it actually started to rain. Even then, we had to make sure it did rain at least a tenth of an inch, or be really sure that it was going to.

All those factors made watering the course especially exciting when a thunderstorm approached. I got to be pretty good at watching the lightning and trying to gauge how far away it was, if it was heading toward the course, and how fast was it approaching. I certainly didn't want to be on the course when lightning was overhead, but I didn't want to pull all the sprinklers off too early and then have to put them back out again. This meant we usually waited until the last possible minute when rain was almost a sure thing to make the twenty-minute final round and pick up all the sprinklers. A few times when the storm died or went around, I did have to put them back out, but in most of those cases, I'd rush around as fast as possible. A few times I was not quick enough.

Driving the Truckster - fast – in a heavy rain and wind storm was not easy. When big, fat, ice cold drops of rain started falling, it got very cold and I couldn't see. With the slippery wet grass, driving was especially a challenge. The real excitement came with the lightning as it got closer and closer. At the front of the storm, the strikes were usually those potent, bright and loud cloud-to-ground cracks – the kind that took my breath away. There were a few close calls, but one in particular I will never forget. I was near #9 Tee and was just bending down to unscrew one of the large Rainbird fairway sprinklers. These were about two feet tall and shot a water stream out about seventy feet. The very instant I touched the metal sprinkler there was an instantaneous flash and boom that almost knocked me over. I jumped back and looked up to see sparks dancing and fading out in a tree at the top of the hill only seventy-five yards away. My heart was pounding, and I quickly scrambled onto the Truckster, leaving the sprinkler there and driving as fast as I could down Country Club Drive toward the clubhouse. I ran into the pump house, shut the pumps off and spent the next five minutes wrestling with the big wheel that closed the main twelve-inch valve. Some of the compressed air was released from the huge water tanks before I could get it closed, and I knew it sounded like a chorus of hissing serpents out on the course as the sprinklers would spin around spewing air. It took me quite a while to settle down, but, finally, I left my dad a note in the shop and went home to try to sleep. That was my second close dance with lightning.

Many nights I spent out on the course watching the sky. With all the books on UFOs Lon and I collected as kids, I was always hopeful I could see something from out of this world. The Northern Lights and

several meteorites put on exhibitions a few times, but the most impressive displays were the lightning bolts. Many nights we needed to wait and make sure it rained enough, so I parked my car out on the service drive on the course to watch the sparks fly in the sky. I became quite a connoisseur, comparing the lightning bolts by color, branches, longevity and spread. I recall many strikes that hit somewhere on the course and one particularly fascinating stroke that seemed to spiral through the sky right toward me.

A couple of years later, when the water system was fully automated, I was back working days and my experience with lightning had another benefit. A thunderstorm was approaching, and it had just started to rain so I was racing back to the clubhouse when I noticed two golfers unwisely standing under a tree. I stopped and told them to throw their clubs in the back and hop on. After saying they'd wait out the rain under the tree, I almost left them there. Back then, golfers were more ignorant about the risks from lightning, but even today, its amazing people will take chances and stay out in a storm. Giving it one more quick try, I mentioned how often trees get hit and insisted they get in. The two golfers relented and climbed in; we headed toward the clubhouse at full LSD speed.

By then the storm was almost fully on us. Then, as you might have guessed, there was a huge flash and simultaneous explosion as lightning struck a tree nearby. I sped to the clubhouse and almost went airborne driving down the ramp into the basement cart storage barn. I didn't see the strike, but one of the golfers did and said it was just across the fairway. Those guys were very grateful and spent the rest of the afternoon at the bar. Later they gave my dad a $100 tip for me. That was my third close call with lightning, but at least it turned out with a good lesson learned.

Flipping Out…

Over many years I had over-confidently driven Trucksters on the course without fear of anything bad happening. It was almost inevitable then that something serious would eventually happen. Late one night I was driving toward the shop after finishing our watering, coming from the Halfway House. Spoon, who was also working that night, was riding on one of the fenders. I was, of course, going fast, driving at an angle up the side of a hill in front of #10 Tee. The grass was wet, and the front tire was slipping sideways down the hill, so I compensated by slightly steering it up the hill in a controlled slide

(called a drift today). It was a natural maneuver that I didn't consciously think about, but was confident with the sliding when the Truckster hit the asphalt cart path. Suddenly, the front tire grabbed, and we instantly changed direction, putting us up on two wheels and going right along the cart path. I tried to brake and turn the wheel out to bring the Truckster down, but there was too much inertia holding the wheel from turning. In an instant, I knew we were going over! I yelled at Spoon to jump, waited for a beat, let go of the wheel and jumped off myself. We both landed safely, but the Truckster did not. In seeming slow motion, the front left corner hit the ground as the back end came up and it flipped entirely over end and landed upside down.

I couldn't believe what had happened. After first checking out each other, we looked over the Truckster. I had hoped by some miracle the damage wasn't serious, but it was. The little fender over the front tire was bent up, and the front left corner of the cowling was bent way back. We struggled with the vehicle and got the Truckster turned over for a better look at the damage. The steering wheel was also bent. I tried to bend the cowling back, but there was still a crease in the metal. The Truckster wasn't even a year old.

After checking the oil, I started it up, and we drove it slowly back to the shop. I was so embarrassed and humbled. But, I was mainly worried that I'd let my dad down. He had given me all this trust and confidence. I went home and woke him up to tell him what happened. He was upset, of course, but was glad that we were okay. I was relieved he wasn't furious with me. I think he realized that I had learned another lesson. This accident caused me to really begin to believe someone was looking out for me.

Surprisingly that was not the immediate end of my night work, but it may have influenced my dad to make a significant change. Soon after that, we began talking about something brand new in golf course operations - automating the water system.

Putting Off That Big Decision…

The summer before my senior year I remember mowing the green on the first hole while looking at our nearby house when I had a teenage epiphany. I was going to college, somewhere, next year. It was a bit late to start thinking about my future: - where would I go to college and what would I do for the rest

of my life. Those questions had crossed my mind before, but at the ripe old age of 16, it seemed like now was the time to make the fateful BIG DECISION that would dictate the rest of my life. My thoughts wandered into 'where to go' and 'what to do' then back to 'I can put it off another few days.' But I really needed to get college applications in, which required a lot of big choices I'd never faced. There were lots of factors in that decision. Some factors in that decision were typical: my grades weren't the best because I was a "smart procrastinator," what school could I afford, and how close to home did I want to live. One major factor was not so typical.

That big question was - should I follow the family tradition? Running this golf course is what my father does. That is what my grandfather did since building the course, even working at the old nine-hole course before that. My uncles were doing the same work on other golf courses. As a little kid, I'd always dreamed of working on the course with my dad, who was the BIG CHEESE; and that dream had finally come true when I was thirteen. I'd had many fun adventures working on and playing around the course, and it was an understatement to say I enjoyed working with my dad. I'd grown up in a house on the course and was quite literally immersed in the game of golf.

Or, should I break away from our family legacy and do my own thing?

With the second tee for my backyard, a lot of people might think golf was in my veins. I could have played the game almost every day. As a

Working on the water system behind 9 Green

217

youngster, my parents enrolled me in junior golf, and every Friday morning in the summer I got up early and went to the driving range for a lesson. We'd play a few holes, but compared to the other kids I felt like I was the worst golfer ever. Their parents were all members of the private country club, but my dad worked there and we rarely played the game. Being a shy kid didn't help, and maybe that was the reason I always looked forward to the end of the lesson and getting back to the clubhouse for a lunch of hot dogs, coke and chips.

I did a lot of daydreaming mowing the grass. By speeding away on the triplex mower to the next green, I was trying to get away from those darn gnats, and leave that Big Decision behind. If it weren't for those gnats, mowing greens would be kind of fun. The hydraulic mowers had three gangs that raised and lowered in sequence when I pushed the foot pedal. I'd gotten really good at the rhythm of raising the units, turning on the apron, backing up, and starting down the line again. Sometimes I worked out a pattern where backing up wasn't necessary, but not very often. I had to stay ahead of the early golfers because if they caught up, it could take forever to finish, and they might get annoyed if their putting surface wasn't mowed.

These mowers made it a breeze compared to the early greens mowers that had to be pushed. I will always remember my dad's story when he tried to mow greens with the old manual-push reel mowers as a kid. My sister Andi and I were both compelled to revisit that bit of history by mowing our tiny front yard with a manual reel mower which needed to be pushed *very hard* to make the reels turn. Neither one of us liked that chore, and I couldn't imagine pushing that hard all day long. Even though I really loved working on the course, no way could I have ever done that. But I think that chore was another of my dad's thoughtful lessons.

These last two paragraphs are an interruption in my written narrative to illustrate my skill at procrastination about the important stuff. So, as cool as the new greens mowers and other new equipment were, I had to quit stalling and get back to that Big Decision…

My Dad and "The Choice"...

Weeks later I was still putting things off. College applications needed to be turned in very soon. I had been thinking about this big decision off and on all summer, not so much where to go to college but

what to do with my life. Did I want to become a Course Superintendent like my dad? On the one hand, my dad had helped start the Turfgrass Management Program at Michigan State. It would be natural, and likely easy for me to get accepted there, maybe even with a scholarship, since my dad was well known and I had plenty of experience. I knew what was involved, managing a staff and a budget, making a course look good in spite of the environment, and keeping members and employees happy. I loved the freedom of driving around the course and working in a grand park-like setting. I liked building and designing things, and a golf course presents opportunities to do some of those creative things. Keeping the grounds beautiful has a lot of appeal. And I liked being outdoors!

What I didn't like was the idea of being tied down to the course, not being able to get away during the spring, summer, and fall, and the requirement of having to get up early almost every day. But then again, that issue came with most any job. Furthermore, I didn't like the aspect of having so many bosses to satisfy and keep happy. I was shy and didn't think I had the personality to remain on friendly terms and be well liked by all the members, yet I knew that was a critical part of the job.

And there were other things that I might enjoy doing. I'd always enjoyed tinkering with electronic gadgets, tearing stuff apart to see how it worked and building things that were different. Over the years, I'd also imagined myself as a scientist, an inventor or a designer. I always liked designing and creating things. I was enamored by the space program since our country was traveling to the moon. I was always having crazy ideas…

But, on the other hand, there was a family tradition. My dad ran this golf course, as did my grandfather before him. I had so much fun working with my dad on the golf course! Growing up I'd always imagined working for my dad, then taking over the club when he retired. My uncles Roy and Les were both superintendents of equally well-respected golf clubs in the state. I didn't want to be the black sheep and break that family legacy. More importantly, I didn't want to disappoint my dad!

So, I knew I needed to talk to my father about this choice. At the time it seemed like an important discussion, but I didn't realize until later just how monumental an event it was. We sat down, and after a long preamble, I told him how much I enjoyed working with him on the golf course and listed the parts of the job I really loved. They were mostly the creative parts of the job... building this, solving that. So I told him that I was considering turfgrass as a career, but was also thinking of other ideas as well, like engineering or landscape architecture. I asked him what he would think if I decided to do

something else; then held my breath. I will never forget what he said... He chuckled... *"Marty, you've had a real good idea of what it's like to be a Superintendent. You know what goes on with the members, dealing with grass and the weather and things. I'd be just fine if you stayed with it, but I'd be really proud of you if you tried something else! You go right ahead..."*

So maybe this legacy stuff wasn't such a big deal to my dad, after all... After that fateful heart-to-heart, I decided to break from family tradition and go to school for electrical engineering. For five more summers and one winter, I continued to work on the course with my dad. We had many more adventures and a few frustrations together. Many times since, though, I've also wondered what would have happened if I had followed in my father's footsteps.

Back to A Day Job...

Once the decision had been made early in my senior year to go to college for engineering, I felt better knowing I wasn't letting my dad down or breaking some family tradition. Still, it did make me realize, as much as any teenager could, my days working on the course with my dad would not last forever. I came to appreciate our time together even more and really enjoyed working on gadgets and schemes with him. We collaborated on various projects, and I had a slew of crazy ideas. Some I've already mentioned, like building the waterfall at the beginning of the ditch, or my abstracted bricklaying for the drinking fountain. Many of the others, like a decorative fountain next to the

Marty getting wired up

practice green in front of the club, never made it to completion. The fountain did get so far as Dad letting me design and build a motorized valve system that could cycle through different spray effects. The gizmo of valves, motors and gears sat on a shelf for years, and I wonder what the superintendent who followed my dad thought about that contraption.

The major project we did accomplish together was the automation of the water system. Ten years earlier the club had installed a modern high-pressure irrigation system. It had all new iron pipes and brass quick-coupling valves running down the center of the fairway, with special Sod-cups in the greens that hid the valves. As I mentioned, plugging in those sprinklers at night was very labor intensive; some low spots or high areas needed a little less or a little more water, but that wasn't practical to adjust during watering rounds. New inventions of a rotating pop-up sprinkler, electric valves and electromechanical timers had recently made it possible and affordable to automate the water system. The technology was brand new, so my dad had visited a couple of courses and became convinced it was an essential next step.

Since automation was brand new, there were only a couple of installation companies in the nation, and they were too expensive for the club's budget. With years of successful "let's do it ourselves" experience, my dad asked me if I thought we could design and install it on our own. Eager to prove myself to my dad as a wanna-be engineer, I immediately said yes. I'd already had plenty of experience

Mark Radebaugh, Dave Couch and Marty Peck laughing at Ronnie LaParl while working with the wire plow rig.

designing and installing residential watering systems as a side job, which helped a lot. We began by figuring out the right sprinkler, valve and controller combination. With the new controller, the duration of each sprinkler's operation could be adjusted, and we decided to place at least four pop-up sprinklers around each green to get better coverage. I drew up plans showing where the controllers would be located, and how many wires needed to be put into the ground and where. My first real, original blueprint!

But then came the first real challenge – how to get all thirty-five miles of wires pulled into the ground to the new two-hundred-fifty sprinklers and electric valves. Conventional trenching would have been messy and time-consuming; we needed a better plan. The best method would be to plow the wires right into the ground – open up a slit through the turf, lay the wires into the slit, and close it up. We looked, called everyone we knew, checked around, but nothing like that existed at the time. So my dad and I designed and built a "wire plow" using a conventional single slit plow, but with a two-inch pipe welded to the curve of the plow as a sleeve. It had a flared guide at the top to let as many as thirty-six wires go into the sleeve at a time.

The next trick was how to set up all these individual spools of wire to unroll into the plow sleeve as we drove along. We then built a trailer with racks of pipes that held the spools, so the wires could be pulled behind the plow. It made for a big, impressive looking contraption when we got it all finished,

Don Ballard takes a break from mowing rough to help Ronnie and Marty pull the wire plow rig through a wet area.

222

and it worked great. We'd start at the controller by pulling the right number of wires through the plow sleeve and anchor them to the control box; then putting the plow into the ground and slowly driving out to and down the fairway past each sprinkler location, drop off a wire each time. It worked almost perfectly; the tricky challenge was juggling spools to make sure we didn't waste wire or run out, and not getting stuck in the muck.

A mysterious large barn is seen out on the golf course to the left behind our house; its foundation had mysteriously blocked the wire-plow. Also in this photo, a shadowy unknown person can be seen right of the center pillar on the porch, watching the new Country Club Hills subdivision under construction in 1924.

I became a regular project foreman, keeping the guys stocked with fittings at each location. After pulling the wires in, we'd dig a hole for each valve and sprinkler, hook them up, test and backfill. Sometimes we did get stuck in the muck and then we'd have to get another tractor. But there was one unusual spot right between #18 Tee and #2 Tee. I was plowing wires and ran into an unexpected obstacle. The plow just suddenly stopped dead and would not move, so we dug around and found what we thought was a huge rock. A little way beyond that was another big rock. Not having a jackhammer or dynamite, we just went up over them and laid something under the wire so it wouldn't get scraped.

Many years later while looking through old photos, I figured out it wasn't really a rock. Seen on the previous page in this early 1920's photo taken from across the street, behind our house to the left out on the golf course, was another barn or outbuilding. It must have been from the old Post family Calmary Farm estate; its foundation would have been right where we ran into those obstacles. Unfortunately, by the time I found this out, it was too late to share the intriguing answer to that puzzle with my dad. Also, in this photo, someone appears to be standing on the porch of our house, just to the right of the middle post watching the construction of the nearby subdivision.

The new automated water system worked beautifully, although it needed an occasional repair due to lightning strikes. The next summer I was still able to go out occasionally at night to make sure the system was operating as it was supposed to, which was even better than being night waterman because there wasn't any real work to do. My dad wasn't one to boast, but the Pro Ron LaParl often commented about the $25,000 we saved the club by installing the system ourselves.

Over the next few years, before I graduated from college, I was officially my dad's Assistant and he left me in charge a few times while he went on work trips in the summer. He'd never had such a luxury before, but it was during one of those trips we had a torrential rainstorm. It was one of those ten-year or fifty-year rainfalls, with five to seven inches, and everything was under water, even the front part of the course.

A giant lake across 6, 13 and 11 Fairways came from flooding rainstorms.

As the storm was winding down, I thought, "What would Dad do?" I started calling places asking to borrow some large industrial

224

pumps. There were only a couple not spoken for, so I picked them up that afternoon and set them out right away. It was critical to get the water pumped off the turfgrass before the sun came out and cooked the grass. I got up a couple times in the night to refill gas tanks and keep the pumps running. We managed to get a lot of the water off the turf by the next day. Unfortunately, the water level was very high in the brook that drained everything away, so the water was up above the dam across the ditch, and some water would fill back in as soon as it was pumped down. By the next day though, we got the water mostly drained off and lost very little grass. My dad was very proud that I'd "saved the day," and he often boasted about that.

Muckin' Around…

Much of the course's back ten holes were built on a peat bog, which caused a lot of work and consternation for my dad and his father. Everyone always called it muck, and a thick layer of it sat on top of a layer of clay, which made digging and drainage a challenge. You could always tell when you were walking on it – if it wasn't squishy, then it bounced like heavy Jell-O. The soil was rich in nutrients and almost always moist, but that meant that the roots of the grasses didn't need to grow far.

Consequently, grass burned easily during hot spells or was flooded from heavy rain, and then the grass cooked in the puddles as the water was heated by the sun. Frequently, patches died and needed reseeding. Whenever there was a significant rainstorm, my dad and I were always down there trying to drain off the water.

It seemed we were always working on some project to help drain that water: trenching, tiling and cleaning out drain tiles or catch basins. Dad frequently talked about the challenges of working in the muck and trying to drain it…

"But that muck was quite a deal. We struggled with that creek and the drainage for a long time. I remember when I first started after my dad passed away, that next fall, we decided to do some drainage down there and we started digging trenches and putting tile in. We dug up quite a bit of tile that was already there and cleaned it out and put it back in with a gravel bed. Which come to find out, didn't actually help much because the muck would seep through the gravel and still get into the tile and still plug it up. But we had quite a time trying to dig a trench in that muck. Why, you

225

took a shovel full of muck out, and you had to have a stone or something over to the side to hit the shovel on to get the muck off of it, because it would stick right to the shovel. And by the time you got back to the trench, why, it had filled up with muck again. The muck where it sat in the ground - why, it was like clay. But then you'd get it loose, and it was like running water, it was like soup. But we had quite a time, we sure did.

"One time, I decided I was going to go across 6 Fairway and put a tile right in front across 6 Green, because we found a tile on each side of the fairway and we wanted to connect them all. So we took the sod off. We started to dig with shovels, but then I got the bright idea we could take the slip scraper, and we could dig this trench with the slip scraper. We started in, and of course working in that muck was just like grease. We got the tractor stuck. Then we got another tractor to pull that tractor out, and we got that one stuck. Then we got another tractor out. I think I had three tractors at the time, and we got the last one stuck. We tried to pull that one out, and then we tried to pull one tractor out with the dump truck, and we got that stuck. Well, now we have a real problem — everything is stuck! So now what do we do?

"We kind of messed around with pushing and shoveling and digging and so forth. We got that truck out, then we got the tractors out. We finally worked around and finagled around, and got them out, and I decided that was a bad idea to try and do it that way. We got all the equipment loose, and then we got to digging this trench by hand, which is the way we should have started in the first place. So we finished up, put the tile in, but we dug it all by hand. Which got into quite a mess, but we got it done.

"Every piece of equipment we had was covered in muck, and we had quite a mess to clean up after it got all done. But by the next spring, why everything was fine. I don't think any of the club members even knew the difference about what happened there. Even the chairman of Greens Committee, I don't think he knew much about what had happened, or what we were doing. But that was always a mess back in there. 10 Fairway, 14 and a little of 9 were always a mess in the spring when the rains came.

"Boy, that drainage was always something else. There was a 12-inch tile under 13 Fairway that went clear across the golf course from that swamp and connected the lake to our ditch. We'd get a good rain, and everything would flood back there. After I was in charge I found what was happening

- the water was running through there from Goguac Lake onto the course and just messing us all up. So, we took some boards, went down, and we boarded up the tile from the lake side of that catch basin, and filled the thing up with a whole bunch of sod and debris. In other words, we plugged that tile up. We plugged up that leak from the lake. And that helped us quite a bit, as far as overflow from the lake.

"But it didn't always help, because we still always had standing water when it rained. And even before when I was a kid, I remember going down there with my folks and seeing only half of number 6 Green sticking out of the water. In other words, the whole back of the course was flooded. The water was clear down 13 Fairway, and of course the lower part of 6, but it was just one great big lake down through there. Which would take a couple of days before it would drain off. When we'd get a heavy rain, Minges Brook would back up and it would run right out on the golf course, both from the diversion channel that diverted into Goguac Lake and from that creek down there on 6 Fairway. The whole course there wasn't much higher than the water table, and when the brook would back up, then the course would get flooded.

"Now, we always had quite a time with drainage down there, but we struggled along with it. I put in three catch basins in that tile that came from 13 Tee into the ditch so we could clean these tiles out. The silt would run into these catch basins and we'd keep digging that out. That helped quite a bit, and we got the drainage going fair, but it was still always a mess down there after a rain. -H.P.

Lifting up the Fairways…

In the late 1960s, a major project was undertaken to alleviate the issues with the muck – by building a drainage pond and raising up the fairways. Since the work was done in the fall, I was at high school then, but when I'd come home every day I'd go out and see the progress. This article from 1966 describes the early planning. My dad recalls the project:

"One year we decided to try to fix that low area across 9, 10, and 14 Fairways, and there was a swamp in between. It's very seldom we could ever get in there and mow anything, and when we did, why it was with a hand outfit. I tried it many times with tractor, the sickle bar, and pretty near every time I tried it, I got stuck.

227

"Dick Cobb come over, who was dredging that whole swamp out west of the course to make channels connecting to the lake and sell lake lots. Well, at the time he was doing that, he took borings through the area between 9, and 10, and 14 fairways to measure the depth of the peat. His recommendation was that we put a pond in; of course, that's kind of what the club wanted anyway. He recommended that you go around the outside perimeter of your pond, and dig a big wide trench and back-fill it with coarse gravel. Then, go in and dig the peat out, and make the pond. But his idea there was to use the gravel to hold the bank of that peat because peat's going to fluff off back into the pond. Well, that looked like too big of a project, so they decided they didn't want to do that.

Planning a 3-Acre Lake

Battle Creek CC Keeps Making Improvements

Pres Kool, Ron LaParl, Harold Peck and Keith Wemmer look over plans for the new lake.

"Well, it was about two years later, why Mr. McQuiston and Dick Brown come along, and they took measurements. But they went to Hoffman Brothers, who were excavators, and they got some figures on what it would take to just plain dig the pond and build a berm around the edge with the peat that come out of the swamp, and fill in 9 and 10 Fairways, and some of 14. Well, it come time for me to go deer hunting, and they had not decided they were going to do this yet, so McQuiston says, "We're going to have a board meeting." And I said, "Yeah. But by the time it goes through, you get things going, why I'll be back from deer hunting."

"So I got ready to go deer hunting, and Mr. McQuiston says, "Hey, with this job pending, and what we want to do, you wouldn't dream of going away and leaving it, would ya?" And I said, "Well, are you going to do it for sure? Positive?" He said, "I'm pretty sure we're going to do it." And I said, "Well, I'm pretty sure I'm going deer hunting!" And I said, "Really, it won't get under motion by the time I get back anyway." I said, "I'll be back in about 10 days anyway." And I kind of fluffed it off. I went deer hunting!

"When I come back, why the first thing I heard was, "Man, you better go down there and see what's going on." Well, I went down, and they had a crane sitting in that swamp that was between 9 and 10 fairways, and he's digging it out. And they were hauling dirt in. Most of the dirt came from an area that had already been stripped when they built the golf course, over south of 5 Fairway. Well, they didn't know that, or I could've explained it to them, but that dirt ended up being mostly clay and became rock hard. But they put a grade across the fairways for drainage, but when you go to drain rainwater on soil, one inch per foot is not very much. Well, anyway, they had that all planned out, and that's what they were doing, and I didn't have much of a voice on anything that was going on because I wasn't there. They said this was the cheapest way they could get it done, which as it ended up really wasn't the cheapest, but...

"Well, they put their fill in, got it all graded off, they hauled the topsoil in. 9 went pretty good, but when they started across 10, they had a problem with these trucks. With all that peat underneath, why as they're driving over, it pumped the water up, and the trucks were getting stuck.

"So they come up with the idea they'd cover the ground with plastic to hold the water back. Well, in theory, it sounded like a good idea, so that's what they did. And they put the plastic sheeting in, but the fill that they put in on top was like road gravel. But okay, they said, we're not worried about drainage underneath, we're going to get surface drainage. By the time I got back from deer hunting, why they had the plastic out and were doing this, and they'd already covered up the drain tiles. And I knew we had a little catch basin there to get to it, but they went ahead and covered that up since they didn't figure it was needed. And later, I had to try and find it, and I never could find that catch basin.

"They got that fairway graded and got the topsoil on. And we went out and had somebody come in with a York rake, and level it all off. We got it fertilized and seeded. This was after deer season, this was in December now, that we got it seeded. Next spring, why we had to locate the quick couplers for the water system. Well I tell you, I had the measurements of right where they were, and so we started digging. But of course, the only way we could dig was by shovels, by hand, and it ended up with pick and shovel because that new ground was just like concrete; it was just hard as a rock. We had about four inches of topsoil on top of it, and the rest of it was just like rock. We had one heck

of a time getting down there and finding those quick-coupling valves so we could bring them up to the surface and water the area.

"But after we got all that done, and we got the sod going, and after it got mowed and everything, well everybody was really happy commenting on that deal. We also put two pumps in a catch basin right there behind the Halfway House, to pump water off the fairway from these tiles we had put in along 10 Fairway, and over along 14 Fairway. And we pump water from there, into the pond. Which from there, it drains through the 12-inch tile that went clear down to the creek, right there at the south side of the 6th Fairway. So I'll tell you, we all figured we got it made.

A happy Harold driving the new Roseman hydraulic-powered rough mower about 1975. On the back cover, Andy Peck is pictured on a new Roseman tractor from 50 years earlier. Both photos were featured together in a Roseman Tractor magazine ad.

"*Well that whole deal did work out pretty good, except the grade should've been more. And a couple years later we had a little problem on 9 Fairway, right to the edge of where they filled, where it was always wet. So I dug a trench right across 10 Fairway, where they had put this plastic in, and ran a 6-inch tile into a catch basin. Mr. McQuiston came along, and he says, "Hey, you were never supposed to dig through that plastic." He says, "That's going to goof the whole system up." And I says, "We have to drain that. That plastic served its purpose because it got the job done, but it's no longer doing any good; it did the job, and we don't need it now." Well, we never did run into any problem from it, and that tile worked out pretty good.*

"*That left the berm around the edge of a pond there behind the Halfway House, between 10 and 14 to deal with. They just pulled the muck out - or the peat - out and piled it up. Piled it up to be hauled, but of course, the stuff is soaking wet there, there's nothing we can do with it. The next year, why the whole deal was, "What are we going to do with this?" It just so happened that Reith Riley was doing a little paving job for us on cart paths and they had this little bit of a bulldozer out there with probably, at the most, a six-foot blade on it. It was just a little bit of a thing. And I went down there, and I climbed on to that little dozer one day. And I said, "Well, I'm going to see what I can do." I had tried leveling some of this off with the tractor, but the wheels of the tractor would spin out and get stuck. So I took the little dozer out and I start pushing this peat around. And I tell you, that worked out pretty good. Not only that, I was having a great time, because I just loved running that thing. Well, it ended up, they left the dozer there and let me use it. And it took me, in between keeping things in shape on the golf course, probably three to four weeks to finish this off. When I got it finished, there was a real nice eight-foot high berm all around. By that fall, we had that ground pretty well covered with grass, which did help an awful lot. The place really looked nice. We got a lot of compliments.*

"*Now, as I look at the pond in 1999, why the pond looks like it's about six inches deep. And there's not much of a berm left around the edge of it like we had originally. All that peat sloughed right back into the pond. And what's going to happen to it eventually? I don't know. Looking back to what Dick Cobb recommended, we should have dug that big wide trench and filled it with gravel. And now we wouldn't have the muck problem down there. Myself, I wouldn't dare put a pair of waders on or go into that pond, as I don't think you could ever get out. But we originally had put pumps*

with aerators spraying up out there. And they looked kinda pretty and kinda nice out there. But I guess they don't do that anymore.

-H.P.

Battling the Creek…

I did get to help my dad with the next big project - filling in the low areas by the creek and cleaning up the creekbed. His words describe it best:

"But the next year Mr. McQuiston decided, "well, we had a lot of fun doing that, so let's go down by the creek on 6 and 13 and fill that area in". We had to build a road to route the trucks hauling fill dirt in around the back of 12 Green and up between 13 Tee, just in front and on down through the rough. Then when they got down to the fairway, they would dump the dirt in there. And, of course, they had a dozer running all the time and spreading it out.

"But earlier we had built a catch basin in the middle of 13 fairway to accept the silt from a 12-inch tile from 13 Tee. Well, I'm down there one day talking with Mr. McQuiston, and I said, "That drains from clear up there at 13 Tee," and I said, "you don't want to just fill that in." And he says, "Nah, that tile isn't doing any good," he said, "we're draining everything right here on the other side of the fairway." And I says, "Yeah, but so far as I see your plan, you're not going to drain any water from 13 Tee." "Oh, no, we don't need to do that," he says, "that's not a problem up there."

"Marty was working at the time, and I said, "Marty, run up the shop and get about a gallon of that dye that we put into the water." I says, "Dump it in that catch basin at 13 Tee." So he did, and pretty quick here comes the colored water flowing through that tile in the middle of 13 Fairway. And I called McQuiston over there, and I said, "Now, do you believe me?" "Yeah," he says, "that does take care of a lot of water, doesn't it?" I said, "It sure does." I said, "We've had to keep cleaning it out for a long time." So they repaired that and went ahead and finished filling in 13. After we finished, we didn't have to close up 6 and 13 fairways after every heavy rain. They could play those two fairways, with no problem. And that whole deal worked out pretty good, as far as I'm concerned, with the exception of the creek, because you can't keep the creek open.

"We also called it the ditch, but it was impossible to keep it clean. The subject came up about the ditch itself, and I made a suggestion that we dig the muck out. We go down to the hard bottom - it

232

was a clay bottom - and dig it out and go about 12 to 14 feet on each side of where the existing ditch was. Backfill all that with the sand or the fill that they were filling the fairway with and dig a new ditch. In other words, grade it out to where it was the same shape of the ditch and everything, but block all that muck on each side, which I thought was a pretty good idea.

"They went ahead and started that, but instead McQuiston says, "We're going to put railroad ties along the edge of this." I had thought we were going to slope the fairway into it instead of an abrupt edge. Well, no, they're putting railroad ties in. So I had a crew down there laying railroad ties. Pretty quick I got cooperation from the crane operator, and he started setting ties for us, which was great. He got them set in there, and he'd punch them in, get them fairly level, and everything. After the railroad ties were in, we had a nice sandy bottom.

Ronnie LaParl (middle) and other workers repair vandalism to #13 Green, with filled-in fairways and the Creek in the background.

"So then when they got all that down, a couple of club members decided to line that creek with rocks that averaged about eight inches in diameter. Of course, I didn't really realize what we could run into. They started hauling these rocks in by the truckload. The deal was we were going to lay them along the bottom of this creek. I had three of my men working, and Mr. McQuiston come along and thought we were going too slow, so he'd started laying some rocks in there. Pretty soon though he'd

233

had enough of that, because here's a man that had retired from Kellogg's quite a long time before that. He was no young fellow.

"He left and the crane operator, who had a big backhoe on tracks, says, "I got an idea. Let me try something." So he takes the crane over to a pile of rocks on one side of the creek, and he picked up a bunch of those rocks and he'd just kind of dribble them across the creek. Then he'd take the bucket and he'd shape the creek. Pound them down and he'd shape the creek with them, with the bucket on that big backhoe. That worked out real good. Well the next day, we had that creek half-filled by that time. I remember Mr. McQuiston come along and he says, "Hey, do you realize how much that crane costs us per hour?" I say, "Mr. McQuiston." I said that because at the time because I didn't call anybody like Jim by their first name. I said, "Mr. McQuiston, when you helped do you remember how little we'd got done, and look how much is done now." He says, "Well I guess that's going to end up being cheaper in the long run isn't it." He accepted that deal.

"But fixing that whole deal with the muck wasn't all too bad. Except for the peat sloughing off into the pond, the fairways turned out to be pretty good. They're harder than a rock, but we got by with it. So that was the big innovation on the whole golf course. Well, for one thing, after a big rain, they didn't have to close the course up anymore. Before, in the spring they would only open up 1, 2, 3, 4, and 15, 16, 17, and 18 fairways, letting them play those top eight holes instead of going on around because it was just plain too wet down back. Over the years, there was a lot of improvement on the course, but this drainage was the biggest improvement on the golf course. My father had been here long enough, and I'd been here long enough to see how big these improvements really are. And boy, I was sure glad to see that done.

-H.P.

Water Works…

The creek with the new rock bed looked great at first, but by the next summer the muck had mostly covered up the rocks and the water was stagnant. All my childhood planning experience helped me come up with a plan, with my dad's guidance of course...

"But come to find out, there was still a problem with the creek because we couldn't clean it out. The muck got to seeping in, and it's still a dirty mess because we didn't have enough flow to keep it cleaned out. After we filled those two fairways, Marty and I came up with the idea to put a dam in and install pumps in to pump the water over the dam, lowering the water level of the creek. When it rained, we could maintain a lower water level across the course there for the tiles to drain in to.

And then I got the idea, I said, "How about if we put an extra pump in there and run the water through a pipe up to the start of the creek, running water through the creek from the other end to get some circulation moving

Harold with granddaughter Allison standing at the Waterfall we built.

through it." Well, that was a good idea.

"We put a pipe in the full length of the creek from where the pump was up to that little waterfall we built at the end. There is a waterfall there now [since removed]. We put that pipe in and we just ran the water through the creek at first. Marty, my son, come along when he came home from school and says, "Why don't we make a waterfall out of this." So we got some big rocks and we put up a pile of rocks and made a waterfall out of it. Really, the thing went across pretty good. I had a lot of compliments on it. Of course, that worked out real good and it helped to get a little flow in the creek.

But now the muck has seeped in and kind of filled it up. Today it's a mess again. I hope they do
something with it pretty soon.

-H.P.

Building that waterfall with my dad's help was one of the most rewarding projects I had on the course. My enthusiasm for building it won out over any concerns he might have had with it being close to a fairway. He brought a load of large rocks and boulders, almost all of which had to be moved using the front-end loader. I had to design and build the rocks into a natural looking arrangement set into a slight hill, with a watercourse that cascaded a few feet down into a pool where the creek appeared to begin. I never heard any complaints that it was too close to play, but it was fairly close to the 11th green and only about 20 yards away from the fairway approach. I'm sure there were occasional balls that bounced all over when they hit the rocks, but I don't think my dad ever had to defend its construction. I finally had the waterfall running that I'd wished for as a kid!

And the Rains Came...

For many years, what we'd previously called "the ditch" with some aversion became "The Creek," because it actually was quite attractive and an asset to those three holes. With the dam and the pumps, Dad had some control over the flooding and Mother Nature. He continues talking about the creek and the flooding...

"That really helped keep the creek clean, which was quite an innovation. And it looked nice, and it got a lot of compliments from club members on that whole project. But we had put two other pumps in that caisson that pumped water over that dam so that we could control the level of the water in the creek because there's a constant flow of water coming into the creek. We found that we didn't need two, because there wasn't that much water normally flowing into the creek. So we used one at a time, but when we would get a storm, then we needed two. I know there was one time we had three or four inches of rain one afternoon. Boy, it really came down too, and Marty and I took a ride around. Well, we had both pumps working, and everything was going pretty good. The water wasn't too bad down there.

"So what happens? The next morning I go down, and the whole thing is underwater. The water is clear up to 6 Tee, and up to the bottom of that slope before the 13 green, and clear across 11

Fairway. And just the crowns of 6 and 13 Fairways were sticking out where they had filled. We had a lot of water down there because Minges Brook couldn't take care of that much rainfall, and it backed up in the night. It backed up right across over the dam and onto the golf course, which-- it's going to do that. Water's going to seek its own level, and there's not a thing you can do about that. But that's what we call 'water over the dam.'

"It did drain down after a day. But after that we had another big storm when I was visiting Marty up in Wisconsin. And I came home, and [Greens Chairman] Mr. Higgins pulled in the driveway right behind me, and he says, "Come on, take a ride. Get in your truck and let's take a ride out on the golf course." So we take a ride down there and, my God, I couldn't believe the amount of water. We'd had at least eight inches of rain in just a few hours the day before. When you get a rain like that, there's not much way you're going to compensate for it. You can't control it. The highway department has problems. The city has problems. Everybody has problems when you get water like that. But, of course, there wasn't a thing we could do about it.

"Even right up there in back of my house, there was a river right across 2, 17, and 3 Fairways from water coming off of Capital Avenue. Of course, I had started out driving around the course, but I couldn't go that way. I had to go back on the service road, but there was enough water running across the service road there next to 10 Tee that I said, "Well, I don't want to go through that. I'm liable to get stuck." But then I thought, "Well, finally, that valley in front of 10 Tee, that big hollow, is going to fill up with water, and we'll finally see some water standing there. Well, this was kind of late in the afternoon. Of course, 9, and 10, and 14 Fairways were underwater. 6 and 13 were underwater too, and I couldn't believe the amount of water even on 7 Fairway. Even before that ditch. There was water all over everywhere. And I thought, oh boy, this is something else now. How are we going to get rid of this?

"Well, the next morning I get up, and, of course, I wake up early cause this is bothering me. We just had so much water. What was I going to do with it? Of course, I knew there wasn't anything I was going to do with it because there was no place to pump it to. Mother Nature's going to take it. So I look out in back of the house, and the river had almost receded across 2 and 17 Fairway. Water was pretty near all gone there. But I get down back, and the creek was higher than ever. Well, there's nothing you're going to do, but just wait until it goes down

"Every once in a while, that day I would go down and check it over. I had put a stake next to the water, and, by golly, I went down about noon, and that stake was about three feet up away from the water. I went down there about 4 o'clock, and the water was about six foot away from that stake, so that meant the water was going down. The next morning when I got up and went down and there was a good flow on the creek, but it had drained off the fairways. It hadn't drained off any place to where we could allow the golf carts to go, but it drained off to where you could at least see the grass. And except for the lowest parts, the grass wouldn't cook in the sun. Let me tell you, it was a lot of rain. That was quite an experience.

-H.P.

Fountain of Youth…

The drinking fountain was another fun project my dad and I built – well, actually, I did most of the work, but my dad in his own subtle way showed me how. Near the far end of the course, there was an old hand-pump with a drinking fountain, where my dad said the log cabin shelter once stood. (It must be where that assault occurred in the '20s since they were "getting a drink.") It was noisy and required pumping for over a minute to get any cold water. My dad and I decided to get an electric pump and use some surplus bricks to build a decorative drinking fountain. I'd never laid brick before and remember constructing this somewhat avant-garde pedestal and basin with an artistic pattern, but to my dad and I'm sure everyone else it just looked like someone's crooked attempt at bricklaying. I laid bricks to build up a three-foot-high, round pedestal around the well pipe then put in a little access door for the pump. We got a small basin for the top, and I surrounded that with some old barn wood spindle pieces and placed some of the bricks at odd angles. Despite that, it lasted many years, as my dad mentions here…

"We drilled a new well over there by where a hand pump for drinking used to be between 7 and 11 Fairways. I got the idea we would hook into the power from the sprinkling system, and we would put a real drinking fountain over there. Marty ran a wire across 11 Fairway to power this little pump on the drinking fountain, and we built that drinking fountain up from brick left over from building the clubhouse. We had to improvise a little bit because it was a pump that was supposed to run underwater, a water-cooled pump, so I had to put the pump in the bucket of water.

"Well since I left, nobody seems to understand what that whole deal was all about. So, they eventually took the drinking fountain completely out of there. We don't have a drinking fountain anymore at all down there. I think it's a shame because that did work out for a long time. It looked nice, built out of that brick from the clubhouse. I had Marty make it, and he was not a bricklayer. He didn't know anything about laying brick, and I said you just keep trying. And he had some of them in kind of any which way.

But it worked out pretty good. We used it for many years. And it ran the water 24 hours a day. Which was okay, we'd run a pipe drain from that into the tile that went under seven and 11 fairways into the creek, so there was no problem about getting rid of the water. Then one time there was a little trouble with the well; we had to drive a new four-inch well, and we had to move the whole thing, but we managed that too. There was often a day when a lot of these things would come up that looked difficult, sound difficult, but we managed to get by. We stumbled over a lot of these hurdles that would come up and made it work.

-H.P.

A Bushel of Pecks...

All three Peck brothers, Les, Harold, and Roy worked their entire careers as Golf Course Superintendents. The three can be seen on the next page with sisters Shirley and Winifred. Harold stayed at the Battle Creek Country Club until he retired in 1988. Roy stayed at the Kalamazoo Country Club and retired in 1985, three years before his death. Les was superintendent at Lansing Country Club, Orchard Ridge in Fort Wayne, Indiana and Wyndwicke Country Club in Saint Joseph; he lived until 1995. The three brothers of golf created quite a dynasty in southern Michigan.

With the three brothers all working superintendent jobs at private country clubs, it became a weekly family tradition for my dad, Harold, his brothers and their wives to get together for Sunday dinner. Fittingly, this was usually at One Country Club Drive, but occasionally everyone went to Roy's house in Kalamazoo or Les' house in Lansing. The wives had a rule at the dinner table about not talking shop, and Mom tried to enforce it by having the offender throw a quarter into a jar, but the golf course talk was inevitable. Their mom, Rena always joined them for dinner at our house and occasionally went to visit with her other sons, but that was rare.

Roy, Les, Jayne and Harold Peck at a National Golf Course Superintendents Association meeting in Boston –
A "Bushel of Pecks"

Rena had strict beliefs about drinking and smoking; she forbid both in the house when she was the matriarch. Later on, she did her best to discourage it, but everyone else in the family smoked and drank as was typical of the era. It must have been difficult for her in the house later when my mom and dad were living there, and she was no longer in charge. Whenever there was a party at the house, my grandma visited with one of the other brothers. However, the inevitable friction was always kept hidden from me as a child.

Growing up with my Grandma Rena in our house was idyllic for me; she was my built-in babysitter and best friend! She was always there to talk to and read me stories. I can even remember asking her why her skin had wrinkles. Although it must have been tough for her to live along with my parent's liberal lifestyle, she never complained. She kept the flower gardens between the house and the 2nd Tee in beautiful condition, working on them into her 80's. Grandma continued to can fruit and vegetables from the garden and even dried and shucked English walnuts. As a little kid, I was always fascinated with a bedside lamp shaped like a golfer that Grandpa had bought for her from a convention. I even still have that special lamp. We were close, and I so regret not asking or remembering more about her life.

Into her '80s, Grandma Rena cared for her lush flower gardens that made a beautiful border between the house and the golf course.

Rena lived at One Country Club Drive until a few years before her death in 1976. Because of her difficulty getting up the stairs, she was moved to a Methodist senior home about an hour away in Grand Rapids. I recall arguing with my dad about the move thinking it unfair to kick my grandmother out of

Rena's children: Shirley, Harold, Roy, Winifred and Les. Harold, Roy and Les were career golf course superintendents.

the house. I bought her a small TV with my own money to ease her loneliness and my guilt. A few years later while I was in college, I had my last conversation with my best friend when she called to try and get me to visit more often by inviting me up for pizza. I thought the request was very unusual because I didn't think she even knew about pizza. A few days later I did make the hour drive to stay by her side and watch her sleep while the rest of her family was gathering. I was the last of her family to speak with her and, to this day, I feel terrible for not visiting her more often.

The rest of her family stayed away from golf, except for Roy's son Ron and Les' son Tim who did work as golf course superintendents. Her step-son Everett had a successful business and rock collecting hobby. I remember visiting Peck's Rock Shop nearby and being given fascinating specimens. I don't remember Phil too much as he died in 1968. Shirley often visited after moving to Connecticut to live near her son Russell. She died in 1997. Winifred married a dentist and moved to Colorado to raise a big family. She still enjoys frequent visits by her five children and many grandchildren.

Harold Peck Day…

Harold had a "Day" on May 3rd, 1973 when the mayor proclaimed it "Harold Peck Day"! There was a big article about him in the paper. In it, Dad said, "I've directed…the rebuilding of all 18 tees into larger and better tees…the removal of 600 elm trees, planted some 1,800 new trees…and seen 10-12 buildings demolished including the old clubhouse and pro shop." He received hundreds of letters and cards from well-wishers, and there was a huge party at the club honoring him. Greens Chairman Bob Nisbet was the MC, and Dad was "roasted" by Pro and great friend Ron LaParl, his brothers Les and Roy, Michigan

Harold is being congratulated by Marty on his "Day".

course architect Bruce Matthews, course owners Daryl Scott and many members and friends. His wife Jayne filled a scrapbook with all the congratulatory letters and accolades he received. His long-haired son even dressed up for the big occasion.

And in 1975, Harold was also honored by the PGA…

"FOR YOUR MANY YEARS OF SERVICE TO THE GREAT GAME OF GOLF"

A Legacy…

Harold loved telling his stories about growing up at One Country Club Drive and working on the golf course, and about the people he worked with. He was pleased that he helped so many others to become Superintendents. He was very proud of his golf course and the magnificent trees, as well as all the beautiful landscaping and gardens like the Rose Garden at the circle at the club entry.

When driving around the course, my dad always pointed out with great pride the many beautiful trees he planted over the years; over two thousand, with many of them exotic and unusual: Tulip, Water Chestnut, Butternut and Catalpa. I know he felt those trees were part of his legacy…

Harold "leading the charge" with the planting of an oversized spruce

"I was just over looking at the chestnut trees that I had planted by #10 Tee. I saw there were a few chestnuts up in the tree, but not very many. But it made me think of when I was a kid, right across from the cottage, there was a chestnut tree. And on down in front of Green's [now Rich's] place, there were two more. They were the sweet chestnuts. Us kids used to pick those up all the time, and we'd just peel them and eat them raw. When I get them now, I still peel them and eat them raw. But there was a time when the Green's man used to rake all that stuff up. He dumped it down the back of where their cow barn was [Stump's Shack]. And when Laird subdivided that area [Cascade Hills] over there, he told me to go over and get any trees I wanted over there, and I found this chestnut tree. We made a regular excavation to get it out and transplant

it over on the golf course. I put it over behind nine green, and I still pick up chestnuts from under it - which is a great deal. It worked out real good.

"We accumulated a lot of trees that we planted around the different areas on the golf course. I got a bunch of oak trees out of that area that Laird subdivided. I planted them on the golf course. But we got quite a few other trees, too. And here I am, back talking about the trees on the golf course, standing right where we planted a bunch of them.
-H.P.

The majority of those trees he planted were an attempt to compensate for the devastating loss of the 800 majestic elm trees that succumbed to Dutch elm disease. My dad said every tee used to have giant elms beside it for shade. It was heartbreaking, and the Greens Committee directed him to plant a couple hundred trees each year for many years. In the hilarious photo on the previous page, Harold is

The spruce tree was to replace a huge elm, but unfortunatly the spruce didn't survive.

"leading the charge" atop a Vermeer planter as they are attempting to save a large spruce tree that needed to be relocated. This was between 14th Green and the Halfway house, where a large elm had once protected golfers taking a break. This was a "Hail Mary" attempt that ultimately failed to save the tree, which was probably too close to the green anyway. Nevertheless, those actions underscore everyone's desperation to replicate the beautifully framed greens.

Moving On...

At the end of my high school years, I had made that fateful decision to go to college; not to become a Golf Course Superintendent, but to become an Electrical Engineer. I am sure my dad was disappointed I did not become one of those who followed in his footsteps to become a course superintendent, but I also know he was very proud I chose a different, new challenge.

Over the ten years I worked on the course, I became good friends with the many other golf course employees. I always enjoyed the times my dad described the evolution of the bunkers, tees and greens, gardens and outbuildings, and particularly what it was like when he was young. I even worked on the course up through the winter of '77-'78 after I graduated from college while my wife-to-be was finishing her degree. My dad had worked for his father, and I had the great pleasure of working side by side with my father for those many years.

The sadness really hit me later after I graduated and moved away when I realized we'd no longer share more of those wonderful years working on projects together. We would both miss working side by side, talking about the grass, the plantings, tournament preparation or battling the effects of the weather together. Looking back, I know in many ways, it was the best time of my life, and I'm pretty sure it was his as well. I wish that camaraderie could have continued forever...

Honoring
HAROLD PECK
Friday, June 17, 1988

BATTLE CREEK COUNTRY CLUB
Battle Creek, Michigan

Harold retired as Greens Superintendent in 1988

THE END OF AN ERA

Leaving the Course Behind...

Harold was Greens Superintendent for another eight years after I moved away. He had a heart attack at age 65 and retired shortly after recovering. He loved working on the course and didn't really want to retire, but my mom encouraged him with the help of a greens chairman who wanted someone younger

> **I haven't missed a pay day in 42 years.**
> *Harold Peck*

running the course. Dad had a grand retirement party, and at least one member called for Harold to be given the title of Superintendent Emeritus. He was given a life lease to live at One Country Club Drive including all utilities paid and a small pension. The club gave them a life membership with a monthly allowance to continue enjoying the dining and social life. My parents enjoyed

A retired Harold contemplates the course from the kitchen, with grand-dog Whimsey

living there for another 23 years!

In the 70's, I helped my dad remodel the kitchen, and we raised the floor in the corner so they could have a nice view of the golf course while sitting at the table. This became their favorite place to sit and talk. After Dad's retirement, he told many of his stories sitting there, watching the world continue out on the golf course that had been his life's work.

But, living in that house all those retirement years did have its drawbacks. My parents did not have the equity most retirees have in a home of their own – they could not sell it and move or use that equity to pay for senior living. My dad lived there all of his retirement years, watching club life go on with someone else in charge of the course. He was a little disappointed that the new Superintendents did not ask him very much about past work or advice, and I know it was difficult for him to watch some of the changes and still keep quiet. Occasionally, he shared his opinions with me, including what he felt were the club's excessive expenses. Extravagance was hard for a man who during his tenure had scrimped and kept costs down by doing projects and all the club maintenance with his staff.

For almost twenty years after retirement, Dad continued his early morning ritual of going down to the clubhouse and making coffee, sitting around with his best friend Ron LaParl and other member-pals, talking about golf, hunting, fishing, and telling his many stories.

Even after retirement, Harold started the coffee every morning with Ron in the Grill Room.

As time went on, it became apparent that my dad was losing his short-term memory, and he was diagnosed with dementia. I knew we would miss those stories about his life. In the late '90s, I gave my dad a pocket voice recorder, and we walked the course one afternoon talking about the history and his experiences. I was thrilled that he took to the idea of recording his stories. His stories from these recordings are a treasured bit of history that is the heart of this book, describing life on the course, his work, and living at One Country Club Drive. He gave us several hours of tales and remembrances, and hearing them now, in his voice, is something that I will always cherish…

My dad slowly faded away as the disease took its natural course, but I was grateful he always knew who I was. If there is a blessing with dementia, it gives you plenty of time to say goodbye. In May of 2011, I was told that Dad had lost the swallow reflex, and it was time to let him go. Anyone who has been close to this affliction knows how terrible it is to watch your loved one wither away, no longer able to eat or drink, and knowing you cannot give them the fluids their body needs because it would only prolong the inevitable. That was by far the hardest thing I have ever had to do in my life! I decided then to try to memorialize some of his life by writing a book, and giving any proceeds from it to the Alzheimer's Association.

Harold watching his golf course through the kitchen window screen of One Country Club Drive

EPILOGUE

The Doll House...

There was one very special project my dad and I collaborated on, but it had nothing to do with the golf course. My mom loved dollhouses and miniatures; she had been creating artistic scenes and settings with them for years. When my dad retired, he fulfilled his promise of

Harold showing the Doll House replica of One Country Club Drive

building her a dollhouse as a home for her collection of furnishings and tiny accessories, and he did it in a big way. He made a large, $1/12^{th}$ scale model of our family home! It was about four feet long and three feet high, with all the rooms accurately scaled. He even made siding, shingles, windows and chimneys from scratch. He decorated all the rooms with paint and miniature wallpaper Mom had picked out, so the Victorian-themed dollhouse might have looked like the original house. I even wired the house and installed lights in every room. We did take one small liberty, building a fireplace in the living room, in order to connect with the fake chimney in the actual house

My mom beautifully decorated the dollhouse with a Victorian Christmas setting from the early 1900s, using hundreds of tiny historical details including early family photos and many custom-made art pieces. Each room had pieces that represented things we cherished growing up and bits of family history. The south side is shown in the photo below; Marty's room is at the upper left, Grandma (and Grampa's) room on the right with the kitchen and living room below, just as it really is. Andi's room, Mom and Dad's room, the bathroom, foyer and dining rooms would be seen from the north side.

Visitors to our house were always taken upstairs to see this family treasure and often spent hours looking through all the details. Although it took days to pack up and then rearrange, the Doll House

The "South" side of the doll house

251

was shown on two occasions at local exhibits, thus taking our home "on the road." Mom was always very proud of that dollhouse, and wanted it to go to a museum. Soon our miniature version of One Country Club Drive will find a new home at the Midwest Miniatures Museum near Battle Creek, with a video walk-through tour available on-line. The dollhouse is a beautiful family project and a perfect remembrance of our long-time family home that will always be where people can enjoy it.

Looking back…

After gathering these words together, I do feel obliged to validate my teenage decision not to follow my dad's golf legacy. Those many years and lessons with my dad on the course did prepare me for what was to come, and I regret nothing about all the hard work and craziness. Many of the unusual experiences I had growing up at One Country Club Drive turned out to be a precursor to my adult life. I have come to realize there are many curious parallels between my childhood and adulthood. These events cannot be coincidental...

Remember the girl I mentioned dreaming about when I was very little, the magical one with blond hair on the horse? I met this beautiful girl named Debbie in college who was full of vitality. She lived to ride horses and reminded me of that special dream. Right after I graduated, we were married, and, of course, had a huge reception where else but at the Clubhouse. I splurged on a five-piece classic band and beer, but our budget only allowed for nibbles and a cake. The staff at the club made up for that with a massive cornucopia of every fancy hors d'oeuvre imaginable, a grand buffet with everything from carved prime rib to shrimp. Soon after we were married, she bought her first horse, and my dream girl with the blond hair still rides her latest horse named William almost every day.

My PortaPott*y never made it into production.*

I graduated from college and went off to become a real engineer, which meant I found myself working in a cubical in a big open office without any windows. I really missed the outdoors and took

frequent breaks just to be near one. Sometimes I found my way up on the roof just to get some natural light. Being an electrical engineer and designing plumbing products for the prestigious Kohler Company was fun, *and* I was still playing with water and wires. I patented whirlpool and spa controls, creating products called the "Autofill Bath System," "Environment" and "Habitat."

It also turned out to be kind of prophetic. In the early '80s, while my wife and I were visiting the lodge of the company's new *River Wildlife* hunting preserve, owner Herb Kohler Jr. joined us for a drink. He was explaining the benefits of boarding our horse at his

My dad was a bit perplexed upon seeing the 2,000 "pot bunkers" at Whistling Straits.

expensive stables to my wife, and I was trying to impress and steer the conversation away from horses when I suggested that a golf course would be a perfect addition to his new resort called *The American Club*. Although I had nothing to do with the outcome, Kohler Co. ultimately built a golf dynasty that includes *The Duke's at St. Andrews* and four championship golf courses in Wisconsin. Kohler's *Whistling Straits* has held a US Senior Open, three PGA championships and is hosting the 2020 Ryder Cup.

My friend Lon followed more closely in his dad's footsteps and eventually became an executive for the nation's top motor parts distributor. The very sad memory of my youth is that our childhood friend

Bobby never found his path to adulthood. We grew apart during our teens and high school, and while Lon and I went to college, Bobby struggled to find himself. Months after I moved away, right before the Christmas holiday, my dad called to tell me that Bobby had died of a tragic accident. I have always regretted our drifting apart; if only we'd remained closer maybe I might have helped him find direction and avoid that fate.

The Victor golf cart we plastered with stickers as kids returned in a new form. A friend called to ask if I would be interested in buying an electric commuter car. It was a little, red, wedge-shaped, enclosed, two-seat, street-legal '75 CitiCar, powered by eight golf cart batteries. The car was popular in the retirement communities of Florida, but it was not working. Repeating my childhood, I built a new controller and souped it up to go nearly 40 mph. For years I drove it to work in the summertime. One day when my wife was expecting our child, I left work to find the little red car had been picked up and turned sideways in the parking spot as a prank.

My street-legal golf cart

Ever since that very short stint as an 8-year-old helicopter pilot, I'd had a fancy to be a pilot, but one expensive (horse) hobby in the family was enough. Nevertheless, dreams die hard. One afternoon at a scuba diving instructor's shop, I was intrigued to find a WWII flight simulator and became thrilled when he said I could buy it. The Link Trainer was an antique mechanical marvel, full of knobs, handles, lights, rotary bellows, and walking beams, powered by a vacuum turbine. Designed in the '40s, the student sat inside while the instructor taught pilots how to fly and navigate using early radio beacons. I built a video monitor into the console, and refurbished the mechanisms and found that it would pitch, roll and rotate up to 9 RPM. A software company hired us to show off their new Apache 64 Helicopter game, a first with pilot's perspective and realistic sound effects. The loud rotor and gun sounds literally woke up the exhibit floor of the 1987 *Consumer Electronics Show* in Chicago as I showed people how to fly and shoot. Later that day, I took my first ride in a real, open-air biplane trainer when one of the

The helicopter flight simulator video game was built from a WWII Link Trainer.

owners invited me for a literal front row seat of loops, barrel rolls and vertical stalls. A few months later, there was another first at the *Personal Computing Show* in London when the simulator and I got our thirty seconds of fame on BBC Channel 1.

My dad's hometown was well-known for its cereal production, and those cereal companies brought the sport of Hot Air Ballooning to town with yearly competitions and air shows. The pilots of the Thunderbirds loved to play golf at the club when they came every year, and always flew just over the treetops of the course and waved at me. The golf course was always a favorite place to launch and land the hot air balloons, and every summer there was a week of much excitement as many balloons floated across and dipped into the lake, or drifted right over the house. My dad collected many bottles of champagne, as the customary gift for giving permission for a balloon to land or take off from your property. Several times I was allowed inside an inflating envelope to take pictures, and both Dad and I took hundreds of photos of all the balloon colors and shapes.

My mom Jayne especially loved the balloons, which gave my sister Andi an idea for their 40th-anniversary party that we kept secret until that day. In 1985 we had a big reception at the clubhouse during the summer (so their hundreds of friends and relatives could attend), and everyone managed to keep our surprise a secret - at the end of the party, when we announced that Harold and Jayne were taking off on a balloon excursion and invited guests out to the practice tee to watch. Our parents were at first stunned and then thrilled while everyone else cheered and applauded. With their friends gathered outside on the tee, they climbed into the gondola and slowly rose up over the crowd. A second balloon launched to follow along and take pictures, and we chased them across the town for the next two hours. It was indeed a perfect occasion and a beautiful memory. For their 50th we had another

Jayne and Harold's 40th Anniversary balloon excursion was launched from the Practice Tee.

party; this one on their New Year's Eve anniversary date when the outside of the house was all decked out with roving spotlights and One Country Club Drive once again was packed full of people. Mom and Dad had 66 great years together.

With my early escapades of building a light show for a rock band and designing stage lighting in the old movie theater, my parents were not surprised I ended up with a career involving lighting. For a few frustrating years, I was engineering manager for a lighting manufacturer, only to be laid off in one of those fortuitous events that turned a potential disaster into the beginning of another great adventure. I started my own business as a lighting consultant bringing the drama learned in the theater into architecture and landscapes. To make it happen required a good dose of the confidence my dad instilled in me, and the creativity my mom instilled, but this last venture has allowed me a great deal of freedom and much satisfaction.

Both my parents were at my historic fire recreation; an event realistic enough to fool the fire department into calling in three alarms. They were also there at my light show production for an NBA home opener, and saw my lighting of the historic space-race rockets on display at Kennedy Space Center. The crazy pretend casino that we put together as kids has evolved into a career creating elaborate lighting designs for large casinos, including one in my hometown. I was very fortunate to have been able to take my thoroughly amazed dad to see it, and you should have seen his eyes light up when he won thousands – of nickels. My lighting design for a local private country club, the River Club of Mequon, was so successful in helping turn the club around that the owner invited me to join, which has

brought me back to my country club roots. And finally, my early interest in model trains and unsuccessful attempts at getting my dad to build a railroad to ride around the golf course helped inspire me to create my "Ghost Train," a bridge lighting project in Milwaukee that realistically mimics a historic train crossing the pedestrian bridge every night.

I was thrilled my parents got to see many of those accomplishments. I like to think that my dad was just a little prouder of me than if I'd followed in the family golf coursing footsteps.

In his later years, as my dad's short-term memory slowly deteriorated, those conversations and memories of life on the golf course became even more cherished. It was fortunate in a way that he was not aware of an ill-advised plan to change the

Putting up lights for Christmas was one of our last projects together.

course to a Links course by cutting down hundreds of beautiful, mature trees he and my Grandfather had planted. Many of those trees had grown to interfere with play and had to go, but most were out of play and cut down just to reduce maintenance. As a result, the course did somewhat return to a barren look similar to its original construction from farm fields, but much of the beauty of the golf holes

framed by mature trees was again lost. I understand a few members resigned in objection, and someone (who will remain nameless) raised the club flag upside down in quiet protest. In the years since, the cutting down of those magnificent trees certainly would've broken my dad's heart.

Finally, not too long ago while musing about this book and the fun I had driving the Cushman Trucksters, I began to look around for one to relive my youth. Trucksters aren't very common, but amazingly a newer one that looked in great shape came up for sale just a few miles away. It wouldn't start, and the dump box was missing the tailgate, so it was a bargain. I brought it home, and soon it was running great. Even more astonishingly, I happened to come across an ad for a Truckster tailgate for sale in a nearby city. It matched so perfectly it could have been the original tailgate. There had to have been some divine intervention (Thanks, Dad!). I drove that Truckster around in the fog one night not too long ago, and it was just like I was a kid back on the golf course. Somebody was looking out for me, again.

I never quit being a "Secret Agent" when it came to finding out when our house was built. A breakthrough in the case occurred when I recently found this newspaper article in one of my mom's many scrapbooks. The article in the *Battle Creek Moon Journal* from October 30th, 1914 mentions that C. L. Post was investing in the property he'd taken over after the death of his brother, C. W., that previous May. The article describes the building of an addition to the main house, and it specifically reports, "a very handsome lodge will be built at the entrance to the grounds," and mentions it will be occupied by the year-round gardener and caretaker. A little later, on January 28th of 1915, another article reveals the hiring of a caretaker, Ernest Drake from Upjohn's Brook Lodge, and his moving to Post's Calmary Farm. That would indicate our house was built between October 1914 and January 1915.

BIG IMPROVEMENTS ARE MADE IN HIS LAKE HOME

C. L. POST WILL HAVE ONE OF PRETTIEST IN MICHIGAN.

New Addition is Being Built, and a Lodge Will be Constructed— Sunken Garden a Feature.

One of the finest summer homes in Michigan is to be located at Goguac lake. C. L. Post is now making extensive improvements on his property at the lake and a large force of men is now employed there.

An addition of considerable size is being built on his home which was built a year ago at the lake. Besides this, a very handsome lodge will be built at the entrance to the grounds, on the main road. This will be occupied by the gardener who will have charge of the farm, and live there the year round.

But finding the answer to that mystery after searching so long now seems to be almost anticlimactic. A house was built, but it wasn't really a home yet, at least not to the Pecks. It was 91 years of family, 91 years of living, working and loving that made One Country Club Drive our home. And I know just when that started – when my Grandpa Andy and Grandma Rena moved in.

Oh, and the leaded glass window with the bullet hole that fascinated me as a kid? I never did find out how the hole got there, but while my parents still lived there I replaced the window with a wood panel. I eventually framed the window and made it, complete with the bullet hole, into a mirror that hangs in our living room - a reflection of our family's history.

I had the greatest pleasure of working for my dad for almost ten years. In those years growing up and working on the golf course, my dad taught me many things: How to be a carpenter, a mechanic, a bricklayer, a plumber, and an electrician…How to grow grass, how to plant trees, and design and plant gardens…How to work with and manage employees…And how to get along with everyone. His greatest, special gifts to me were creativity, problem solving and confidence. He taught me many things, but mostly that I could tackle whatever I put my mind to.

And you know what? I did something else that I think my dad would be proud of.

You see, I wrote this book...

Thank You for Reading!

PostScript...

One day not so long ago, while I was putting these words together, my friend Mark Radebaugh called. He was standing next to the house at One Country Club Drive watching a giant excavator taking bites out of it! Slowly, inexorably, the house I grew up in, the house my dad grew up in, and the house where his parents had raised seven children, was being demolished. He gave me a blow-by-blow account as they were putting the pieces into a truck and hauling it away. In tears, I asked him if he could get to the white pedestal at the top of the stairs where I had always suspected something was hidden, which might hold details about the construction of our house. He said, "It's gone, the whole upstairs is mostly gone, and there is nothing left at the top of the stairs. There's just a little corner of the attic left above your parents' bedroom." I was shocked! I guess I'd always dreaded the inevitable. In the years since my dad had died and my mother moved out, the club had fixed up the house so employees could live there. I had thought, had hoped, the house would always be there.

A few days later, a box was delivered. In it, my friend Mark had sent me the fancy doorknob from the front door, and the house number above it – '1'. Except for these memories, that's all that was left...

"But it wasn't our house. It was never really our house. But it will always be our *home*!"

- Marty Peck